LISA BRASSARD MAYER

SILENT VICTIM RUNNING FREE

Outskirts Press, Inc.
Denver, Colorado

Silent Victim Running Free
A True Story About One Woman's Struggle To Survive The Abuse, Deception, And Cruel Acts Of One Man And His Family, And Her Quest To Help Her Children And Find Happiness
All Rights Reserved.
Copyright © 2008 Lisa Brassard Mayer
V4.0

Outskirts Press, Inc.
http://www.outskirtspress.com

ISBN: 978-1-4327-2115-2

Library of Congress Control Number: 2008923149

Outskirts Press and the "OP" logo are trademarks belonging to Outskirts Press, Inc.

PRINTED IN THE UNITED STATES OF AMERICA

INTRODUCTION

I decided to write this book to help the many women who are being victimized by abusive men. I've been through a most horrible ordeal that one cannot believe could exist in a seemingly happy relationship. The majority of the public would probably have seen my marriage to this monster as perfectly happy and healthy. Some have witnessed his true nature and a few friends actually heard him abusing me. Those friends were afraid to say anything due to fear of retaliation. My family had suspicions, but lack of proof because I remained silent to ensure their safety.

The silent victim tries to make everyone think that all is well, when in actuality, every day is spent trying to survive both mentally and physically. I'm hoping that by writing this book I'll make other women realize that they aren't alone and that they'll find the strength to escape the feeling of entrapment.

Many people ask the same question about someone being abused, such as "Why doesn't she leave her husband (or boyfriend) if he abuses her?" You'll hear many hurtful comments, such as "She's stupid for staying" or "She deserves to be beaten for staying in that relationship." Only the victim of abuse knows the answer to why she won't leave and understands the seriousness of the situation. The real answer to that question is "fear." Society doesn't know what it's like for a woman to be threatened with a knife and told that she will be killed if she leaves. One couldn't imagine how you feel when your husband says he'll take your children to a foreign country if you leave. Fearing that my children would disappear was my biggest fear of all. I prayed to God every day that he would keep my children safe with me. I told myself I would "tip-toe" around and "do as I was told" just to keep peace and keep them safe.

Ultimately I learned that there are no reasons to stay in an abusive relationship. I pray that all victims find the strength and courage to leave their abusers and that God keeps them safe.

CHAPTER 1

Scars of the Past

"Oh my gosh", I cried! "Sahir is coming! I have to hide or he's going to steal Kadin and Kazem! Sarim and April are with him!"

Every time I hid, they seemed to find me. There was no escaping, and all I could do was cry. My body was overcome with fear, and no matter how hard I tried, I simply couldn't run. Sahir was getting angry, and I feared for my life. I cried for help, but nobody was there.

"He's taking the kids! Please, someone stop him!"

Next thing I knew I woke up. My heart was pounding so fast. Was I having a heart attack? I got up to use the bathroom, and my arms got all tingly inside. I felt queasy, and I thought I was about to faint. Staggering, I made it back to bed, and I just lay there wondering if I was dying. I soon felt the tingling in my lips, and realized I just had an anxiety attack. I only knew this because I was in the hospital a few years back for the same thing. At that time I also thought it was a heart attack. The doctor had told me that when your lips tingle, it's a sign of an anxiety attack.

These reoccurring nightmares and anxiety attacks are only two of the many scars my ex-husband Sahir left me with. It was only three weeks ago when I had

1

my last episode, and I know it's only a matter of time before it happens again.

In addition to all of the nightmares, I also live in constant fear. There isn't a day that goes by that I don't worry about my family's safety. Sahir has so much animosity toward my family and me. He blames his actions on everyone but himself. The numerous threats he made against my mom and my brother cause me to worry about them constantly. The only comfort I have is from knowing that my brother at least lives a great distance from him. My mom, on the other hand, lives only ten minutes away. Sahir has threatened my present husband because I'm no longer a piece of his property, and he's jealous that I'm happy. Past threats of abduction have left me worried sick that my two youngest children will be kidnapped and taken out of the country.

In addition to the emotional scars, there are physical ones as well. I have a constant sick feeling caused by all the kicks in the stomach that I endured, and also from all the worrying that I do each day. There's also the chronic Vertigo that I was left with from all the head trauma Sahir inflicted on me. I truly believe without a doubt that if Sahir had been given the chance, he would have finished the job. He definitely would rather see me dead than alive and out of his control.

One thing Sahir never anticipated was that I would eventually escape his control. Even though he was able to physically control me all those years, he never succeeded in controlling my heart and my mind. I knew that if I had lost everything I believed in and all that I felt, I'd be nothing more than an empty shell. My love for my children and my family gave me the strength to hold my head high, and to hold onto hope and persevere.

I wrote my story to inspire other women to hold onto the hope that there is a light at the end of the tunnel. Hopefully it will also open their eyes to the "red flags" that some men possess. These are the warning signs of a typical abuser. It's important to remember that jealousy is not love, but rather about control. Any woman is vulnerable regardless of race, religion, family upbringing, etc. Recognizing these warning signs and staying away can be the difference between life and death.

CHAPTER 2
The Early Years

In the early years, my childhood was normal. I was born in Kew Gardens, New York and lived in Queens until the age of four. My parents decided to move to Long Island so my brother and I would grow up in the suburbs where it was quieter. They bought a house in a nice new neighborhood, hoping to give my brother and me a good environment to grow up in. I met a lot of new friends, and I was happy we moved to such a beautiful place.

Two of my best friends were Melinda and Linda. We spent almost every day playing together. There were many street games, such as kickball and spud, which we organized with the neighborhood kids. Melinda and I joined the same pool club in the summers where we both were a part of the swim and tennis team. Her sister, Mary, also joined the swim team when she was old enough.

We spent many summers at the club. It was a great place! They held a lot of activities and contests, such as scavenger hunts and diving for pennies. They held bingo and arts and crafts. At the end of the year trophies were given out. I earned many swimming and tennis trophies there. I also enjoyed the diving boards. We had some crazy diving contests, which were fun. Sometimes I'd get too crazy on those diving boards and get hurt.

Many wonderful memories are planted in my mind from those summers. My mom used to make us snack trays each week. She would make my brother Corey and me each a tray every week. We had the responsibility of rationing our sodas and treats so it would last the entire week. We were told that if we ran out, that was it until the following week. We were careful to ration properly. I don't think either of us ever ran out.

One of the best things that I used to love about the pool club was the cute lifeguards who worked there. I was a typical teenybopper who had crushes. Like any girl, I got in the habit of discreetly watching them, and at times it got me into trouble. My interest in cute guys and perpetual clumsiness didn't mix well. One good example was when I fell onto the tennis courts. I was walking on a four-foot ledge that stood next to the courts. I turned my head to look at one of the lifeguards, and the next thing I knew I fell off. I landed on the courts flat on my butt! How embarrassing! Aside from my little accidents, my summers were the best.

Life had its bright side, but there also was a dark side. Ever since I can remember, I was plagued with OCD, also known as Obsessive Compulsive Disorder, and low self-esteem. I can't remember when it started, but I remember it as early as when I was five. In kindergarten I used to sit there staring at the buttons going down the front of my teacher's dress, thinking how disgusting they were. I started having such an aversion to them. I stopped wearing anything with buttons. I didn't want to touch or even think about them.

I don't know what started my quirk. My mother

seems to think it might stem from the death of my grandfather. She said that I used to sit on his lap playing with the buttons on his vest. I don't know about that theory since he died when I was six. Who knows, maybe I sensed something was going to happen to him. I was close to him, and loved him very much. When he died I was too young to comprehend the true meaning of death, although I remember kneeling in front of his body at the wake and feeling sad. I'll always have fond memories of him.

As time went on, my neurotic habits increased. I had many compulsive habits. They ranged from excessive throat clearing and eye blinking to repeating certain words. The more stress I was under, the more frequently these repetitions would occur. I became increasingly self-conscious, and my self-esteem was low. I hated being abnormal. I always asked myself why I couldn't be like everyone else. I tried to control my behaviors as much as I could, but it was hard. I didn't want anyone thinking I was weird. If someone mentioned something about my habits, I became embarrassed and flustered. I said many prayers to God, asking him to help me stop these strange compulsions. The pressure of these urges got so bad at times, I would ask God to please let me die. I was so unhappy about who I was. I felt like I just didn't belong in this world and that I was suffering.

The years went by, and I tried dealing with my problem the best I could. I became shy and the self-consciousness increased. I joined the band in school hoping to come out of my shell. As shy as I was, I actually did a duet with another flute player named Wanda who later turned out to be another best friend. We performed many concerts together, and although performing in front of an audience is hard for someone shy like myself, I enjoyed it. By the time I reached junior high, the shyness started to escalate and so did the problems.

I had a good band teacher in junior high, but he was strict. When something didn't sound right, he started singling everyone out. He would make each person play his or her part in front of the entire band. I always knew my part, but had a lot fear playing in front of everyone. I was so scared that my head would start shaking. Try playing the flute when your head is shaking! I started getting so nervous that I wanted to quit the band.

I remember one night before a test where we were going to be graded on playing our part alone. I lay in bed the whole night thinking about how I didn't want to wake up the next morning. I even said a prayer begging God to take me that night. The next day I was shaking so much during the test that I couldn't play. I started crying in front of the other flute players. The teacher was sympathetic. He knew my nerves were the only thing that kept me from playing my part, so he gave me a good grade.

When my nerves got so bad that I couldn't stand it anymore, I decided to tell the teacher I was going to quit band. I'm so thankful that my teacher believed in me, and he wouldn't let me quit. He promised that things would get better.

My love for sports along with my decision to no longer feel sorry for myself and overcome shyness led me to join a sports team. I knew being on a team meant that at times the games would be played in front of an audience. I wound up going out for field hockey, volleyball, basketball and softball. Volleyball was probably the hardest, since it was the first indoor sport I went out for. It also drew a larger number of spectators. The more games I played, the more relaxed I became. The sports teams helped me become more outgoing and increased my self-esteem.

During my second year in high school I met Joe. He was my first serious relationship. He was handsome and sweet and always made me laugh. We spent nearly every day together in school and after. We got along well in the beginning, but after the first year tension grew between us. My dad didn't believe in serious relationships at so young an age, (which I now understand), so I always tried to downplay the seriousness of how I felt. The more he tried to forbid me to go out with him, the more tightly I held onto Joe. Eventually Joe felt cramped, and we began arguing every day. After two years of going together, our relationship fell apart.

Being a parent myself now, I understand just what my dad meant. I feel foolish about the way I dealt with things as a teenager. Back then you couldn't tell me anything. After all, I was seventeen, and I knew everything, right? Wrong! My oldest son and daughter are now young adults, and I sometimes chuckle at things they do because it reminds me of myself when I was that age. I try to always be there for them, but at the same time, let them make their own decisions even if I don't agree with them. Life is learning from your mistakes. It's hard when you're a parent and you love your children so much that you want to protect them from falling. I learned that to survive in this world, you have to fall a few times. I've got to say that I have fallen more than a few times and hard! Whew!

In August 1980, I left for college. I decided to live on campus at Stony Brook University so I could experience what it was like to live on my own. I turned eighteen and felt like I was on top of the world! I thought it was great that I had finally become an adult and was able to do whatever I wanted. I went to a few parties on campus where there was a lot of drinking going on. I never liked the taste of alcohol, but I wanted to fit in with the crowd. I probably went to a total of four parties, all of which I got pretty buzzed and little sleep. After the last party I got so nauseous and tired that I decided it wasn't for me. I hated feeling sick, and never developed a taste for alcohol.

During the school year I began dating a guy named Ken. We started out as friends in the beginning. He was kind and always had a sense of humor. We probably should have stayed friends because I wasn't ready for another serious relationship, and I think I always tried to make myself feel like I had deeper feelings for him than I ever had. After a year I ended the relationship because I couldn't pretend anymore. Ken was hurt from the break up and I felt guilty. I never wanted to hurt anyone, especially someone as nice as he.

During the summer after my first year in college, I decided to lose weight. I always had a weight complex, and to top it off, my gynecologist said that I had "a little more than the average person" when I asked if I was overweight. I was 5 ft. 5 1/2 in. and weighed 130 lbs. After he made that comment, I was determined to lose weight. I started a diet that would later turn to anorexia.

In the beginning of my diet I only cut out junk food. I wouldn't snack between meals. It wasn't more than one week later when I began cutting my portions down. I started losing weight, and I was so happy. I felt great, and for the first time I looked slim. It wasn't long before I dropped down to 115 lbs. This is when I should have stopped, but then the weight loss wasn't enough.

My eating habits went out of control. I started skipping meals and sometimes ate only cereal for dinner. I started counting every calorie I consumed. I was obsessed with my weight. I began eating vegetables out of the can because I was so hungry. I knew they wouldn't make me gain weight. I began taking diet pills higher than the recommended dosage. My health began deteriorating in front of my eyes, and I was turning into an emotional wreck.

I met a new friend at school named Ted. He was a true friend who helped me a lot during a tough time in my life. He tried to help me battle my anorexia by offering much support when I needed it, and he never judged me. I never got to thank him for all his support, but I'll always remember everything he did for me. True friends are hard to come by, and I was lucky to have found him.

In the fall of the second school year I met Tim. He was my assistant manager at the place I worked. By the time I met him, I was a mere 94 lbs. and my anorexia was at its worst. I was weak, and each day was a struggle. Regardless of how I looked, he was kind to me and didn't judge me because I was anorexic. We dated for about a year, got engaged and one year later married. I think back then I was more in love with the idea of getting married. I always wanted to grow up too fast. I feared being alone and, being in such bad health, made a hasty decision. I had no idea what love was all about.

My parents were worried about me and advised me to go to a psychologist for my anorexia. I agreed as I was never in denial about my problem, and wanted to put an end to my illness. I was tired of being cold and shaky. I wanted to clear my head of the obsessive thoughts about calories and weight. I still didn't want to gain weight, though. The one thing I was lucky about is the fact that I never made myself throw up. I had such a fear of that. It was probably one of the lifesaving factors in my life.

I began seeing a therapist my parents had found. He was nice, and I felt comfortable talking to him. The only problem was that he didn't specialize in anorexia. During our sessions he began telling me about all these diet recipes his wife had made at home. It was his last comment that made me realize he wasn't going to help me. He said that maybe I should eat a light meal at night or perhaps not at all. This made me drop out of counseling.

I made up my mind to help myself. I think that the real kick in the butt came when I saw my mom crying while she was listening to a Karen Carpenter song. Karen Carpenter had died from anorexia at a young age. My mom was afraid that I, too, was going to die. I've always loved my mom so much, and it killed me to see her so sad. It was the first time I ever saw her cry.

Little by little I ate more and gained some weight. It bothered me to gain the weight, and I still had my eating quirks, but at least I was getting healthier. I wanted to have children, and I knew that, unless I was healthy enough, it wasn't possible. The anorexia had made my menstrual cycle stop. When I reached a healthy 120 lbs. I began menstruating again. Tim and I both agreed to begin a family.

In the beginning of 1986, I became pregnant. I was excited and looking forward to having a baby. Tim and I told all our friends and family the good news. I was feeling queasy, but glowed with the thought of a part of me growing inside. I just couldn't believe it. I had six weeks of feeling wonderful, and suddenly it all withered away.

I remember going to work that day feeling fine. Everything went well except the usual twenty-four hour a day morning sickness. When I returned home in the evening I went to the bathroom and I noticed some spotting. Panicked, I called the doctor, who in turn gave me an appointment for a sonogram the next day. I was scared that something was wrong with the baby. I didn't sleep too well that night.

The next morning I went for the sonogram and a physical exam. I was so upset to hear the news that the doctor couldn't see the fetus on the sonogram. He could see the sac, but what happened to the fetus? He said it didn't look good, but decided to wait and see what happens. Even at that point I didn't give up hope. I was sad, but it didn't sink in that I was probably going to miscarry.

I went home and later in the night, I started getting contractions and bleeding heavily. I was crying, and in my heart I knew I was going to lose the baby. When I reached the hospital, it wasn't long before I miscarried. I was so depressed and couldn't stop crying. The doctor looked at me and truly felt the pain I was feeling. He reached over, held my hand and said how sorry he was.

It took Tim and me some time to heal and mourn the loss of our baby, but three months later I became pregnant again. I was scared to tell anyone at first because of the miscarriage the first time, but eventually we both began telling everyone. After a couple of months had passed, I felt myself slowly relaxing and not being so fearful of losing the baby. At about twenty-six weeks into the pregnancy I had a sono-gram, which came out normal. It was at that time I found out I was having a little girl.

Our baby was born March 4, 1987. She was the most beautiful baby I had ever laid eyes on. I stared at her and couldn't believe how precious she was and that she was a part of me. We named her Kayla after a famous model because she was so beautiful. Not only was our new baby Kayla beautiful, but she was a great sleeper. I was lucky that she loved her sleep. This gave me time to rest. She actually began sleeping through the night regularly as early as one month old.

I was truly blessed to have a beautiful healthy daughter and sixteen months later I was blessed once again. This time we had a beautiful baby boy. We named him Timmy after his father. Timmy arrived three weeks early, but he was still a healthy 6-lbs. 15 oz. I was so happy and again amazed that he was a part of me.

Having two babies so close in age was hard in the beginning. They were both in diapers, and Timmy had a formula intolerance. He had projectile vomiting, which made it difficult. After having a baby, your hormones are all out of whack. I found myself over-whelmed and depressed. I loved my babies so much, but I was exhausted and started to have anxiety.

To add to the stress, my husband Tim started to have pressure at work. It appeared as though his em-ployer felt that he was making too much money, so they tried to find reasons to fire him. There were other former employees who also claimed they fell victim to that. The tremendous pressure that Tim was under put a huge strain on our marriage. We just couldn't see eye to eye on anything anymore. It got to the point that we argued every day. I became stressed and felt a wall going up between us. Things got so bad that our marriage crumbled.

In the fall of 1990 I told Tim that I was leaving him. A couple of weeks before we separated, I met Sahir. He wasn't the reason why I left Tim, but rather the boost of courage I needed to leave an unhappy marriage. This was when I was about to make the worst mistake of my life. It was a path that could have led to my death.

CHAPTER 3
The Beginning

After I told my husband Tim that I was leaving, I stayed in a motel temporarily until I found an apartment. I was lucky to find a studio apartment, which I could move in right away, and the price was reasonable. I decided not to let my children know at that time what was going on between Tim and me. I didn't want to upset them, and I felt they were too young to understand. We worked it out that I would stay with them at home during the day, and at night they would stay with their dad.

When I first met Sahir, he seemed nice. He worked at a gas station where I often purchased the gas for my car. He was handsome and polite, and had the most incredible accent. He was born in Turkey and had been in the U.S.A. for only a couple of years. I was barely out of a bad marriage when I began dating Sahir. At that time, I was extremely vulnerable and probably not ready to start a new relationship.

In the beginning things were good between us. He was nice to my children and me, but his brother Sarim and his brother's wife April became jealous over our relationship. His parents, who lived in his native country, were angry that he was involved with an American. They wanted Sahir to marry this girl from his

15

country. When he told them he didn't want to marry her and that he loved me, all hell broke loose. Sahir and his family began fighting like little children. He was constantly on the phone with his mother arguing, and at home arguing with his brother.

About two months after Sahir and I had started going out with each other, the fighting between him and his family got so bad that he wanted to go back to his country. I was so heart broken over the thought that he might return to his country and not come back. I decided to have a talk with Sarim. I desperately tried to get him to accept me and put an end to their disputing. I was successful, and Sahir and Sarim agreed to work things out. Sahir's parents, on the other hand, still resented me. Sahir lived with Sarim, April and one of their sons, Omer. Sarim's other son lived in Turkey with his grandparents. His son who now resides in the United States has gone back and forth living in both countries at different times. He probably never did well in school due to his parents' lack of showing love toward him. They also never seemed to provide him with any care and stability in his life.

Sahir began inviting me over to his brother's house. Sometimes he would invite me over for dinner; other times just to see each other. The cruel behavior slowly began. One night Sahir invited me over to see him. In my mind I was looking forward to a nice evening with him. As soon as I got to his brother's house, he said, "Sarim and I are going out. You can stay here and keep April company."

I was so outraged. I asked myself, how could someone invite his girlfriend over, then leave for the night? I told him nicely that I would rather go home than sit there with his brother's wife. First of all, I went there to see him, not his brother's wife. Second, his brother's wife wasn't even nice to me. At some time Sahir had told me that she was extremely jealous of me. Sahir looked mad when I told him I wanted to leave, so I grudgingly stayed. They went out drinking, and I was now stuck babysitting his brother's wife.

I decided to make the best of it even though I was hurt over the situation. April and I spent the night playing cards, which lasted a couple of hours. I soon grew tired and decided to wash up for bed. While I was in the bathroom, Omer wanted to come in, but I told him he couldn't because I was changing and that I would see him when I was finished. He was mad that I wouldn't let him in the bathroom, so he urinated all over Sahir's bed. I told April what her son had done, and she just looked at me. She never offered to clean it up or even confront her three year-old son about what he did. I was now furious. I cleaned up the mess and decided to go to my apartment.

I politely told April, "When Sahir comes home, could you please give him this message? Omer urinated all over the bed. I cleaned it up, but the bed is still wet and I can't sleep in it, so I'm going home. Tell him he can come to my place later if he wants to."

April agreed to give him the message. When I got back to my apartment I went right to bed. I lay there thinking about whether or not April would actually give him that message or if she would just lie about the whole thing because she was jealous. From what Sahir told me in the past, she was known to lie. It was getting pretty late and Sahir hadn't come over to my apartment, so I decided to go back and see if he had returned home.

As it turned out, he was home and upset that I left. Just as I feared, April had lied to him by telling him that I left because I was mad that he went out. She didn't say anything about Omer messing up the bed. I told Sahir everything that had happened that night. Sahir seemed a little better after I explained what happened. I was pretty upset about that evening, but decided to hold in all my frustrations and forget about it.

On many occasions April displayed jealousy toward me, which increased as time went on. It could be as simple as a dirty look or as bad as some evil plan that she carried out just to hurt me. I had sensed her animosity toward me from the day I met her and not long after that did she actually admit to me that it was true. She approached me one day out of the blue and said, "Laurie, I have to admit that I've been jealous of you. I'm so fat and you're so thin and pretty."

I was shocked that she would just come out and say that. I told her she shouldn't be jealous of me and that there was no reason to be. I also told her I never tried to make her jealous.

Even though we talked about the jealousy issue that day, things didn't get better. Sahir asked me to move in with him and his family in April 1991. I agreed to move in with them, but I didn't have a good feeling about it. This meant I was going to be around them all the time, and I'd have to be subjected to more cruelty. I think the only reason they asked me is so I would drive Sahir to and from work every day and they wouldn't have to. (Sahir didn't have a license).

The first real problem that arose after I moved in was the lack of privacy and respect for my property. Their son Omer was spoiled, and they always let him do whatever he wanted. I had a little refrigerator in Sahir's and my room. Omer would always go in there without asking and eat whatever he felt like eating or drinking. He would also touch everything in the room and break things. When Sarim and April refused to do anything about it, Sahir and I put a lock on our door. April got extremely insulted and she said to me, "When I saw that lock on your door, I just wanted to rip it off!"

I told her the lock was to keep Omer out because he touched everything in our room. She just gave me a dirty look and said nothing more about it. My room was now safe, but I couldn't save my dishes in the kitchen that Omer tossed off the balcony and broke. April found the dish tossing amusing. She just sat there watching him and laughing. She did nothing to try to stop him, and she never apologized.

During the day I was lucky to have some peace and quiet. I would stay with Kayla and Timmy at their father's house until he returned from work. Usually it was until about 6:00 pm and sometimes until 11:00 pm. I also worked part-time at McDonald's, so it, too, gave me an escape. Sometimes I would have to bring Kayla and Timmy to Sarim and April's place, which I wasn't thrilled about due to Omer's poor behavior. I didn't want them to copy any of the bad things that he did.

Toward the middle of the month Sahir received a call from his younger brother Sharif. Sharif told Sahir that he wanted to come to the U.S. He tried to get a Visa in Turkey, but he was unable to because it's difficult, and few are able to get one. Sahir and Sarim made a plan to pay someone to obtain an illegal visa. They needed $15,000 to purchase this visa and, of course, they didn't have the money. I found out about their plan when Sahir and I were at the mall shopping. He sat down with me in the food court and told me that he had a favor to ask of me. He explained the situation about Sharif and wanted to know if he could borrow money. He also promised that Sharif would work in the U.S. and pay me back. I had a bad feeling, but being a person who's too trusting and has a big heart, I said yes. I felt he was sincere and that he would see to it that I'd get my money back. I gave him $2800, which was every last penny I had. Then to top it off, Sarim asked to open some credit cards in my name so he could take cash advances. I was stupid enough to agree. He took about $6000 in cash advances. What was I thinking?

At the end of the month Sharif arrived in the U.S. He seemed like a nice guy. He didn't speak any English, but based on his facial expressions he seemed to like me. I'd always go out of my way for him to make him feel welcome. Anytime he needed a ride somewhere or needed clothing, I'd accommodate him. Sahir and Sarim got him a job at a gas station almost immediately, so I believed Sharif was going to pay me back the money.

Things began to get worse after Sharif arrived. Sahir and I had even less privacy. Every night when we finally went to bed there would be a knock at our door. Sarim and Sharif wanted to play this Turkish tile game, called, "Okay." This game would go on into wee hours of the night. Sometimes they would play it in the day, too, and it would go on for hours. It got to the point that I never had any time with Sahir. They began playing that game every free moment they had. I started to resent it. I told Sahir how I felt, but he would just make excuses that they kept asking him to play and that he couldn't say no. Other times he just wouldn't care at all, and he would get annoyed at me for mentioning it.

I no longer had my apartment to retreat to, and Sahir always expected me to stay in the house and wait for him. I was so bored and frustrated at the situation. I was tired of enduring April's nasty remarks and Omer's poor behavior. I felt sorry for Omer because he was so neglected. It was bad enough that they would always let him do whatever he wanted, but when Sarim had enough and lost his patience, he would repeatedly smack Omer in the head. Seeing Sarim hit him made me so ill, and I knew I couldn't do anything about it.

I had also seen Sarim repeatedly smack April in the head when he was mad at her. The worst thing about it was that April thought this behavior was perfectly normal. She went as far as to say that she used to be a compulsive liar, but Sarim fixed her of that. (She was referring to his beatings). Little did I know at this time that not only was I soon to be a victim of physical violence, but ten times worse.

CHAPTER 4
The Abuse Begins

In the beginning of May 1991 Sahir asked me to marry him. I had a lot of red flags about Sahir and his family, but I put on the blinders and said I would marry him. I thought I loved him, and I figured things would get better. We agreed to have a civil ceremony only inviting my parents, Sarim, April, Sharif, Omer, and their friend who was living with us, Omar.

I was excited about the wedding so I went to my mom's school where she taught to tell her about it. After I told her, she looked so serious and disapproving. She tried to talk me out of it, saying that I was going from the frying pan into the fire. She tried to warn me about the difference in culture. I didn't have any knowledge about their customs and how women were treated. Deep down inside something didn't feel right, but nonetheless, I disregarded my mom's advice and even my own gut instincts. My parents said that they wouldn't attend the wedding ceremony, and at that time I was hurt. I thought that maybe when the time came, they would change their minds.

Preparations for the ceremony were few, but Sahir needed a suit, and we needed wedding bands. Time was short so I asked Sahir if we could buy the rings on his day off. He agreed, but when the day came he said he was going to play "Okay" with his brothers. He said he'd go shopping when they were done. I was already annoyed since he promised me we'd go, and I also knew they'd be playing for hours.

By the time they were finally finished, the store only had only one hour before they closed. We had to quickly purchase some kind of ring, and the moment wasn't a romantic memory. He quickly purchased an inexpensive band for me (price wasn't important to me, but the attitude and the manner in which he purchased it was). He was too cheap to buy one for himself and decided to borrow his friend's ring. It was a ring his friend used in a phony marriage to acquire a green card.

Sahir, too, had a phony marriage in Turkey in an attempt to acquire a visa so he could come to the U.S. The department that issues visas could see right through his plan, since the woman was more than twenty years older than Sahir. They had him on a list with a red flag next to his name in case he ever tried it again. Sahir was still able to get a job on a ship even though they had him in the computer as a possible flight risk. He managed to jump the ship when it docked in New Jersey and his brother, already waiting there for him, picked him up and sped off.

About three days before the wedding, Sahir began to get cold feet. He started saying that he wasn't sure if he should get married. My feelings were hurt, and I was beginning to think that his brothers pushed him into marrying me so he could get a green card. I was almost to the point of calling it off myself. I had enough of his lack of caring about my feelings. When Sahir saw that I wasn't happy, he apologized. I accepted his apology but my uneasiness grew. Still, despite my growing doubts, I married him.

May 22, 1991 was the day I signed my life away. We had the ceremony at the town hall as planned. My parents didn't show up, which on that day had hurt. I know now how hard it must have been for them, knowing that I was making a big mistake. They must have felt helpless when they knew they could do nothing to stop me. Today I have no ill feelings about them not coming, and I understand their decision.

The ceremony was short, and after it was finished we proceeded home. I thought it was going to be a nice day for a change. April had cooked and bought a cake for later, but immediately after we finished eating, Sahir and his brothers decided to play "Okay." It was bad enough how much they played that game, but right on our wedding day? I was fuming! I spent the entire day alone in our bedroom crying, realizing I made the biggest mistake of my life marrying him. I couldn't believe what a fool I was! I thought of the old saying, *you made your bed, now lie in it!*

It was about 8:00 at night when they finished, and April called me into the kitchen so we could cut the cake. I wasn't in the mood, but I figured I'd make the best of what was left of that day. We did a little dancing, which kept my mind off of my sorrow and anger that I had building up inside. I kept telling myself that I wasn't going to have another failed marriage. I'd try to be the best wife so my husband would be happy.

The following month Omar's parents planned to visit from Turkey. They were going to stay with us a few weeks. When they arrived, Sahir, Omar, Sarim and Sharif planned for all of us to take a trip to Niagara Falls. They planned to rent a ten-passenger van so we could all fit in one vehicle. We'd stay overnight and return the next day. When the time came, they needed money for the van. Of course, they didn't have the money and once again used my credit card. It cost about $450 and again they promised to pay me back. Borrowing from my credit card was starting to become a habit of theirs, and I began to wonder if they were ever going to pay me back.

The morning of the trip they still hadn't made arrangements of what they were going to do with their dog. They had gotten the dog only about a week before from someone they knew. It was a German shepherd that must have been mistreated at one time. He had a bad hind leg and was extremely nervous. Back then I didn't know why they got the dog anyway. They never liked dogs, and they didn't even take care of their own son. I couldn't imagine they'd treat the dog any better. It was just as I expected. They decided to lock the dog in the basement with a bowl of water and a big bowl of food. I felt bad for the dog, but knew I couldn't say anything.

We left for the trip early in the morning. Kayla and Timmy were unable to go because they were sick. I was sad they couldn't come, but something inside me said that it was better they didn't go. Every moment with Sahir and his family was tense. I always felt I had to watch what I said and that they were always judging me.

We drove many hours without stopping, and I asked Sahir if we could stop to eat. He just kind of brushed me off, and when we did finally stop, they only stopped so they could eat their Turkish delights. It consisted only of their Turkish cheese and olives, which I disliked. The cheese had a rancid smell and an awful taste. Sahir knew that I didn't like what they had, and I don't believe that April did either. He still disregarded my feelings, and they went back on the road.

We drove for quite some time until I was so hungry I was starting to feel sick. I hadn't eaten all day, so I finally pleaded with Sahir to please stop to eat something. They finally agreed to stop at McDonald's. I figured we'd sit down and eat and also stretch our legs a bit, but I was wrong. Sahir and his brothers demanded we take the food in the van and eat while driving. I get nauseous sometimes in the car if I concentrate on something, and especially if I eat while the car is moving. I had no choice. It was either eat under those circumstances or starve. I was already dreading this trip, and it was only the beginning.

We arrived at Niagara Falls at about 10:00 pm. It was cold that night, and, of course, they didn't make reservations at any motel so we could get some sleep. We drove around all night and just waited for morning. Luckily, they at least stopped for coffee and a bite to eat early in the morning. By this time I was exhausted and not happy.

Later in the day, Sahir and his brothers found a motel room. I was so happy because we'd been up all night and I was tired. My happiness was cut short when Sahir told me I was going to sleep in the room with April and Omar's mother and he was going to sleep with the guys. I was shocked! First of all, I thought that I should sleep with my husband. Second, I didn't even know Omar's mother (she didn't even speak one word of English), and April was the wicked witch of the east.

I quietly told Sahir I wasn't happy with the idea and explained why. He got angry and said that he didn't care how I felt, and that it was going to be that way whether I liked it or not. I said nothing more about it and just felt sad. Sahir just walked away with Sarim and sat by the lake.

When I turned in the direction of Sahir and Sarim, I noticed Sahir talking. He seemed upset, so I went over. I tried to apologize to Sahir just to make peace even though I knew I did nothing wrong. I was snubbed by both of them, so I walked away in tears.

Sharif saw me and assumed that Sarim made me cry (at that time Sharif thought highly of me because I did so much to help him). Sharif walked over and punched Sarim in the face! I couldn't believe it! Why would he resort to such violence? Also, why didn't he ask what was going on instead of assuming? I quickly stopped Sharif and told him that Sarim didn't do anything (by that time Sharif knew a little English). When Sharif realized he made a mistake, he became mad at me. I felt so bad, and I started blaming myself. I wished I had never complained in the first place and just stayed in the room with April and Omar's mother.

When I returned to the motel in tears, Omar's parents just gave me a cold stare. I knew they didn't understand English, but I apologized anyway. I ran off to be alone and sobbed quietly to myself. I thought about how it was the worst trip I had ever been on, and I couldn't believe how crazy this family was. I just wished I could go home. I had witnessed two brothers being violent and began seeing Sahir's temper flare. I didn't have a good feeling inside.

After a short while Sahir came looking for me. He told me that he got a separate room for us. I was relieved, but I could see that Sahir was furious and that worried me. He dropped me off at the room and went drinking with the guys. I spent the whole night alone in the room until early in the morning when he finally returned.

Sahir walked in extremely drunk. He drank so much that he got sick two times. All I said to him was that I wasn't happy about the situation, and suddenly he began smacking me hard across the face. I ran in the bathroom and cried hysterically. I couldn't believe he struck me! I stayed in the bathroom for some time before I came out, and when I finally did, he was sleeping. I was so overtired that I cried myself to sleep. It was the first of many times that I did just that.

The next morning we headed back home. It was a quiet ride. Everyone was exhausted from getting so little sleep. I tried to sleep in the van for the majority of the trip. I was still upset about everything that went on the day before, especially about the smack in the face. I was so angry with him for what he had done to me, but I still forgave him. I don't even remember if he ever apologized to me or how we made up.

When we arrived home that night, everyone was in for a surprise. Sarim and April got what they deserved for leaving the dog locked up and neglected. The dog must have gotten so anxious about being left in the basement that she broke down the door. She scratched and chewed away at it until she got through. The entire living room and dining room was in shambles. The dog had peed and pooped everywhere. She tore up the couches and whatever else she could get to.

This was only the first time they mistreated the dog. Numerous times I came home to find the dog tangled in a chain that was strangling the poor thing. Luckily, I got there in time to free her. It wasn't long before they got tired of the dog, drove somewhere far away and just let her go. I had hoped that someone kind would find her and give her a good home.

Sarim and April weren't the only ones to be cruel to animals. Sahir always claimed he loved animals. He had many pigeons in his back yard that he seemed to love. He would ask Sarim and April if they could feed them while he was at work or occasionally let them out to fly. They appeared to be bothered by his request and eventually refused to care for the birds.

One evening I heard Sarim and Sahir yelling at each other in a heated argument. I was in the bedroom, and they were in the living room. They made their way to the outside where the screaming continued. After a period of time Sahir returned inside. When he came into the bedroom, he had blood on his shirt. I panicked, thinking Sarim had hurt him. When I asked him what happened, I was again shocked at his answer. He told me that he got so mad at Sarim because he and April couldn't even do him a small favor of caring for the pigeons. He said that he felt bad because he got so mad that he ripped off the pigeon's head! I wanted to report him for animal cruelty, but I knew he would find out because I was the only other person who knew about it.

Sahir kept assuring me he was sorry and that something like that would never happen again. He said he didn't know what came over him and that he wasn't that kind of person. I was beginning to wonder.

CHAPTER 5
Trip To Turkey

Tension grew between Sahir and Sarim. April took Sarim's side even though it had nothing to do with her and she knew nothing about the situation. She would constantly make nasty remarks to Sahir and me. She wasn't even nice to Sharif because she resented him living there. Sahir already had enough of Sarim, but what tipped the scales were April's nasty remarks. He definitely wasn't going to have a woman treat him like she was better than he was. Sahir and Sharif decided to find an apartment together. I was glad that we were no longer going to live with Sarim and April. Sahir also promised that Sharif would start to pay back the money he owed me.

In September 1991 we found an apartment not far from Sahir's workplace. It was a two bedroom one bathroom apartment in a private home. The day we signed the lease, Sahir displayed jealousy toward the new landlord, Jason. He kept putting his body between Jason and me every time Jason tried to speak to me. Jason is a Greek man who was always respectful and polite toward us. I guess it was his custom to kiss the hand of a lady. He proceeded to kiss my hand, and I thought that Sahir was going to blow a fuse. Boy, if looks could kill! The jealousy that filled the room was so obvious, but Jason didn't say anything about it. I was so embarrassed about Sahir's behavior.

The day we moved in we met the tenants of the second apartment in the house. Their names were Adrian and Carlos. Adrian's parents lived with them and they, too, were nice people. When Carlos stopped by to ask us if we needed help moving our belongings, Sahir became jealous once again. He made me go into the bedroom and told me to stay there until Carlos left. He refused Carlos's help because he didn't want me near him.

After Carlos left, Sahir told me he didn't like him, and that anytime he came by in the future, to go into the room. He forbid me from saying hi to anyone but Adrian. I knew that unless Sahir was there, I wouldn't avoid our new neighbors, and I would most definitely says hello.

I ran into Adrian one day, and we had a lengthy chat. She was a nice lady and I felt comfortable talking to her. During our conversation she mentioned that her mother thought I was a snob because many times I didn't say hello. Adrian said she had defended me by telling her that maybe I was just shy. I confided in Adrian about Sahir's jealousy and how he forbid me to say hi to them. I also told her to please apologize to her parents for me and in the future, if Sahir is next to me, I'm unable to say hello. Adrian said she sensed Sahir was jealous and that Carlos had told her that Sahir was behaving strangely when he came by to offer a hand with our moving in.

I eventually also had a chat with Carlos. I explained the situation to him. He, too, was understanding. I was glad to make new friends with nice people, even if it meant I had to be secretive about our friendship. I felt so isolated not being allowed to have any friends, and I grew lonely.

Now that we moved in and Sharif no longer had a ride to work (he, too, had no license), I would have to drive him and pick him up. His hours were from 6:30 am till 11:30 pm! Sahir said I would also have to drive to his work mid-day and bring him something to eat. Sahir's hours were from 6:00 am till 9:30 pm. Sharif's work was about eight miles away and Sahir's five miles. I began driving almost eighty miles a day to drop off, pick up and bring food to the two of them. I was so tired that when I went to visit my parents or grandmother during the day I could barely keep my eyes open. I found myself practically falling asleep behind the wheel when I was driving. I was slowly becoming physically and emotionally drained.

During this time Sahir was notified by a lawyer whom he had hired to obtain a green card. The lawyer told him that since he came into the country illegally, he'd have to return to Turkey and re-enter legally. When the time came, I'd have to go with Sahir to the Turkish consulate. I had mixed feelings about going. I was excited to see a different country since I had never traveled out of the U.S., but I was fearful of how I would be treated by his family. I knew they disapproved of me because I'm American, and they wanted him to marry a Turkish woman. I was also worried because I had also already witnessed the horrific behavior of Sahir, Sarim and Sharif. What if the rest of his family was just as violent?

Another problem concerning the trip was the fact that I would miss Kayla and Timmy so much. I had never been away from them that long before. I wasn't the only one who had concerns. When I told my parents about the trip I could tell they were anxious. Even though they didn't say anything, it was evident through their facial expressions.

In the summer of 1992, we received a call from the immigration lawyer. He told us that an appointment was made at the Turkish consulate in Istanbul, Turkey for November 6, 1992. Sahir booked a trip right away. He decided that we would leave October 25 and stay in Istanbul until November 7. We would then take a bus to his parents' house, where we'd stay until December 4. When he told me we'd be in Turkey five weeks I began to panic. I asked him if we could make the trip a little shorter, but he was adamant about the five weeks. All these thoughts ran through my head. How was I going to survive there for five weeks? What if his parents hated me and treated me in a bad way? I told myself I'd always keep a smile on my face and try to make a good impression on them. They didn't speak any English except for the younger sister who knew nothing more than a few phrases. The only way I'd be able to communicate to them was through Sahir's translations and my facial expressions. I knew it was going to be a long trip.

Sahir and Sarim were still angry with each other at this time, but they slowly began talking again. Sahir told Sarim about the trip to Turkey, and Sarim agreed to drive us to the airport. Things had been quiet since we moved into our own apartment, and keeping a distance from Sarim and April had made life a lot more peaceful. I was going to miss the peacefulness, but at the same time I was glad they weren't fighting anymore.

October came quickly, and soon it was time to leave. I was both excited and worried at the same time. When we got to the airport, I already missed

Kayla and Timmy. I didn't want to go, but I knew I didn't have a choice. I wouldn't even be home to spend Thanksgiving with them. This thought made me even sadder than I already was.

We had a nine-hour non-stop flight to Turkey. It was a smooth flight, and we arrived about 1:00 pm in the afternoon. Things already started rocky when some crooked security workers at the airport searched our luggage. As they searched our bags they tried to get some jeans from us. Lucky for us, when we told them "no", they backed off. They could have made trouble for us if they wanted to.

When we left the airport we stopped to visit one of Sharif's friends. I was nervous and shy. The friend and his family didn't speak English, and the mom kept staring at me. She constantly smiled at me and seemed nice, but the staring made me uncomfortable.

A combination of being so nervous and traveling such a long distance caused my bladder to be totally full. I asked Sahir to ask the mom if I could use the rest room. She smiled and showed me where it was. When I walked in I was surprised and confused. I was used to our toilets back home, and when I saw nothing but a hole in the floor and no toilet paper, I was shocked. They had only a faucet near the floor with a small pail under it. I thought, do you take off your pants or do you just squat over the hole? I figured that the urine would splash on my pants, so I took them off. How would I wipe myself? Lucky for me I had tissues in my pocketbook. After I was done, I tried to rinse the paper down the hole with the water, and it wouldn't go down! I began panicking, thinking I might have clogged their drain. After many attempts, the paper finally seemed to go down. It was a strange experience. Whew!

After spending a couple of hours at the friend's house, we left to go to our hotel. I was glad because I didn't want to have to use their bathroom again!

By the time we reached the hotel, it was late afternoon. We were tired from the time change. Turkey is seven hours ahead of New York, so we had jet lag. We fell asleep at 6 pm. By 2 am we were wide-awake again. We tried to walk around the city, but nothing was open because it was the middle of the night. We were bored because everything was closed, and there was nothing to do but wait for morning.

Breakfast was served in the hotel about 6:00 am. Turkey had a different breakfast than what I was used to. They served Turkish cheese, olives, tomatoes and cucumbers. I wasn't used to eating vegetables in the morning, and the cheese I knew I already didn't like because I tried it before. The only thing I did like was the bread, so that was the only thing I ate.

Later that day Sahir's brother Sabih and his sister Ipol were to meet us in Istanbul and stay with us in the hotel. They planned to travel back to their house with us after the appointment. When they arrived, Sabih gave me a friendly hug and a warm welcome. He seemed pleased to meet me and eager to show me around the city. Ipol, on the other hand, smiled and said hello, but her eyes told me there was jealousy and disapproval in her heart. Despite those negative signals, I smiled and always made her feel welcome in my presence.

That second night in the hotel was rough. The weather was unusually hot and humid that week. It reached 83 degrees during the day and was muggy in the evening. The hotel room had no air conditioning, so we kept the windows open at night. Unfortunately the windows had no screens, and we were literally eaten alive by mosquitoes! Sabih and Ipol got it the worst since they were sleeping by the window. They had bites all over their faces. To top it off, during the night I spotted a huge cockroach climbing up the wall! Yuck! I have such a bug phobia, and those bugs are disgusting! Needless to say, I had trouble sleeping that night.

In the morning we were tired from a sleepless night. Sahir overheard the hotel owner talking on the phone to pest control. She was complaining about how they sprayed the hotel and still they had a roach problem. All I kept thinking about was my fear of having one of those things get into my luggage. Oh, gross! Sahir chose this hotel because it was cheap. I agree that it would have been too expensive to get a top quality hotel, but this one wasn't clean. The bathtub was covered in grime. I hated stepping into such a filthy tub, but it was the only way I could wash.

We spent the day walking around the city. There were nice sights to see. It was a beautiful city with many shops. Sahir told me that the people in Istanbul were more liberal in dress codes for women than in his city and other places. From what I observed, some women dressed more liberal, while others dressed like strict Muslims. The majority of women wore long coats and scarves on their heads. Others were extreme and wore black robes that covered everything except their eyes. There were some who didn't wear anything over their heads.

While I was walking through the city, it seemed like every man I passed would stare. I don't know if it was because I dressed differently and they knew I was from the U.S. or for some other reason. Sahir noticed them looking, and it infuriated him. He became so jealous that he started yelling at me in front of Sabih and Ipol. He told me I wore too much make-up and that was the reason they kept looking. I wiped off my lipstick, but I told him I wasn't going without any make-up. As it was, I wore little to begin with. Even if I didn't wear any make-up, he would find something else to complain about.

All day he made remarks about it. I just kept hoping he wouldn't lose control of his temper. Sabih and Ipol kept looking at Sahir puzzled as to what the problem was. I don't know what he told them, but I often wondered.

One of the most disturbing things I saw in the city, which was heart-breaking, involved children. There were homeless children who rolled out dirty mattresses and slept on the ground at night. They had nowhere to go and no parents to take care of them. It was sad to see them live the way they did. It's an image in my mind that I often look back on and wish that things were different for those poor children.

The day of the immigration appointment had arrived. Sahir and I were both nervous because the lawyer told us that the officers usually asked a lot of questions, and they also could deny Sahir re-entry into the U.S. if they wanted to. We were relieved when things went smoothly. They didn't interrogate us as I pictured. We had nothing to hide, but due to the way Sahir had entered the U.S. in the first place and the fact that his previous phony marriage was on record, he had the greater risk of being denied a green card. Sometimes they have tough officers working, but we were lucky to have a nice one. He just asked some routine questions, and we showed him some wedding and family pictures. Thinking back now, I wish they had denied him a green card. I would have saved myself from a lot of grief.

The next day we took the bus and headed for Sahir's hometown. My stomach was beginning to hurt from being constipated. I was extremely dehydrated from not drinking enough water. I didn't want to drink too many fluids while we were in Istanbul because I didn't want to use the city's public rest rooms. They were dirty squat toilets with no toilet paper, so I only used the bathroom in the hotel room. It had been nearly a week since I had a bowel movement, and I was starting to feel sick. By the time we reached our destination, I was nauseous and had severe pains in my stomach.

When we arrived at his parents' house I was surprised by the condition it was in. It was an old house that looked like a hollowed boulder from the outside. I felt so sorry for his family that they lived in such poor conditions. I knew they didn't have much money, but I never pictured their house as run down as it was. Sahir and Sarim were always sending money to their parents, so I never imagined that their place would look as bad as it did.

When we went inside we received a warm welcome from Sahir's parents and younger sister, Tezer. Despite how sick I felt, I smiled and gave them a big hug. I tried to make a good impression, and although I felt sick, I tried not to show it. Sarim and April's younger son, Ogan, came over and hugged us as well. He'd been living in Turkey since he was eight months old. I don't know how Sarim and April could leave their child in another country, although I think Sahir's parents took much better care of Ogan than Sarim and April ever would have. Had he been in the U.S., he would probably wind up neglected and abused just like Omer.

We sat down and Sahir had a lengthy conversation with his parents. He hadn't seen them in more than five years so he had a lot of catching up to do. They told him about a new house they wanted to buy. They saved all the money Sahir and Sarim had sent them, but they were still about $600 short. I felt so sorry for them living in such a shack that I offered to take a cash advancement from my credit card so they could buy the house. They were so happy, and they jumped at the offer.

After a few days, I finally went to the bathroom. I still felt sick, and I didn't recover until two weeks later. During this time I still tried to keep on my feet, but at times the pain and nausea got severe. Sahir's family just glared at me while I was in pain and nobody showed any concern about my condition.

I began seeing signs of resentment from his family. Washing yourself in their house was an involved task. His mother had to boil water because they had no running hot water. The fact that I have long hair made it harder. To rinse the shampoo out of my hair, I needed Sahir's assistance. It entailed pouring a pot of water over my head. Sahir agreed to help, but what I later found out was that Sahir's family ridiculed him for helping me. They claimed he was acting like a woman. Sahir was upset about it, and as a result his attitude changed toward me. I could sense the tension growing inside him.

About ten days later, Sahir's family moved into their new house. It was brand new and much nicer than where they were living before. They seemed excited, and I was happy for them.

It wasn't long before they wanted more. During our stay we paid for all the groceries for the entire family. We only had a limited amount of money, and it was going fast. The only thing I bought for myself was a few cans of Diet Coke. I didn't mind so much about the groceries because I knew they didn't have much money, but then they began taking advantage of us. Every conversation they had involved money. I quickly learned the Turkish word for money because they mentioned it so much.

Toward the latter part of our visit they decided they wanted brand new cabinets. It would cost $400 and they asked Sahir for the money. Sahir told me about it when we were about to go to bed. He already told them yes and gave them the money. I was flabbergasted! He didn't even discuss it with me. Our money was nearly depleted, and I was afraid we wouldn't have enough to get home. When I told Sahir how I felt, he began smacking me hard across the face. Not only was I was in pain, but I was also humiliated. I started to cry, and I just wanted to go home. I couldn't believe that he had hit me again and, just as I had done in the Niagara Falls motel, I cried myself to sleep.

In the morning I had trouble facing his family. I wondered if they heard him smacking me. Smacking women in the face seemed to be normal in their family. Sahir used to tell me stories about how his father always beat up his mother. On one occasion I had also witnessed Sabih smack Tezer in the face because she didn't iron his clothes. What kind of family is this? I had never witnessed so much violence in a household. I was missing home and couldn't wait to return to the U.S. I wrote a sad letter to my parents and told them to please eat a piece of turkey for me on Thanksgiving. I can imagine that they started to worry about me because I sounded so depressed in the letter.

When we finally returned home on December 4, I

40

was so happy to be home again. The trip was rough, but overall I thought things went smooth with Sahir's parents and that they liked me. Even though there were little incidents here and there, they hugged me when I left, and they seemed okay.

When we walked in the door to our apartment, Sharif was sitting there. We said hello, and when Sahir left the room, things turned bad. Sharif said to me in a sarcastic tone, "So, Laurie, how's my country? How's my family?"

When I heard those words in his unfriendly tone, my stomach dropped. I immediately called Sahir back into the room. I told him there was a big problem and explained what had just happened. I was surprised to hear Sharif talk to me in that way, and I was puzzled. I was wondering what prompted him to treat me like that. Sahir questioned Sharif and soon an argument broke out.

As it turned out, Sahir's family in Turkey called Sharif numerous times during our visit to complain about me. They didn't like me because I'm American. They didn't like the fact I drank Diet Coke (which I paid for myself). They also mentioned the inconvenience of my bathing regularly (they washed once a week). Of course, they had no problem taking my money. I could have been a saint and they still would have found something wrong with me. I was so hurt when Sahir told me this. All the time we were there they smiled in my face, but they were secretly stabbing me in the back at the same time.

I later found out that we had been doomed from the start. Sarim had told his parents many negative things about me even before we arrived in Turkey. As a result everyone in Sahir's family already disliked me before they even met me. After Sharif and Sahir finished arguing, Sharif told Sahir that he was moving out and going to live with Sarim.

The next morning Sahir called his mother and began screaming at her. They were on the phone for about an hour arguing back and forth. Little was resolved, and Sahir got off the phone in a rage. He told me that he no longer had a mother.

This was just one of many fights he had with his family. All the family members constantly fought. They were always jealous of what the other had. Unfortunately, like April, I was caught in the middle of their quarrels. Sahir told me that from the beginning no one in his family liked April. While it's true I don't care for her, I don't think they should have judged her before they actually knew her. The first time she went to Turkey everyone said bad things about her immediately after she arrived. They hated the fact that she is American, and they didn't like her physical appearance.

Regardless of how they treated me, I still tried to get Sahir to make up with Sarim and his mother. I hated what they did to me, but I told him they are still his family. I didn't like to see family split apart. They were all stubborn, though, and Sahir didn't speak to them for some time.

A few days later Sharif moved out and things quieted down around the house. The good thing about Sharif moving out was that I didn't have to drive to his work to bring him food all the time I could finally get some rest instead of running around like a chicken with no head.

I began feeling sad and used. I had done so much for Sharif since he arrived in the U.S., and in return he spat in my face. When he finally decided to get his license I let him practice in my car. I drove him to and from the test two times (he failed the first time). I even insured his car in my name because his insurance was too high. He later got into an accident and the people in the other vehicle tried to sue me for $2,000,000!

I was now beginning to have doubts about him paying back the money he owed me. How about all the money he owed on my credit cards? How would I ever get the money to pay them off? I kept wondering about how I could have been so naive.

CHAPTER 6
Sahir's Temper and Violence Escalates

Sahir began treating me as if he owned me. Ever since we got married, he regarded me as his property. He became extremely jealous of all males who talked to me or even if they just said hello. I wasn't allowed to wear skirts above the knee or shorts of any kind. He told me that if he caught me wearing them, he would smack me. If I had a different opinion about anything, he would accuse me of being bossy, and he would get angry. He told me that he wanted me to be a Turkish woman, demanding that I keep covered up and do as I was told.

Sahir would reinforce these rules by using scare tactics, such as telling me he would hurt my family or that he would kill me if I ever tried to leave. He even went as far as sticking a knife to my throat. I began feeling like Pinocchio, nothing more than a puppet on a string wanting to be real.

I remember the first time that Sahir displayed extreme jealousy. Sahir, Kayla, Timmy and I went to McDonald's for a bite. While we were there, I ran into one of my former high school classmates, Mike. We used to play softball together and we hadn't seen each other in years. Sahir was in the bathroom when Mike and I said hello. I introduced Kayla and Timmy to

Mike and asked how he was doing. We chatted for less than three minutes and when Sahir saw us talking, he had an angry look on his face.

I introduced Sahir to Mike and explained to Sahir how Mike and I were former classmates. After seeing how jealous Sahir was, I hoped that by introducing them to each other Sahir would realize that Mike was nothing more than a friend. I then politely told Mike I had to go because our kids were hungry. As we walked away, Sahir started giving me the fifth degree. In a jealous tone he demanded to know where I knew Mike from. He didn't believe we were old friends. I once again explained that we knew each other from high school, and I told him that we played softball together with many of our friends. Sahir then went into a jealous rage. He didn't believe a word I said so he proceeded to follow Mike into the bathroom. I was so embarrassed by Sahir's extremely pathetic behavior. I was scared to think what he might say to Mike or if he would go as far as to punch him.

When Sahir returned I frantically asked him what he said to Mike. He said that he yelled at him and questioned him about where he knew me from. Thank God, Mike calmly answered Sahir. He told Sahir about our softball games and explained that he just said hi to me and nothing more. He said that he didn't mean to upset anyone.

Sahir was always looking for a confrontation, and I was thankful that Mike didn't feed into it. All I could think about was how sorry I felt that Mike got verbally attacked by Sahir. What was Mike thinking after all this? Those thoughts ran through my mind for a long time, and I knew I might never get the chance to apologize to him.

When we got home Sahir was still irritated. He kept

questioning me about Mike. He then told Kayla and Timmy to watch TV and that he and I were going in the other room to talk. Seconds after Sahir closed the door, he began hitting me in the head and pulling my hair. He went into a rage of jealousy. I pleaded with him to stop, but it was to no avail. He continued smacking me in the head and face and knocked me onto the bed. I tried kicking my feet to keep him off of me, but he was too strong. I was only about 108 lbs. at the time, and he was a muscular 180 lbs. Sahir then proceeded to throw me to the floor where he began kicking me in the back, legs and stomach. This beating went on for a solid fifteen minutes and didn't end until I began choking and gasping for air. He had kicked and punched me so hard that I felt like I was in a torture chamber.

I lay there quietly sobbing as Sahir left the room. I heard Sahir tell Kayla and Timmy not to worry and that we were just talking. Knowing that they might have known what was going on worried me. I didn't want them to know because it wasn't something a child should have to be exposed to.

I tried to calm down and come out of the room so I could check on them. The only thing they asked was if I was choking in the room. I told them was that I was choking because I had something in my throat. I don't know if they believed what I said or if they were too scared to admit they heard everything. Nonetheless, they never made mention of it again. I then told Sahir I hated him for what he did to me, and I didn't talk to him the rest of the day.

After this incident, I was confused. I was extremely angry at Sahir, but I still loved him. I was also fearful of him, and I hated the control he had over me. He was like Dr. Jeckyl and Mr. Hyde. One minute he could be sweet, and in a second he could be a raving maniac. What was I to do? Even if I wanted to leave, I would always remember his words, "I'll kill you if you ever try to leave!"

The next day Sahir tearfully apologized. He said, "Laurie, I'm so sorry. I don't know what happened. You just got me so angry. I promise it won't happen again. I'm not that kind of person. It's this country that made me this way. I was never like this in Turkey. I just have so much stress."

This was only the first time I heard those words from him, and it certainly wasn't the last. I accepted his apology and felt that he truly meant it. He was upset about what he did, and he shed a lot of tears so I felt he was sincere. In days to come I found out just how wrong I was.

Beating me up came easier and easier for him. He would eventually apologize after each incident to make me believe he was sorry and that he would change. You never knew what would trigger him off. It could be something as simple as teenagers that he saw in a TV movie. He would get jealous over anything to do with teenagers because he would always picture what it was like when I was a teenager. He would accuse me of having many boyfriends, and he would then call me a hooker. Whenever I came to visit him at his work, he would make me face the wall, and I wasn't allowed to say hi to any men who walked in. He even got mad at his 92-year-old male customer who began a conversation with me! The beatings he subjected me to ranged from mild to severe, and he always beat me when no one was around. This way there were no witnesses. There are certain beatings I'll never forget because of the severity of the pain he inflicted on me.

One of those severe beatings sticks in my mind because of the end result. I don't even remember what triggered him off that day because there were so many times he got extremely angry, so it was hard to keep track. During his rage that day he smacked me hard with the palm of his hand, hitting me right on the side of my cheekbone. My face had a huge bump on it and my eye turned black and purple. He panicked because he knew someone would see it. Sahir never wanted anyone to find out because he knew he could get into trouble.

I had to work the next day, but Sahir didn't want me to go. I finally convinced him to let me go by promising him that I'd tell everyone that I fell in the shower. If anyone questioned me about it, I promised to tell him or her I hit my face on the soap dish that was sticking out of the wall. Sahir could care less how he hurt me; his only concern was that someone might find out about the abuse.

After things calmed down and I stopped crying, the only thing Sahir did was look at the terrible black eye he had given me. His only reaction to it was a hard laugh because he thought it was so funny.

When I went to work the next day everyone asked how I got the black eye. I didn't tell anyone the truth. I kept my promise to Sahir and told everyone I fell in the shower.

One of my friends at work said that one of the employees went around telling everyone she suspected my husband had done it. Even though I gave everyone a logical explanation as to how I got injured, I felt that people probably knew the truth about it. I wanted to tell someone how it really happened, but I was too afraid. I was frightened of what Sahir would do to me if I told someone and he found out.

Having no freedom and living in constant fear kept me walking on eggshells. Things were building up inside me, and I was tired of holding it all in. I desperately wanted to tell someone about the abuse.

It was hard putting my feelings aside and working like nothing had ever happened. Every time I would try to do my job, someone would ask about my eye. I had one man actually ask me in a joking laughter, "What happened, did your boyfriend punch you in the eye?"

I didn't think it was funny at all, but I had to pretend to laugh so no one would get suspicious about what really happened. Another thing I also had to put up with was Sharif's laughing when he stopped by to say hi. I was surprised to see him at first because He and Sahir weren't talking to each other (I later found out they had put their differences aside). When he saw my black eye he asked what happened. When I told him the "falling in the shower" story, he thought it was so funny that he burst out laughing.

When I returned home that evening, Sharif came over to visit. Sharif told Sahir that he just couldn't figure how I could fall in the shower and hit my eye in that manner. He went as far as to stand in the shower trying to reenact the accident. He probably knew the truth and that's why he kept asking. I don't know why he had to know. It wouldn't have made a difference. That whole family always thought that spousal abuse is normal and perfectly acceptable. My parents, on the other hand, would be upset. To keep them from worrying, I avoided seeing them for a while. I didn't want them to see my eye. It looked bad, and I knew they would become suspicious. They definitely would have trouble believing my "falling in the shower" story.

A couple of weeks later, Sharif finally made a payment toward what he owed on my credit cards. As it turned out he only gave me enough to pay the interest for that month! He gave me not one penny toward the principal! I said nothing and hoped things would change in the months to come. During this week I finally visited my parents. My eye was still healing, but it was only a little yellow versus the black and purple that it was two weeks before. When they asked about it, I decided to give them the same story that I gave everyone else. My mom kind of raised her eyebrow in suspicion, but I stood by my story. I hated to lie to them, but I didn't want them to know. I knew they would report him, and I feared for their safety. Sahir had always made threats against my family, and I loved them too much to let anything happen to them.

Sahir's jealousy continued to increase as time went on. Now that we had our own apartment, I began bringing Kayla and Timmy over to our place during the day and on weekends. The big problem was getting them there. Sahir refused to let me pick them up at their father's house or vice versa. Sahir was extremely jealous of their father and he forbid me from having any contact with him. He agreed to let me meet Betty, their father's girlfriend, half way.

Betty and I began meeting at a bank located at the halfway point. There we dropped off and picked up Kayla and Timmy. There were times that Betty couldn't make it and their father had to do it. Sahir would become furious even though I didn't speak to their dad. Every time I went to pick the kids up or drop them off, he'd time me to see how long it took. When I returned home he'd interrogate me about who I met at the bank and why it took so long.

Sahir became obsessed with the thought of Tim. He started making bad remarks about him. He knew that Tim was Irish, so he started calling him the Irish Mother Fucker. He would even say that in front of Kayla and Timmy. I would always ask him to not say things like that in front of them, but he would just get angrier.

I made the mistake one day of picking a four-leaf clover up for good luck. I didn't think Sahir knew the correlation between shamrocks and Irish. I didn't dare make that mistake again. Sahir went as far as forbidding Kayla and Timmy to use their last name around him. He also would get mad at the color green because he knew it was an Irish color. I remember how mad Sahir got when Kayla won a ribbon at school for field day. She only had a green one because that was the school color. It was getting so ridiculous. On that same day Kayla and Timmy accidentally left their Catholic religion book on the floor and Sahir saw it. He yelled at them and told them that he didn't want to see that "poison" lying around.

Sahir claimed to be a Muslim who hated the Catholic religion. He wanted me to convert and become a Muslim, but I refused. I told him I couldn't change what I believed in and that I also knew nothing about his religion. His wanting me to convert was just another control issue anyway. He didn't even practice his own religion. While we were married he never went to a mosque and rarely celebrated any of the holidays. He even admitted to drinking wine, which he later told me wasn't allowed.

I grew so tired of Sahir upsetting Kayla and Timmy, and I felt so helpless. I instructed them to keep their religion books and Irish things hidden and to try to ignore his nasty comments. They agreed to not use their last name in front of Sahir. Kayla and Timmy were always wonderful kids. They loved me so much and always tried to keep peace. I have such guilt about what they endured in the past, and I wish I could erase all the bad memories they had.

Sahir took his abuse one step further. His desire for power over me led him to do another unspeakable act. One afternoon he decided that he wanted me to have anal sex with him. When I told him that I didn't want to because it was too painful, he tried to force himself on me. He threw me on the bed and pinned me down. The only thing I could think about was how scared I was that he was going to hurt me. I desperately tried to get him off of me, but he was too strong. Holding my two wrists with his one hand, he proceeded to attempt to sodomize me. I squirmed and struggled with all my might. This had gone on for some time, and as a result, I began to get tired. Panicking that I wasn't going to be able to hold him off much longer, I feared the worst.

As I was about to give up, things suddenly did a turn around. As strong as Sahir was, he, too, got tired, and to my surprise he actually gave up. I hated him for what he did to me that day, and I felt violated. After that incident, the thought of him touching me made my skin crawl.

CHAPTER 7
Pregnancy And The Birth Of Kadin

fter the attempted sodomy by Sahir, I no longer had any desire for him sexually. I hated to even think about him touching me. If I had my way, I would never have gotten close to him again. Regardless of how I felt, I knew it was impossible to deny him sex. Knowing that I would just get beaten up, I continued having sexual relations with him. During those encounters I would place my mind elsewhere. I would try to imagine that I was having sex with someone else. Each and every time I would feel disgusted after, and I wished he would simply go away.

In May of 1993, I became pregnant. I've always loved children, but with this pregnancy I was worried. Knowing the way Sahir and his family treated women, I thought about the terrible life the baby would have if it were born a girl. I also knew Sahir's jealousy and irrational thinking. I feared that if the baby was born with blonde hair and blue eyes, Sahir would think the baby wasn't his. My paternal grandmother had blonde hair and blue eyes, so the possibility was there. I found myself praying for a dark hair, dark eyed baby boy. Normally, having a baby is a special gift that brings so much joy into one's life. It's not supposed to be a time of worry, stress and negativity. The way I was feeling was definitely not normal. Despite my worries, I was still looking forward to the baby and tried to put my fears aside.

I once again had 24-hour morning sickness just as I had with my other two pregnancies. It was hard working with food while being as nauseous as I was, but I needed the money. Two years had passed, and Sharif was still only giving me enough money to pay the interest each month on the credit card bills. Reality kicked in, and I realized he was never going to pay the money back.

I decided to work more hours so I could pay it off myself. I began working 30 to 38 hours a week, which gave me less time to spend with Kayla and Timmy. It was hard not being able to see them as much, but I didn't want my credit to go down the drain. Once the baby was born, I wouldn't be able to work, so this was my only chance to get the cards paid off.

At 26 weeks into the pregnancy I had my first sonogram. The lady doing the test told me that she could tell me if the baby was a boy or a girl. I wanted it to be a surprise, but I was so worried about how the baby would be treated if it were born a girl. I just had to know what it was. Finding out wasn't going to change the outcome, but at least I would have time to prepare myself if it was a girl. When the lady told me the baby was a boy, I was so relieved. Even though I still had to worry about the baby's hair and eye color, at least I didn't have to worry about the gender issue.

Months went by and I worked hard. It was a physical job, and I was exhausted. I made good payments on the credit cards, and the principal slowly went down. It felt good to not owe so much money to the banks, but I resented the fact that I had to work so hard during the pregnancy because of Sahir's family. Sahir did nothing to help me pay the money back, and in addition to that, had the nerve to ask for more money. Ipol called from Turkey and said she was getting married. Sahir wanted to send her $500 as an engagement gift. All the money I made the next few weeks went to Sahir so he could send it to his sister. I was so angry with him, but I knew it was better to keep quiet.

By the time I was 7 1/2 months pregnant Sahir's anger was building inside. He would constantly say negative things about Sarim, April and his mother. He told me he was so angry with his mother that he wanted to smack her.

One evening he decided to drink beer because he was so full of rage. He was one of those drinkers whom one beer would turn into six and the end result would be a loss of self-control. The drinking would intensify his rage. I let him know I was concerned about his excessive drinking that night. He became extremely angry and started yelling at me and telling me to stop being bossy. I became familiar with that look in his eyes, so I proceeded to the bedroom to leave him alone.

A few minutes after I got into bed, he stormed into the room. He was angry that he couldn't find his cigarettes. He kept demanding that I tell him where they were. I refused to admit that I knew where they were because he kept screaming at me. The next thing I knew, he grabbed me by the hair and dragged me out of bed. When I fell to the floor he grabbed my ankles and dragged me to the living room. I began screaming and crying because he was hurting me. While I was on the living room floor, Sahir began kicking me in the back with all his might and wouldn't stop no matter how many times I pleaded with him. He then jumped on top of me and began repeatedly smashing the back of my head on the floor. I became so dizzy that the room began to spin.

Sahir finally got off of me and started raging and screaming about how I got him so angry. I now feared for the safety of our unborn child. Dizzy from the beating, I quietly crept to the phone to call my mom. I didn't want him thinking I was going to call the police because I feared he would grab the phone and possibly kill the baby and me. Sahir thought I was bluffing and that I wouldn't actually call anyone. When my mom answered I told her in a crying voice to call an ambulance. Frantically she replied," Is he beating you? Oh, my God, Joseph, he's beating her!"

I was so scared, and all I could keep telling her was to please call an ambulance. My mom then said to hang up so she could call the police. At that point Sahir became quiet. He didn't know about the police, but it was obvious by the look on his face he feared that he was in trouble because my mom now knew.

Soon there was a knock at the door. When Sahir opened the door an ambulance and the police were standing outside. The only visible evidence of him abusing me was an abrasion above my eye. I had bruises all over my back and legs, but they were hidden under my clothing. Sahir learned to hit where it didn't show. After giving me a black eye from a previous beating, he began hitting me in the head rather than the face. The police kept asking what happened, but with Sahir standing there I was too afraid to say anything. He would surely get back at me if I told, so I kept telling the police that I fell. The police were frustrated. They knew I had been beaten, but they couldn't arrest him unless I admitted what really happened.

The man in the ambulance was kind to me. When he asked if my husband beat me up, I didn't answer. I just kept crying. It was a safe way of saying yes. He probably knew that I would have said no if Sahir didn't do it. The fact that I kept quiet was a tell tale sign that Sahir had caused my injuries. Unfortunately, no one could take action without my testimony. The only thing I told the man was that I was afraid I was going to lose the baby.

I confided in one of the doctors in the hospital, however, of what really happened, but I told her I didn't want anyone to know. The doctor told me the only thing they could do is monitor the baby for a while. No one ever checked my body for any bruises, and I certainly was too frightened to show them. Had they done this, the police probably would have had enough proof of abuse, and they would have arrested Sahir.

I lay in the hospital sad and confused. I didn't want the baby having a father who was in jail, but yet I was fearful that one day Sahir might kill me. I thought that maybe he would change after this incident.

Soon the hospital decided to release me. The baby seemed fine, which was a relief. The nurse told me that my husband was in the waiting room, and she asked me if I wanted him to come in. Hesitant, I said yes. Sahir came in and said he was so sorry. He told me that Sarim was going to drive us home, (he finally made up with Sarim because he had no one else to call). I wasn't thinking clearly and didn't know what else to do, so I went home with him.

The next few days I remained dizzy. This was the second time Sahir had smashed my head on the floor. The first time was during another of his severe beatings. He hit my head so hard and so many times that I was dizzy for months. Every time I would lay my head down or get up, the room would spin. Some days my sense of balance would be off. It's a condition that comes and goes, and I fear I'll have it for the rest of my life.

Sahir kept apologizing just as he always did after he beat me up in the past. I wondered if this time he really meant it. Would it only be a matter of time before he did it again? I was hoping that maybe since the police were involved that it was enough to scare him and that he would change.

About 2 1/2 weeks before the baby was due, I left my job because I knew the baby could come early. Timmy was born three weeks early, so it was possible that this baby could also be early. When I left my job, I was happy knowing I had accomplished what I set out to do. My credit cards were all paid off, thanks to my hard work.

I needed to buy some last minute items before the baby was born, so I decided to do some shopping. While I was at the store I ran into one of Sahir's customers. She was the wife of a doctor. When she saw me, she made a remark about how I looked. She asked Sahir if the baby was okay and said that my belly looked too small considering I was 8 1/2 months pregnant. When I heard this, I started to worry about the baby. I knew Sahir had severely beaten me about one month before.

Worried about the baby, I went to the obstetrician. She, too, said that I was carrying small so she ordered a sonogram. She also said I had been working too hard and that I should take it easy. By this time I had grave concerns about the baby's condition. I started to blame myself, thinking that the excessive work was the cause.

A day or two later I went for the sonogram. I'll never forget what a day it was. I had to drive all the way to the hospital, about nine miles from where we lived. It's not that the distance was so terrible, but rather the conditions I had to drive in. It was snowing hard that day, and my windshield wiper motor died. The visibility was extremely low, so I had to keep stopping.

I knew I couldn't wait until another day for a sonogram because there might be something wrong with the baby. I was frantic, and what should have been about a twenty-minute ride, turned out to be forty grueling minutes of sheer agony. Visions of me getting into an auto accident and fear of losing the baby filled my brain. I was so thankful when I finally made it to the hospital.

A couple of days after the sonogram I found a message from the obstetrician on my answering machine. The doctor said that the baby was retarded in growth and that he only weighed about five pounds. When I heard the message, I began crying hysterically. When I called the doctor back she told me to take it easy and stay off my feet. She also ordered a second-level sonogram to see what the problem was.

When I went for the test I was so nervous. I prayed that my baby was going to be okay. After the test was finished, the lady who did the sonogram told me that she didn't know what the other doctor was talking about. This new sonogram showed that the baby was already about seven pounds and he was doing just fine. I was so relieved to hear her say that! I wondered how the sonogram could have been so messed up. I was upset that the hospital gave me a scare by making such a bad mistake. Nevertheless, I was so thankful my baby was going to be fine. Rather than dwelling on their mistake, I counted my blessings instead.

The baby was born February 26, 1994. He was a beautiful healthy baby boy who we named Kadin. (Sahir actually named him. I had no say in the baby's name). I thought about just how wrong the doctor was about Kadin's weight. Kadin weighed 8 lbs. 1 oz. at birth! He was actually the largest baby out of all of my children. I was so happy he was born healthy and that he had brown hair and brown eyes. I let out a deep sigh thinking I didn't have to worry anymore about Sahir accusing me that the baby wasn't his.

I soon realized I was totally wrong. When the nurse left the room, Sahir looked at me and had the audacity to ask if Kadin was his child! Words cannot describe how I felt at that moment. I was so hurt by his words that I felt like lying to him and saying that Kadin wasn't his child.

Sadness and anger soon turned to fear due to past experiences with Sahir's irrational behavior. Was he going to constantly accuse me of pretending that he was really the father of Kadin? With a forced smile on my face, I told him that Kadin was indeed his child. I hated pretending I was happy when in actuality I was miserable. In time I came to realize that I was going to have to pretend a lot just to survive.

When I arrived home from the hospital, the only thing I wanted to do was rest. I was physically drained and wanted some quiet time with Kadin. The minute I walked into the door, however, April showed up with Omer by her side. She told me Sarim had sent her over to our house to help, and that she was going to stay the entire day.

My stomach hit the floor upon hearing those words! Oh my, God! I thought. I politely told her she didn't have to stay and that I would be just fine. She just told me to shut up. They were her favorite words to use as a way of telling you she was going to do it anyway. In my opinion those choice of words are low class, and I hated it when she used them. No matter how many hints I dropped, she just didn't get the message that I wanted to be alone. I knew that day was going to be a long torturous one.

Omer hadn't been there more than five minutes, and he was already getting into trouble. He was touching everything he wasn't supposed to and making a mess of things. April just sat there totally ignoring him and letting him do as he pleased. I spent the entire day watching him and running after him. I also had to make lunch and dinner for April and Omer while she did absolutely nothing.

By 7:30 pm I became so exasperated that I told her I had to pick up Sahir at work. It was true that I had to pick him up, but I was supposed to go there at 9:30 pm. I told her I was going early because I needed to get some fresh air. The truth was that I needed to get away from her! Thank goodness she decided to go home rather than follow me to Sahir's work.

I wound up having to sit for two hours inside the office at the gas station where Sahir worked. It's not something I would have chosen to do, but at least I could sit down instead of having to chase Omer.

I had a rough time the first month after Kadin was born. Kadin wasn't a good sleeper and he didn't like being in his crib. Every time I would nurse him and try to put him in his crib, he would cry. I told Sahir we should let him fuss a little before rushing right in so he could learn to soothe himself sometimes. It would also give him a chance to get used to the crib. Sahir became angry and demanded I pick up Kadin every time he made a little fuss. He believed that a baby should never cry. I knew Sahir would lose his temper if I disagreed with him, so I did as he said.

I began picking up Kadin every time he cried. This went on all night long, so the only sleep I got was the few times I nodded off when I was nursing him. Sometimes I would be lucky and Kadin would sleep an hour or two here and there. I finally decided to take a nap after I dropped Sahir at work in the morning. Kadin usually slept at that time, so I would sleep from 7:00 am until 10:00 am. I also decided to nurse Kadin in our bed and let him sleep the night there. I believe that children should sleep in their own beds, but Sahir never gave me any other choice. Sahir didn't object to Kadin being there because in his country it's a normal practice.

In time I even went as far as to tell Sahir that the doctor told me it was healthy for a baby to cry, but it was of no use. After a couple of attempts to try to change his mind, I gave up and Kadin remained in our bed.

CHAPTER 8

Vertigo And Attempting To Reach For Help

In the summer of 1995 my dizziness became worse. Every time I laid my head down or looked up at something, the room began to spin. It would cause me to be nauseous, and I had trouble getting up. My sense of balance was off every time I got up from a lying position. Most of the time the dizziness would only last a few seconds, but it happened all the time. Some days I would have it bad where I had trouble walking, and it would last for several hours.

I was becoming worried that I had a brain tumor, so I finally decided to go to the family doctor. At this time I still wasn't ready to tell anyone else about how I got my head injury, so when I went to see the doctor I told him I fell on the ice and hit my head. He referred me to a neurologist for further diagnosis.

When I called to make an appointment with the neurologist, the receptionist told me that the next available appointment wasn't for another three months. I desperately needed to go, so the only thing I could do was suffer from the dizziness and wait.

During the next couple of months I suffered quite a bit. Nothing I did relieved the terrible dizziness I was experiencing. I dreaded laying my head down at night to go to sleep, and getting up in the morning was no better. The only thing I could do was to avoid looking too high up. This would avoid some of the daytime vertigo. As for the imbalance, there were some bad days and some not as severe. On the worse days I avoided standing because it was impossible to keep from falling down.

In October my appointment date finally arrived, but I waited so long that I was no longer having symptoms. I knew the dizziness would eventually come back, but it would be difficult to diagnose without having symptoms during testing. I went to the appointment anyway because the doctor's office was so busy, and I knew it would be a long time before I'd get another appointment. I took Kadin with me to the doctor's office, and while I was waiting to be called into the examination room I had some time to think. I was tired of walking on eggshells and living in fear. I wanted to reach out for help in the worst way. I was so scared, but I decided to tell the doctor the truth about what happened.

The first thing I asked the doctor was if everything I told him was strictly confidential regardless of what it was. After he told me that he wasn't allowed to tell anyone what I said without my consent, I began telling him the truth about my head injury. It felt so good finally letting out what had built up inside me for so long. The doctor asked if I wanted someone from social services to come to speak with me. I hesitated because I didn't know much about social services, but a few moments later I agreed to speak with them. The doctor told me he first had to run some tests, but after he was finished he would send for someone.

The tests turned out just as I suspected. The various tests the doctor performed should have triggered the dizziness, but since I was no longer having any symptoms, nothing happened. As a result, the doctor was unable to make a diagnosis. He decided to send me for a MRI and refer me to an ear, nose and throat specialist to see if there were any abnormalities.

After the doctor completed the tests, he left the room to speak with social services. Immediately after he left, I started to panic. What if Sahir found out I had told someone? He would be furious, and surely he would retaliate! I became so filled with fright that I changed my mind about speaking with anyone.

Quickly, I bolted out the door and left the examination room. As I got in line for the payment window, I overheard the doctor telling someone that I must have changed my mind and left the building. I tried to hide behind the other people waiting in line so no one would see me.

While exiting the office, my heart was pounding uncontrollably. By the time I reached the car, I was unable to catch my breath. After a few moments I calmed myself down. I was disappointed at myself for not having the courage to get help. Going back home to the place where I had to walk on eggshells and be a prisoner was something I dreaded.

About one week later I went for a MRI with the hope that the test would show what kind of injury I had sustained from Sahir smashing my head on the floor. I didn't want to get dizzy anymore, and I guess in my mind I had hoped they would find something serious so Sahir would get in big trouble. The fact that I was still not having any symptoms caused me to be skeptical about anything showing up on the test. There was a chance, however, that they would find out what was wrong with me. I remembered how debilitating it was when I got those dizzy spells so I would do anything to find a way to prevent their re-occurrence.

After the test was completed, the technician told me that nothing abnormal had shown up. I was relieved that I didn't have a brain tumor, but still disappointed that I didn't know why I was getting so dizzy and that Sahir once again got away with beating me up.

A few weeks later I went to see an ear, nose and throat specialist (ENT). This was my last hope in finding out about my dizziness. I was more confident this time that they would get to the root of the problem because the symptoms had come back.

The doctor did various tests, which triggered the dizziness. He diagnosed me with BPPV, which is short for Benign Proximal Positional Vertigo. He told me I was too young to have Vertigo and that usually elderly people get it. He also said that a person could get this type of vertigo from a head injury. I already knew my condition was the result of my head injury, but I was glad to hear it from a professional.

The doctor treated my Vertigo with some kind of machine, which is supposed to disperse these particles that settle inside the inner ear. He also told me about exercises that could be done as a treatment.

By the time I left his office I was still getting Vertigo, but it was a little better. The machine and exercises were only a treatment rather than a cure. The dizziness could still come and go.

I went home that day and attempted to do the exercises that the doctor had told me about. They made me feel so dizzy and sick to my stomach that I gave up. I was now feeling down and thinking I was going to have this disability for the rest of my life. Having this condition made me start to resent Sahir, and I wanted to leave him in the worst way. How could I ever leave without him finding me and killing me? Would he kill me next time he got into a rage? I just sat there on the bed and wept.

The next year or so I spent tip-toeing around just to keep things quiet. I was miserable, but I was going to try anything to prevent any incidents from occurring. Kadin was getting older and was now beginning to understand his surroundings. I wanted him to feel safe and secure, and I certainly didn't want him to copy his father's abusive behavior.

Regardless of how quiet I kept, Sahir still had his moments. His language became increasingly vulgar. Some of his favorite words were *mother fucker*, *bitch* and *shit*. He would constantly use those words in front of Kadin, and when I tried to politely ask him to refrain from using those words, he would get annoyed at me. Even women with children in public who heard Sahir swearing told him that he shouldn't use those words in front of his child. Sahir would just get angry and say something nasty back at them. It got so bad that Kadin started to copy Sahir. I was glad Kadin couldn't say the word correctly because it was embarrassing when he blurted it out in public. I tried to teach Kadin not to use foul language, but it was extremely hard because his father didn't set a good example.

During this time there were no severe beatings because temporarily Sahir was able to semi-control his temper. He knew that Kadin could now talk. If Kadin were to witness domestic violence, he might tell someone, and Sahir didn't want to risk getting into trouble. There was still that tense atmosphere which, in my heart, I felt Kadin could sense. You could tell by the look in his eyes. Even though his father didn't lose total control, he would still grab me by the neck from time to time if something angered him. This would always send me into sheer panic, as I knew the grabbing by the throat was the first thing he would do at the start of a rampage.

I quickly learned how to apologize even if things weren't my fault and how to talk to him if I needed something. Asking his permission for everything like he was some powerful person, and I was the slave, was the key. It could be something as simple as wanting to go shopping with my mom. I had to lower my pride and do whatever it took to get some breathing space.

My parents would ask me to go out to eat while Sahir was at work just to get me out of the house. Even though they didn't know about any other abuse except for the incident when I was pregnant, they could see his jealousy and control over me. I had to downplay the type of restaurant that my parents wanted to take me to, and I had to plead with him to let me go. He would still get jealous, but he allowed me to go with them. It was hard having to act like a slave, and I hated it, but I knew I was going to have to outsmart him if I was going to survive.

I also began lying about who would pick up and drop off Kayla and Timmy when they came back and forth between houses. Even if Tim drove them, I would just tell Sahir that it was Betty. I hated to lie, but it saved me from possible physical harm and mental badgering. I began living my life in survival mode.

From time to time I would run into our landlord Jason, and Adrian our next door neighbor. Since Sahir wasn't home, they would chat with me for a while. On different occasions, they both told me how sorry they felt because in the past they heard Sahir beating me up. They heard me crying and pleading for him to stop. I always wondered why they didn't call the police. I wished they had, but I didn't blame them because I knew they were scared. I enjoyed talking with them when Sahir wasn't home because I felt isolated. Speaking with them gave me an outlet and a chance to be around other people.

I was also glad that he allowed me to visit my maternal grandmother. We were always close, and she was a wonderful person. She was one of the few people who Sahir wasn't jealous about. Nearly every day she would be looking out her window waiting for me to visit. We would spend many hours chatting with each other.

My grandmother, along with the rest of my family, would be careful about what was said in front of Sahir. Everyone avoided mentioning Tim's name in front of him. They all knew Sahir was extremely jealous, and they didn't want to cause any problems for me. My grandmother cared about me so much that at one time, she actually called my phone and left a lengthy message on the answering machine just to erase a message that Timmy left. Timmy had accidentally mentioned his father's name on my machine, so my grandmother went out of her way to cover it up.

Sahir's irrational behavior began affecting my whole family. When he went to my family's holiday gatherings, everyone was tense. My entire family not only avoided mentioning Tim's name, but also things of the past that involved me. Every holiday I had to worry whether or not someone would slip and accidentally say something Sahir didn't like.

In time Sahir became increasingly jealous of our family gatherings because he knew there was so much love in our family and he, on the contrary, always bickered with his family. He didn't like how close we all were. He slowly started coming to the holidays less and less, which for all of us was better since we didn't have to walk on eggshells when he wasn't there.

Sahir suddenly began celebrating some of the Turkish holidays because he was so jealous of how my family always got together and celebrated. He started to pick and choose which Muslim practices he would follow, where previously he never practiced any. He certainly didn't choose to stop drinking when he was angry. He continued to argue with his family over money and other issues, and his fury was on the rise. He was like a ticking time bomb waiting to explode.

CHAPTER 9
Fourth Pregnancy And The Birth Of Kazem

The landlord who leased the property to Sahir's boss decided not to renew the lease. Sahir and Sarim spoke with him about starting a gas station and convenience store business of their own. After several meetings, the landlord agreed to lease them the property.

Since the gas station was already doing business, they concentrated on that first. Sahir had worked there for years, so he knew everything about that business. The only difference was that he was now half owner.

The gas station made good money, so it wasn't long before they started construction on the store. The building used to be a restaurant, so they had to reconstruct the inside. They had a good friend who did construction for a living, so cost was minimal. In no time the store was ready to do business. From the day it opened it drew in many customers. The store turned out to be a successful business, which made a lot of money.

In the beginning Sarim and Sahir worked things out between them. Sarim would be the one to make the business dealings, while Sahir and April would deal with the customers and take care of the inside of the store. I, of course, wasn't allowed to work in the store because Sahir was too jealous for me to talk to anyone. Sahir and Sarim hired a couple of Turkish guys to pump the gas at the station.

In March of 1996, I became pregnant with my fourth child. I was once again happy about being blessed with another baby, but all my worries started to fill my brain again. Those same fears I had when I became pregnant with Kadin started all over again. Would the baby be a girl? How about the hair and eye color? I got a knot in my stomach as I once again prayed to God for a dark hair, dark eyed baby boy.

My nerves were immediately shattered when I began thinking back to the time when Sahir questioned me about whether or not Kadin was really his baby. I was already having 24-hour morning sickness, which didn't help. I also had flashbacks of Sahir beating me when I was 7 1/2 months pregnant. A cold sweat came over my body as those terrible thoughts ran through my head. I knew I was going to have to keep things quiet for the next nine months to ensure the safety of my unborn baby.

One day in late April the safety of my baby was unexpectedly compromised by someone other than Sahir. After deciding to stop at my parents' house for a visit, I got in the car with Kadin and proceeded to drive to their house. The possibility of what was about to happen was the farthest thing from my mind.

As I was traveling down a major highway, I suddenly got this vision as I was approaching the intersection. It was one of those "what if" type of thoughts. The exact words that ran through my mind were, *What if someone suddenly drove right in front of me at the last minute?* I don't know why that popped into my head. Maybe I sensed something.

A second before I entered the intersection, a car drove in front of me. It was a busy intersection, and I had no way of avoiding the car. I had a feeling of unavoidable doom come over me just before our cars collided. With a 50-mph impact, I crashed into the side of the other vehicle. My legs smashed into the dashboard, and my chest hit the steering wheel. I had trouble breathing, and I knew that my right leg was broken.

Panic started to set in as I wondered if Kadin and my unborn baby were okay. In excruciating pain I turned around to see if Kadin was hurt. He was crying, but seemed to be more scared than anything. He had no apparent injuries and when I asked him if he was okay, he nodded yes. I was so glad he wasn't hurt and thankful that the day before I had installed a clip on his seat belt that kept the car seat from moving around. It probably saved his life.

Immediately following the accident a man came to my aid. He was a nice man who kept me calm during the whole ordeal. He stayed there until the ambulance arrived and filled out a witness report to show that the accident was the other driver's fault. I asked if it were possible for him to let Sahir know that I had been injured in a car accident. Without hesitation the man agreed, and he asked where he could find Sahir. He then immediately drove to Sahir's work. I'll always be grateful to him for everything he did to help me. In my eyes he was a Good Samaritan, and I'll never forget him.

By the time Kadin and I arrived at the hospital, I was so upset. I kept thinking about the baby and how I was afraid that something might have happened to it. The nurse told me I was unable to x-ray my chest because of the pregnancy, but that it was necessary to have my right knee x-rayed. I kept asking the nurse what risks were involved concerning the baby, but the only answer she gave me was, "It's not like a drink where you can say whether or not you want it. You have no choice."

After repeated failed attempts to get a real answer, I finally asked the doctor when he came into the room. He said I'd be covered with something to help protect the baby and that the risks were minimal. I don't know why the nurse felt it so hard to say that. She didn't belong working in the ER. She was cold and treated the patients liked they were chopped liver. I was glad that she wasn't the one doing the x-rays. The x-ray technician was much nicer and a lot more sympathetic to the situation.

The doctor examined me and felt confident that the baby was okay. He said I was lucky because I was in the early weeks of my pregnancy. Being that the baby is so small in the early weeks, it's protected during that time. I was so happy to hear the good news. My knee on the other hand wasn't so good. The x-rays showed that I had shattered my knee. In addition to that, the doctor suspected I had cracked my sternum even though he couldn't take x-rays. There was nothing he could do for my sternum except tell me to wait until it healed. I needed reconstructive surgery on my knee, but since I was pregnant, it was impossible to get it done. The doctor decided to splint the knee and see if it improved. I was in so much pain, and I kept worrying how Sahir was going to react with me in this condition.

When I got home from the hospital, I was barely in the door when Sarim and April were already on the phone with a lawyer. They never even asked how I felt or whether or not I wanted to even involve a lawyer. I was flabbergasted by their indifference to my feelings or physical state. Knowing their thinking from past experiences, I could safely guess that their intention was to try to get their hands on money no matter how low they stooped. They probably figured that if I won a lot of money from my case, they could find a way to get it from me.

They wound up getting a lawyer whom they had hired in the past. This made me even more suspicious knowing that he may be in cahoots with them. Sahir went along with their idea, so it was impossible for me to express how I felt.

When the lawyer arrived, he asked me a lot of questions about the accident. He took down all the information and had me sign a retainer. After he was finished, Sarim suggested that I file loss of wages due to inability to work. I asked him why he was thinking of that since I wasn't employed at the time of the accident. He said that he would pretend I was working for him. I told him I refused to commit fraud. I could see Sarim getting annoyed, and I knew Sahir was going to start pressuring me as well, so I also told Sarim that I didn't want to get into trouble.

Seeing that my explanation wasn't helping, I quickly asked the lawyer if I could get into trouble by doing what Sarim had suggested. Even though I already knew the answer, I figured that Sahir and Sarim couldn't argue my point after hearing it from the lawyer. As it turned out, the lawyer had to be truthful, and I was successful in having them forget the whole idea. They weren't too happy about it since it was a lost opportunity for them to get their hands on more money.

After a long stressful day, the lawyer, Sarim and April finally left. Shortly after, Sahir offered to stay home from work a week or so to help me. The only reason was because the lawyer had suggested finding someone to assist me at home. Sahir was much too jealous to even think about the possibility.

Sahir was nice to me the first few days he was home. I was unable to raise my leg on my own, so getting in and out of bed and the shower was impossible without any help. Sahir actually assisted me without complaining. That was pretty much the extent of his help, however. Hobbling around on crutches, I still did pretty much everything I normally did even though I was in constant excruciating pain.

Sahir's little bit of helpfulness didn't last long. My condition became a burden to him, and after a short time he went back to work. My mom began picking me up and bringing me to her house to help out. Regardless of how much pain I was in, Sahir still demanded sex. Within a couple of days after my accident, he expected me to satisfy him. I couldn't refuse, knowing just how temperamental he was. I was so disgusted with him that I would just close my eyes and try to get it over with.

I began going to physical therapy for my knee. Most of the time my mom would take me there, and occasionally Sarim and April would drive. Sahir hated when I went there for two reasons. One was that he was jealous of whom I might talk to, and the other because he hated the fact that people would be touching my leg. He also didn't want to stay home to watch the kids while I was gone. In his eyes it was a woman's job. He would try to make me feel guilty by constantly complaining about it. Every time I would go I would have a hard time concentrating on what I was doing. All I could think about was how angry Sahir was, and how I had to hurry back home.

After two weeks of physical therapy, my leg wasn't improving. The constant pain and difficulty putting weight on it prompted the doctor to do surgery. Since I was pregnant he would only be able to give me a local anesthesia and do an arthroscopy. An arthroscopy is an exploratory surgery where they stick a small camera inside to see what's going on. It's a procedure where they can also remove bone fragments if any exist. Desperate to alleviate the pain and improve the condition of my leg, I consented to the operation.

This was the first time I ever had to have surgery, so I was nervous. I wasn't too thrilled about having a spinal and being awake for the procedure. I would have preferred to be asleep, but because I was pregnant it wasn't an option.

The surgery only took about twenty to thirty minutes, but it seemed a lot longer. My blood pressure was so low that it caused me to feel faint. The thought of them cutting me open made me feel weak. When the surgeon was finished I was extremely glad.

I was able to go home the same day, although I wished I could have stayed overnight. I knew I was going to have to run around when I got home because Sahir always expected me to do everything regardless of how I felt. The only thing he couldn't force me to do was drive. My leg was in no condition to drive, and it would be out of commission for months to come.

When I arrived home that afternoon, the pain was more than I could bear. The only thing I was allowed to take was Tylenol. My leg hurt so much that I had tears in my eyes. The pain I was experiencing was even worse than childbirth.

When Kayla saw me crying she got scared because she thought Sahir had yelled at me for something. Seeing her frightened like that made me realize that she, too, was walking on eggshells. She had never witnessed Sahir beating me up, but she still must have sensed something was wrong. It was likely that she felt the intensity of his control over me and that she had seen his displays of jealousy. While she never witnessed any extreme physical violence at that time, on numerous occasions she had seen him grab me by the neck when he was angry. Thinking back to the McDonald's incident, I realized that she must have known that Sahir was beating me up behind closed doors. Kayla had eating quirks since she was five years old, which I previously linked to my own eating disorder. I was now starting to realize that a lot of it had to do with anxiety.

Timmy also displayed some signs, too, which took me years to figure out. He began exercising excessively to the point where he was doing 500 sit ups a day. I couldn't figure out why he was doing so many. It wasn't until years later that I realized he wanted to become strong so he could protect me.

For the next few months I continued going to physical therapy. At this time I started to develop stomach problems which made me nauseous and gave me a lot of pain. I figured it was caused by the pregnancy and that it would go away after the baby was born. I was in pretty sad shape, and my parents were worried about me. My mom knew how depressed I was. She would take me clothes shopping and I would show her all the different outfits that I liked. I would then let out a depressing sigh and tell her how I wished that Sahir would let me wear them. I was feeling so sad over the fact that I had no life and that there was no way out.

Sometime during the summer, the insurance company paid me about $5600 for my totaled car. As soon as I received the check, Sahir told me that Sarim wanted to borrow the money for the business. I didn't trust Sarim, and I would soon have to buy another car, so I was reluctant to lend him the money. Sahir insisted I lend it to Sarim and told me not to worry because he would make sure Sarim would pay me back. Boy, I had heard that one before! I had no choice but to give Sahir the money.

About two weeks went by and Sarim had not yet returned the money. Sahir told me he was going to take the money from the business because he knew it was the only way I was ever going to see it again. It wasn't that he cared about me getting back my money, but rather he needed transportation. Sahir sensed that Sarim hated driving him everywhere, so he needed me to drive him. Seeing that my leg was getting stronger, he knew that I would soon be able to drive again. He realized the only way it was going to happen was if I had the money to buy another vehicle. Sahir was too chicken to learn how to drive himself, so that money was his only ticket to ride. When Sarim found out Sahir had taken the money back, he wasn't happy. The tension between the two was on the rise.

Shortly after getting the money back, Sahir and Sarim went looking for a car for me. Sarim wanted me to get a cheap unreliable car, probably so he could get his hands on the rest of the money. Sahir found a used mini van, which was in better shape, and I had just the right amount of money to purchase it. Shortly after purchasing the vehicle, I began driving. I was still in a lot of pain, but I didn't want to give up trying. I was tired of constantly being in the house. Sarim and April weren't too impressed that I bought the mini van. They even made a comment to Sahir about me having to buy the more "expensive" one.

Toward the later part of the summer, Sahir got into another heated argument with Sarim. I don't recall the exact issue, but it had to do with money and the business. Sahir became furious with Sarim, and even though he was half owner of the business, Sahir walked away from it. He told Sarim he wasn't going to do business with him anymore. I knew Sahir would never walk away from what he put into the business, but I also knew how stubborn Sahir could be when he was angry. It was obvious that it would be some time before he made up with Sarim and went back to the business.

Sahir began talking with Omar who also was an-gry with Sarim. He was presently still living with Sarim and April and wanted to move out. He asked Sahir if he could move in with us. Sahir wasn't thrilled about Omar moving into our apartment. His jealousy about having a man living so close to me bothered him. Despite his jealousy, Sahir agreed to let Omar live with us, and the only reason he agreed is because he knew that he needed an ally.

The idea of having Omar live in our apartment was hard for me, too. We had two small bedrooms and only one bathroom, which was located inside the spare bedroom. Since I was pregnant at that time, I had to urinate a lot, which meant I would al-ways have go through Omar's room to use the bath-room. Another problem was that the spare bedroom was Kayla and Timmy's room when they were with us, so they were going to have to sleep in the living room. I mentioned to Sahir how uncomfortable I was having Omar there, and he agreed that when the baby was born he would tell Omar to move out.

After Omar moved in with us, things turned out even worse than I expected. It was only a short time before problems arose. One problem was that it was already crowded in our apartment to begin with, but to add to all our clutter, Omar had about ten garbage bags full of his things, which sat in the corner of the room. There was also a lack of privacy. Kayla, Timmy and I weren't comfortable walking in his room to use the bathroom, especially at night. It's hard to relax when someone is right outside the door. Another problem was Omar's lack of good aim. Every time he used the bathroom he would urinate all over the toilet seat and floor! He wouldn't even lift the seat when he used the toilet! Every day I had to clean and mop the bathroom three to four times and it was frustrating!

On top of all these problems, a nightmare occurred. It was totally unexpected and horrifying. Kayla and Timmy were rolling around on a fold up chair/bed we had in the spare room. When they were done playing, I lifted it to straighten it out, and to my shocking surprise there was a loaded gun underneath it! I couldn't believe Omar would leave a gun right there where the kids could reach it! What if it had accidentally gone off while they were playing? I was so upset that I was stuck for words. I immediately put the gun out of Kayla and Timmy's reach and called Sahir at work.

Sahir confronted Omar about the gun and the only reply that Omar gave was, "Don't worry, the gun has a safety on it. It's not dangerous."

What a dumb reply! I was wondering if he had

any brains upstairs. Sahir told Omar that we didn't want the gun in the house. Even though Omar claimed he got rid of it, not a day went by when I didn't worry that the gun would turn up somewhere in our house. Luckily, we never saw it again. Sahir was starting to regret his decision to let Omar stay with us.

Omar helped Sahir find a new job by recommending him to a friend who owned a gas station. They immediately hired Sahir, not only because he was a friend, but also because of Sahir's experience. The station was farther away, so I had to do more driving back and forth. When Sarim heard that Sahir got a new job, he attempted to work things out between them. Sarim had difficulty running the business alone, and he knew that he needed Sahir. Despite the attempt, Sahir wasn't ready to give in.

Things at home became tense due to the resentment Sahir and I had developed toward Omar. Omar was always bad with money. I don't know what he ever did with all the money he earned, but he was always broke. Desperate for money, he asked Sahir if he could use my credit card to charge some gas. Without my knowledge or consent, Sahir gave him my credit card number. When he told me what he did, I couldn't believe it. I was so angry inside. I had worked so hard paying back all the charges his family put on my cards in the past. Now, to top it off, Sahir gives his friend my card. I had to calmly explain to him that Omar couldn't be trusted because of his money problem. Sahir said not to worry and that Omar only needed to fill his gas tank that one time. I had such an uneasy feeling about the situation, but I didn't want to push the issue and have Sahir fly off the handle. I decided to remain quiet and hope for the best.

A couple of weeks went by, and I received the statement for my credit card bill. To no surprise there were three charges on my credit card that Omar made. Two were gas fill ups and one was a cash advance. I immediately told Sahir about the charges, and to my amazement he actually listened. He agreed to let me change the number on my credit card. He then confronted Omar about the extra charges he made. Sahir was now so angry with Omar that he decided to kick him out of our apartment. Broke and having nowhere to go, Omar decided to move back to Turkey.

After Omar moved out Sahir became depressed about having no one in his family to talk to. He constantly said negative things about all of them, and his mood and state of mind worried me.

I was in my seventh month of pregnancy when Sahir's temper finally got out of control again. It was one afternoon when something set him off. I don't recall what it was because it was usually over nothing. He grabbed me by the throat so hard that I couldn't breathe. He attempted to lift me by my neck while he was strangling me. I frantically tried to gasp for air, but he held my neck so tight that I was unable get any. I passed out from the lack of air, and the next thing I knew Sahir was throwing water on me to revive me. He panicked, thinking I wasn't going to wake up and that he would be in trouble.

Sahir started to laugh when I came to in an attempt to downplay the seriousness of the situation. He tried to make a joke of it so I wouldn't tell on him. Of course, he then started the apologizing again and telling me that I just made him so mad. I was so upset at him that I actually told him I wanted to divorce him. He threatened me and said that he would take the kids to Turkey if I ever left. He also said that I would never see them again. I was petrified upon hearing those words! The thought of losing my children was more than I could bear. I refused to talk to Sahir the rest of the evening, so he slept in the spare room that night.

In the morning Sahir approached me with tears in his eyes. He said he was so sorry and that he didn't want to lose me. He promised he would never hurt me again. I don't think I totally believed him because he had said that so many times in the past, but I accepted his apology and hoped he would change. His words about taking the kids if I left kept ringing through my head. I was going to do anything to keep them from disappearing.

On December 5, 1996 our second child was born. He was a beautiful healthy baby boy. Sahir had already decided many months ago that the baby's name would be Kazem. Like our first child, I had no say in the matter.

Immediately after I gave birth, Sahir's mother entered the delivery room. She was visiting Sarim and she somehow was able to sneak into the room. I was surprised the nurse had allowed her to come in right after the delivery. I was a little upset that the nurse didn't ask me whether or not I minded having visitors. I was extremely exhausted and would have preferred waiting until the next day. Nonetheless, I still greeted her with a warm smile and made her feel welcome.

Sahir's mother told Sahir that Sarim was downstairs in the waiting room. He wanted to make amends, and he had a gift for Kazem. Sahir still refused to speak with Sarim even though I tried to get him to forget their differences. After a short visit, Sahir's mother went home with Sarim.

I was scheduled to have a Tubal Ligation after Kazem was born. I was happy with the four wonderful children that I had and didn't plan to have anymore. Sahir and I had discussed the matter months ago, and he didn't object to me getting the procedure.

Shortly after Sahir's mother left, the nurse came into the room and told me that the doctor decided to do the Tubal Ligation right away rather than waiting until the next day. I was tired, but thought it better to get the surgery over with. The nurse wheeled me downstairs to prep me for the surgery. Just as she was about to put a catheter in me, another nurse came in and said that they would have to do it first thing in the morning. I didn't mind the change in plans because this way I could get some rest.

First thing in the morning the nurse walked into my room and said that an emergency surgery had to be performed. This would cause a delay in my operation. I was starting to get hungry because I hadn't eaten since early the day before. I was hoping I wouldn't have to wait too long. I was also nursing Kazem so I was quite weak from being so hungry.

As the day went on, the nurse came in about every hour constantly changing the information on the surgery. One minute she would tell me the surgery was still on for that day, but that it would be a little delayed. The next minute she would tell me it was canceled. It was driving me crazy, and I was so hungry that I felt like I was going to faint.

At 5:00 pm my parents came to visit. I was so light-headed that I had trouble seeing them. I broke out in tears because I was so weak and frazzled. My mom immediately told the nurse that I hadn't eaten in 25 hours, and she pleaded with her to do something about the situation. Since it was too late for the surgery, they rescheduled it for first thing next morning and finally gave me something to eat. I never thought I could be so hungry! The doctor also decided to keep me in the hospital an extra day so I could recuperate after the surgery.

When morning arrived I waited for the nurse to come in and take me for the Tubal. At about 9:00 am she came in and told me that the surgery would be delayed again. I became extremely upset knowing that I might once again wait the entire day and possibly not even get the procedure done. I was hungry and didn't know when I was going to be able to eat. I decided to wait it out and try not to get myself too crazy.

Three more hours went by and still I got the run around. I finally called my mom and in a tearful voice told I her what was going on. Whimpering, I told her I couldn't take another day of not eating and playing that "on off surgery game" that the hospital was playing. My mother immediately called the hospital and complained. To my surprise, within minutes of her phone call, the nurse came in my room to prep me for surgery. My mom was such a lifesaver!

I initially decided to have the surgery without the use of painkillers because they usually made me feel sick. The only thing I planned to have was a spinal. Early in the procedure, though, I started feeling pain and pressure on my stomach, and I started to panic. No sooner than I told the surgeon, something was put into my intravenous. Boy, was I in "lala" land! I was glad they gave me something for the pain after all, because I then didn't feel a thing!

After that episode everything went smoothly, and it was over before I knew it. I felt good after the procedure, and I barely had any pain. I was extremely surprised that the pain medication didn't make me queasy. Another thing I was surprised about was the fact that the nurse even remembered to feed me right after the procedure. I was happy to have it over with, and I could now enjoy some quality time with Kazem.

CHAPTER 10
Increased Health Problems And More Surgeries

The day I returned home from the hospital I was tired, and the doctor had advised me not to drive for two weeks, since I just had surgery. Regardless of my condition or the instructions given to me by my doctor, Sahir requested that I pick up his mother so she could visit. Not only did he have me drive to Sarim's house to get her, but also he sent me to Pizza Hut to get some pizza for dinner. After her visit I also had to drive her back to his brother's house. I spent the entire first evening home running around like a chicken without a head. I didn't dare complain about the situation, as I was familiar with the consequences of saying anything. Even if I was able to say something, I wouldn't have had the strength.

The first month was an exhausting one. I made many attempts to put Kazem in the crib, and he wouldn't sleep at all. He would cry the minute I put him in there, and Sahir once again expressed his belief that babies should never cry.

After one month of getting virtually no sleep, I decided to let Kazem sleep in our bed. I was so tired that I was like a walking zombie. I was still driving Sahir to and from work, but in addition to driving him, I also had to load and unload my two-year-old and new-born baby. I felt bad for Kadin and Kazem that they had to go back and forth in the cold weather.

I became so drained that toward the middle of January I became sick. I got a bad stomach virus, which left me unable to move. Lucky for me, Kayla helped take care of Kadin and Kazem, and the worst of it only lasted a day.

On top of everything else, I got the worst news ever. My mom called and said that my grandmother was diagnosed with lung cancer. I was so devastated to hear the bad news. I was always so close to her that ever since I was a kid, I always worried about her dying one day. When she lived with my parents, I used to check on her before I went to bed to make sure she was breathing. I couldn't bear the thought of losing her.

A few days later my mom told me that the doctor was going to try radiation to shrink my grandmother's tumor. My grandmother was already going on eighty years old, so there was only so much they could do for her. I prayed that I would have at least another twenty years with her. I knew that was asking a lot, but I loved her so much and cherished every day with her. Even though I was skeptical about how success-ful the radiation was going to be, I wasn't about to lose hope.

Sometime within the next month or so, Sahir finally made up with Sarim. Sarim pleaded with him to come back to their business. He told Sahir he couldn't run it without him. This boosted Sahir's ego, so Sahir quit his job and went back with Sarim. I used this opportunity to ask Sahir if Sarim could drive him to and from work because it was hard on Kadin and Kazem going back and forth every day. Knowing what a power trip Sahir was always on, I asked him in a kind and needy voice, which to my surprise worked. I didn't expect he would agree, and I felt a weight lifted off my shoulders when he did. It might have been a small weight, but anything helped.

I was once again feeling ill due to my vertigo and stomach problems. The pain and nausea would get so bad that I couldn't move my head at night. In addition to that, I also had so much pain in my knee that it kept me limping and gave me difficulty with stairs. I decided that rather than sit there suffering, I was going to have to do something about my problems.

The first thing was to take care of my knee problem. When I talked to the doctor about the lack of improvement in my knee, he suggested another surgery. This one would be a little more extensive. It would involve another arthroscopy, and in addition to that a lateral release. A lateral release would be a procedure to enable my knee to move around more freely. I agreed to the surgery, hoping it would improve my knee.

Toward the end of May I went to the hospital for the operation. The doctor still gave me a spinal even though I requested to be put to sleep. He felt the anesthesia would go into my breast milk if I got anything more than the spinal. I even checked with the pediatrician to see if my breast milk would be safe for Kazem if I had regular anesthesia. The pediatrician told me that once the anesthesia wore off, it was safe for the baby to drink because it wouldn't sedate him. Regardless of what the pediatrician said, the orthopedist refused to give me anything other than the spinal. Since I didn't have a choice, I figured I'd make the best of it.

The procedure only took about forty minutes, and everything seemed to go well. I once again went home the same day and knew I'd be running around as soon as I stepped in the door. I had a lot of pain after the surgery, and I got a negative reaction from the spinal. To top it off, I had a migraine headache, which didn't go away even after taking Advil. My mother brought me to her house so I could rest a bit. She knew that when I returned home I was going to have to run around taking care of everything, and that Sahir would offer little help.

About a week or so after my surgery, I continued going to physical therapy. When my leg became strong enough, I was able to drive myself once again. Going to therapy became more stressful mentally. Sahir's jealousy increased again. The thought of a man touching my leg consumed his mind to the point where he began timing the visits. When I returned home from a visit, he'd get angry and ask why I took so long. During every physical therapy appointment I concentrated on hurrying home rather than improving my knee. I'd sometimes ask to skip certain exercises just so I could get home faster. I think the physical therapist sensed something was wrong at home because he had a certain look on his face although he never pried into my affairs.

I was growing tired of Sahir's unwarranted interrogations. I felt like no matter what I did I'd have to explain myself. I was always faithful to him and never gave him any reason to be jealous, so I would always ask myself why he wouldn't trust me. I didn't know how much longer I could go on like that.

As time went on, I resented the fact that Sahir had all the freedom, and I was a prisoner who had absolutely nothing. He could wear anything he wanted and go any place at any time he pleased. There were numerous times when he even went to Manhattan with Sarim and Sharif looking for hookers. Sahir would tell me he was looking for a hooker for Sharif and that he was going to sit in the car and wait until Sharif finished with his business. He'd wind up staying out all night and never even call to let me know he wasn't coming home. I found their behavior disgusting, and I didn't believe Sahir's story for a moment.

By that time my feelings toward him had diminished so much it didn't matter to me if he'd been with another woman. I had actually wished he would cheat on me so I could get enough courage to leave. I figured that if he cheated on me, he couldn't say anything if I left him. In my mind, I also felt that if he found someone else, he would leave me alone. The only thing that did concern me, however, was the chance that he'd contract a sexually transmitted disease and give it to me. It worried me so much that I even had Kazem tested for AIDS after he was born. In my heart I knew there was a good chance that Sahir slept with a hooker, although I never had any proof of it.

Sahir's trips to the city became less frequent in months to come. Sharif found a girlfriend named Deb, a customer of Sahir's. I think Sharif used Deb more for sex than a serious relationship. Even though she was his girlfriend, he would tell her he was going to marry a Turkish girl one day. He would also tell her that the Turkish girl wouldn't have as big of a heart as she had, but would be more beautiful than she.

Deb and I became friends. She would constantly tell me how Sharif dumped on her. Most of the time I'd see her crying about how Sharif treated her. I felt so sorry for her, and I had often wondered if he physically abused her just as Sahir was abusing me. She always denied it when I asked, but I felt as if she just kept it hidden.

In my opinion, Sharif would also have used her for a green card if he could have. Deb was still legally married, so it wasn't possible. He wound up marrying a drug addict instead who needed the money. It was another of Sahir's customers from the gas station. Sarim and Sahir paid her $5000 to do a phony marriage to acquire the green card. Sharif and the girl never lived or spent time together.

To add to Deb's stress, April became jealous of Deb just like she did when Sahir met me. She started bad mouthing Deb when she wasn't around. Sarim sided with April like he always did, and they began treating Deb like dirt. Deb would always ask me what she did to deserve that kind of treatment. I had to explain to her that she did nothing wrong, and that April's jealousy was the cause. Deb finally decided to keep her distance from Sarim and April and not let their blabbering bother her.

Even though Deb and I were friends, we didn't spend much time together. She was too busy working and constantly running around catering to Sharif's every need. From time to time we'd chat a bit, and I confided in her about Sahir's temper. I don't think I got into real detail about how abusive he was. I was careful what I told her. Even though Sharif didn't have deep feelings for her, it was evident that she loved him. I was afraid she'd tell Sharif everything I told her. After dealing with Sahir and his family for so long, I learned not to be too trusting of people, especially anyone connected to them.

In November of that year my knee was still giving me problems. I couldn't seem to get rid of the pain and still had trouble walking and descending stairs. I wasn't satisfied with the orthopedist whom I was presently seeing. He didn't have much of a personality, and the only thing he could ever tell me about my knee was that it would get better. It certainly wasn't the case. It was already 1 1/2 years since the accident, and there wasn't much improvement. A friend had recommended a different orthopedist whom he knew. I decided to give him a try in hope that he had an alternate solution to improve the condition of my knee.

When I met the doctor, I was impressed with his personality. He was friendly, unlike my previous doctor who was cold as ice. He was ambitious and gave me a sign of hope that there was a chance he could help me. The doctor suggested another surgery that would be even more extensive than the previous two. It was another Lateral Release, which would enable my kneecap to move even more freely than before. He was confident that it would be a good solution to my problem. I quickly agreed because I was ready to try just about anything. He scheduled the surgery for the end of the month, and to my relief the anesthesiologist agreed to put me to sleep during the procedure.

The day of the procedure started out rocky in the morning. Sahir was in one of his moods and was yelling at me for no reason. He was on his jealousy kick again about the doctor being a man. He didn't like the idea that I'd only have a hospital gown on and nothing underneath. Sahir got pretty heated just before I left. Thank God my dad arrived to pick me up before things got any worse. My dad saw me in tears and knew right away that Sahir had done something to make me cry. He kept asking me to leave Sahir, but I knew it wasn't that easy. Even though my dad didn't know about all the threats and abuse that was going on, he knew about the incident when Sahir beat me while I was 7 1/2 months pregnant with Kadin. I'm sure that in his mind, he suspected there were more.

When we arrived at the hospital I told my dad not to wait around. I knew he'd just be sitting there and that there was nothing he could do, so I told him I'd call when I was done. I remember sitting in the waiting room feeling so alone. Everyone had loved ones supporting him or her, and the only one I had was a raving lunatic at home who only cared about himself. I had to hold back the tears because I knew if I started to cry, I'd never be able to stop. That was a time that I needed a hug.

The surgery was done within an hour, and the doctor told me everything went well. After a couple of weeks of healing, he wanted me to resume physical therapy. He was confident that my knee was going to show signs of improvement. His positive outlook and warm personality helped me think positively. It was the first time since my injury that I believed my knee would get better. It was always like a breath of fresh air to be around someone as kind and sympathetic as the orthopedist. Unfortunately I knew that I'd soon have to once again go home to a dangerous madman.

CHAPTER 11

Sabih Comes To America

On April 29, 1998 Sahir's youngest brother Sabih came to the United States. Sarim and Sahir were able to pay someone in Turkey to get an illegal visa. It was a guy they knew who worked in immigration. He had connections and was able to obtain the visa for the right amount of money. I don't recall the exact amount, but I remember the cost being in the thousands. Sarim and Sahir wanted to bring their sisters to the U.S. as well, but it was difficult to obtain a visa for young girls, which made it impossible to get one illegally.

Sarim and Sahir were glad Sabih came to the U.S. because now they had another brother who could help run their business. Their mother, on the other hand, was becoming increasingly resentful and jealous because she wanted her boys to live in Turkey with her, although she still liked the money Sahir and Sarim frequently sent to her. It wasn't long ago that we helped pay for her new house, and she was already looking at another new house to buy. The more money that was sent to Sahir's family in Turkey, the greedier they became.

Sabih was the only one in Sahir's family, aside from his younger sister whom I only met in Turkey, who was always nice to me. Regardless of whatever quarrels went on between Sahir's family members, he always smiled at me and spoke in a polite manner. When Sabih first arrived, he didn't speak any English. Sahir would have to translate so we could communicate. Even though I couldn't understand what he was saying when he spoke Turkish, I could understand through his gestures that he was trying to be friendly. Eventually he did learn to speak pretty well in English. Regardless of how nice Sabih seemed, I remained cautious about getting too close to him. He was still from the same family, and I had witnessed his temper in Turkey. He smacked his sister pretty hard when he was mad at her.

On different occasions I witnessed the severity of not only Sahir's temper, but also his brothers' tempers. Sahir and his brothers opened a second gas station and hired some Turkish workers to pump the gas and work the cash register. One evening, a group of three guys in their late teens came into the store looking to buy cigarettes. They gave the cashier a hard time before they finally left. When the worker told Sarim and Sahir what happened, they became furious. They promised the worker they would track the guys down and beat them up.

Sahir and Sarim kept their promise. One night Sahir came home and told me that he and his three brothers found the teenagers who were bothering the worker. They jumped the three teens and began punching them in the face and head so hard that they left them bloody. Sahir said that one of the teens was in such bad shape that he must have gone to the hospital. I was horrified upon hearing about their act of violence. It was true that the teens did something wrong, but they definitely didn't deserve to be beaten up. Also, no one has the right to beat someone to a pulp. Sahir and his brothers should have let the police handle the situation.

After hearing what happened I wanted to call the police and report the incident. I felt sorry not only for those kids, but also their parents. They must have wondered who could do something so terrible to their sons. I wondered if the teens were okay. The fact that I was unable to tell a soul what had happened that night left me feeling helpless. Sahir knew I was the only other person he told. I didn't want to think about what he would do to me if I called the police and he found out.

This wasn't the only incident involving the beating up of another person. On a different occasion, another incident occurred at the same gas station. Sharif was the one working alone this time. He, too, was bothered by someone, except this time it involved only one guy. Not only did Sharif grab the guy and pin him against the wall, but he also repeatedly punched him in the face. He beat him up so severely that the police actually arrested Sharif rather than the guy. The guy's face was all bloodied up, so the police didn't have any trouble telling that Sharif had assaulted him. Sahir and his brothers thought they were so tough beating people up. Sahir always told me that everyone else was "Chicken Shit." He seemed to like that phrase a lot.

As a result of Sahir and his brothers beating up the teenagers, Sabih sustained an injury to his hand. He broke his knuckles and needed to go to emergency. April was instructed by Sarim to take Sabih to the hospital and give false information so the hospital bills would be paid. April pretended that Sabih was Sahir and filled out all the paper work under Sahir's name.

I found out about the insurance fraud when a hospital statement came in the mail. Knowing that Sahir didn't have a hand injury, I was puzzled as to why the hospital sent the statement. When I questioned Sahir, he told me the story. Somehow it didn't surprise me that they would do something so low. I had hoped Sarim and April would get caught in their fraudulent plan, but they never did. I was once again in no position to open my mouth. They would know I reported them since no one else knew about it.

The health insurance fraud wasn't the only time they committed such an act. Somewhere around the same time I had knee surgery, April got into a car accident. She wasn't injured in any way, but she pretended that she hurt her knee. After the accident she decided to go for surgery so she could file an injury lawsuit against the other driver.

Sahir had informed me of Sarim and April's plan. He told me Sarim said that April didn't get hurt in the accident and the only reason she was going to have the operation was to get money from a phony lawsuit. I also knew this to be true because of a previous conversation that I had with April prior to the accident. She told me that she had suffered with arthritis in her knees ever since she was a kid. It wasn't difficult putting two and two together. Further evidence of this was the fact that April's only treatment was an arthroscopy to eliminate the arthritis in her knee. This was actually the second car accident where they sued for phony injuries. I'm surprised that no one ever investigated them, and I wish someone had.

In addition to their fraudulent schemes with insurance, they had also done some crooked business dealings in the past. Sahir had told me of instances where Sarim had switched the gas in the tanks at the station. He had run out of super unleaded, so he siphoned the gas from the regular unleaded tank and put it in the super-unleaded tank. As a result, the customers were paying for super, but only getting regular. Sarim and April had also collected many cigarette coupons and sent them to the companies for reimbursement even though the cigarettes were never purchased. I'm sure there were many other illegal things they did that I didn't know about. Since Sahir was in business with Sarim, I had always worried about Sarim and April's crookedness. If they did something illegal with the business, I didn't want to be held accountable. I had no clue as to how they did their other business dealings, and I didn't care to know. I was glad that even though Sahir was half owner, the business was in Sarim's name. I didn't want any part in it and the less I knew, the better.

As the months passed Sabih had a run-in with Sarim and Sahir. He felt that Sahir and Sarim were using him for the business. He didn't like the fact he had to work the graveyard shift and that he was working so many hours.

When he finally got fed up, he got another job at some other gas station. Finding another job gave him more free time, so he finally found a girlfriend, which was something he so much desired. She had two children from a previous marriage, which didn't seem to matter to him. Sabih always loved kids, and it seemed as though he treated them as his own. It looked as if he was sincere about how he felt about his girlfriend, unlike Sharif who used Deb.

I don't know how bad the argument was between Sabih and his brothers because nothing was discussed at our house. Whatever discussions they had took place at Sarim's house. From what I could see, they were angry at Sabih's decision to work elsewhere, but they were still talking.

As fall approached my grandmother's condition took a turn for the worse. The radiation had shrunk her tumor temporarily, but it began to grow again. I felt myself falling apart when I heard the bad news. I didn't know how much time I had left with her, and I was extremely sad knowing that I might lose her soon. The thought of her dying was more than I could stand. Losing her was something I had feared for so long. I didn't know how I was going to go on without her.

By Thanksgiving her health began to deteriorate. She was often asleep, so I tried to visit every day and talk to her when she was awake. One of the last times she was fully awake during one of my visits, Sahir actually came with me. My grandmother knew in her heart that Sahir was a jealous man, and she always worried about me. She was always careful of what she said to him even on the visit that day. She looked Sahir right in the eyes and said, "Don't fight anymore." She then looked at me and said, And don't you be stubborn, too."

She knew that Sahir was the only one responsible for his actions. She only said something to me so she could get her point across without making him feel singled out. She knew his temper and feared what he would do behind closed doors if he got angry. Sahir actually laughed after she said it because he knew the point she was trying to make. I was surprised that he didn't get offended and angry as he usually did.

As my grandmother's condition worsened, I couldn't get her off my mind. One day I decided to clean out some of the toy totes we had at home to keep myself busy. I came across an alarm clock my grandmother had given Sharif when he lived with us. It was an old clock she no longer needed. Sharif had trouble waking up at that time, so she told me he could have it. When Sharif moved out, I let the kids play with it so it was no longer in good shape. I was going to throw it away, but a thought came to me. It was one of my superstitious thoughts that were caused by fear and the OCD I still suffered from. I felt if I threw my grandmother's clock away that her time would be up. After that moment of thought I clung on to that clock so tightly and put it back where I found it. I wasn't ready to let go of my grandmother.

By Christmas my grandmother was in grave condition. She barely opened her eyes and ate almost nothing. She only had a sip of water now and then. Seeing her cling to life made me depressed. I thought back to the last thing I told her before she could no longer communicate. I told her I couldn't live without her. Thinking back, I realized how selfish it was to tell her that. It seemed as though she was holding on because she knew I needed her.

By the beginning of January she was no longer eating or drinking anything. She wasn't receiving any hydration intravenously because that was her wish. She came down with an extremely high fever due to dehydration. I had seen her suffer too long, and I loved her too much to see her continue to suffer. On the night of January 9th I prayed that her suffering would end and before I went to bed I threw her clock away. It was one of the hardest things I ever had to do. It hurt so much that I cried hysterically.

That night at about three o'clock in the morning she passed away. I was crushed from losing her, but happy that she was no longer suffering. I felt good knowing God was watching over her. I knew she was probably in heaven with my grandfather whom she missed so much.

The next couple of days my family held a wake for my grandma. To my surprise, Sahir attended the wake on one of the days. Seeing her lifeless body lying there was hard for me. I already missed her so much. We went to a Chinese restaurant to eat something after the wake was over. It was the first time that my grandmother wasn't there with the rest of the family. I felt such emptiness inside without her, and I could barely eat a thing. It was one of the saddest moments of my life. I felt like she left me behind, and I wanted to go with her.

Sahir refused to go to the funeral, and I was just as glad. I paid my last respects to one of the most special people in my life and without Sahir there, I could do it in peace. I think my grandmother would have preferred him not to be there, too. Many people attended her funeral because she was a wonderful person who touched the lives of many. She'll be greatly missed, and remembered by all who knew her.

CHAPTER 12
The Final Year

The landlord decided to have his son move into the apartment that Adrian and Carlos lived in. I was sad that I wouldn't see my friends next door anymore. I knew Sahir would never allow me to visit them. It was easy to sneak a visit while they lived right next door, but with Sahir keeping such close tabs on me, it would be impossible to sneak a visit elsewhere. I don't think Adrian and Carlos were too happy about the move either. Not only were they happy living in that house, but they also spent a lot of money putting in wall to wall carpeting. They never expected that the landlord would tell them to move out.

Shortly after Adrian and Carlos moved out, the landlord's son, Colin and his girlfriend Lea moved in. Sahir became even more jealous than before. Colin was a strong-minded young man in his early twenties. Sahir didn't like the fact that Colin was a young guy living next door and also hated the fact that he was Greek. Sahir was always prejudiced of everyone who wasn't Turkish, and even more so about certain nationalities. He had this ridiculous qualm over the situation with Cyprus. He didn't like Greek people because he said they're trying to take Cyprus from Turkey. He would even go as far as insisting that the Greek salads

I ate were actually Turkish salads. He talked about it so much that I couldn't stand to listen to it anymore.

Sahir would even make remarks about my own heritage and the heritage of some of my family members. He would brag about how Genghis Kahn invaded China. My mom is Chinese, and he was always so jealous of her because she's an independent person. He would always tell me that she was trying to break us apart. He didn't like it when I went shopping with her, and although he didn't forbid me to go, he was angry every time I went. He also would make negative remarks in front of me about Jewish people even though I have Jewish relatives. Things he said were hurtful, and the only thing I could safely do was tune him out. At one time I actually had the courage to tell him of my disapproval over his prejudiced behavior, but he just laughed at me and continued his racism.

In April of 1999 Sahir decided to take the kids and me to Disney World in Florida. I was excited because we never took a family trip together that included Kayla and Timmy. Sahir would once in a while do something nice, but it had to be his idea and under his control. From previous experience, I knew going to an amusement park meant I would have my usual restrictions. I wasn't allowed to wear shorts or sit next to anyone other than my children on a ride, and there was to be absolutely no talking to any men other than Sahir. The control Sahir had over me was something that I hated, but at least the trip got me out of the house and around other people. It also made me happy knowing that the kids would be able to have some fun.

We left for the trip right at the start of Easter break. We anticipated that it would be the most crowded time of the year to go, but it was the only time we could get everyone together. Kayla and Timmy would be off during the summer, but Florida is too hot at that time. Sahir planned a one week vacation so we could also go to the other parks.

When we arrived at the motel, everyone was excited. The first couple of days went smoothly. Sahir was in a good mood, and I was careful not to set him off about anything. Even though I took extra care in watching every step I took, I knew in my heart it was only a matter of time before something would change Sahir's good mood.

It wasn't long before my inner feelings came to pass. We went to a breakfast buffet one morning. During the course of our brunch, Kayla and Timmy put some bacon and sausage on their plates. When they went to sit down, Sahir saw that they had pork on their plate and became angry. They didn't realize that it would bother Sahir if they ate it. They knew he didn't eat pork (one of those Muslim teachings that Sahir chose to follow), but they never figured it would upset him if they ate it in his presence. Sahir became so angry that he made them sit at another table. They apologized to him, but he ignored the apology and remained angry. I was so sad to see them look so puzzled and excluded. I wanted to sit next to them, but I knew Sahir would lose it if I tried. Sitting in that restaurant seemed like an eternity. When the brunch was finally over I was extremely glad. Lucky for us, Sahir calmed down when we arrived at the park.

The rest of the day was calm, with little or no trouble, but by evening Sahir's temper heated up once again. I don't know what flared him up, but he wound up screaming at me in front of the kids. They looked so frightened and never said a word. To my surprise Sahir actually apologized to Kayla and Timmy. He told them he loved me and didn't mean to yell. I don't know if he said that just so they wouldn't tell anyone about his temper or because he really meant it, but whatever the reason, he actually remained calm the rest of the trip. He even changed our flight and extended the trip for four days more.

The day we were to fly back to New York was hectic. The flight was early, and I myself had to get four children dressed and ready. I was the one to drive and get the rental car returned. Having to do everything without Sahir lifting a finger was difficult. By the time I finished and got in line to check in, the plane was leaving in thirty minutes! When I saw the huge line I almost fell over. I feared we weren't going to make the flight. All I could think was, what are we going to do if the plane leaves without us? We have four children with us and Sahir is going to freak out!

When we finally reached the check in, the man told me that the plane just left. After hearing him say that, I was ready to cry. The man suggested we check with Delta to see if they could take us (we were booked with U.S. Air). When we spoke to the people from Delta, they were extremely nice. They said they were full, but they could put us on standby. If someone didn't show up, they would take us at no extra charge. I began praying for an opening.

As the time approached for boarding of that flight to begin, I became nervous. Sitting at an airport until the following day would be nearly impossible with four children. Just then we were called to the counter. They had a space for us! I was so happy and grateful to them. They did us a great favor that I'll never forget. We got home only a couple of hours later than we planned, and I was so relieved when we walked in the door.

A couple of weeks passed, and the stress caused by Sahir's controlling temper was slowly building inside me. My stomach problems became so bad that I decided to go to the doctor. When I went to see our family doctor, he suspected that I had IBS (irritable bowel syndrome). He referred me to a gastroenterologist for further evaluation. I hated going to doctors, but I could no longer live feeling the way I did. I was always pretty healthy before I met Sahir, but after I met him everything seemed to go downhill.

When I met with the doctor, she agreed that the symptoms were typical of IBS, but she told me she would have to run a series of tests to rule out anything else. The first two tests she scheduled me for an endoscopy and sigmoid. The endoscopy involved sticking a camera down my throat to see if I had an ulcer. The sigmoid involved going into the colon to check for polyps. It's similar to a colonoscopy, but not quite as extensive. I wasn't thrilled about doing the procedures, but I knew it was necessary.

My mom took me to the hospital the day of the tests. Sahir stayed home to watch Kadin and Kazem. The doctor only sedated me during the procedures, but everything went smoothly. The only thing she found from the testing was that I had gastritis (erosion of the stomach lining). I was thankful I didn't have an ulcer.

Shortly after lunch I arrived home. The minute I walked in the house Sahir yelled at me and asked why I took so long. He then asked, "What were you doing for so long? Were you having a party over there?"

Sahir then rushed out the door with his friend and left me home with a huge mess to clean up. I felt like I was just hit by a Mack truck. I wanted to cry, but I didn't want to upset Kadin and Kazem, so I put my mind somewhere else and worked on cleaning up the mess.

In the midst of going for all my testing and taking care of my health, I received a phone call from my lawyer. The insurance company from the driver who caused my accident wanted to settle. The amount they offered me wasn't quite as much as I thought I should get considering all the pain and suffering I had gone through.

After much thinking, I decided to settle anyway and put the money toward a house so my children would have a better place to live. Our apartment was much too small, and some new houses were being built right around the corner from where we presently lived. They were reasonably priced and were selling out fast. I was lucky that I went down there immediately because I bought one of the last lots they had. The house wouldn't be finished until the latter part of the year, so it gave me some time to get myself healthy again before the move.

In May of 1999, the doctor sent me for a test to see if my gallbladder was functioning properly and whether or not I had any gallstones. The test came back negative for gallstones, but showed that my gallbladder was borderline dysfunctional. I had to make a decision as to whether or not to have it removed. My paternal grandmother had trouble with her gallbladder and required surgery to have it removed. Based on family history and more importantly my desire to try anything that could possibly eliminate my nausea and pain, I decided to have the surgery.

Several days before the surgery Sahir had another fit of rage. He locked me in the room and proceeded to punch me in the head. I began kicking desperately to get him off of me. He hit me so hard that I couldn't bear the pain. Sahir suddenly snapped out of his fury when Kadin knocked on the door. I was lucky that he didn't want the kids to find out about his beatings. I don't know what else he would have done to me had Kadin not knocked on the door. Knowing that Kadin and Kazem might have heard what was going on was upsetting to me because I didn't want them exposed to Sahir's violence. I prayed that if they did hear something, they wouldn't understand what the commotion was about.

After Sahir's attack on me I went into the shower and began sobbing. I spent the entire time trying to think of a way to leave him without the kids disappearing. Not one single possibility as to how I could do that came to mind. Feeling helpless, I cried even harder.

The day of my surgery Sahir invited Omer to stay overnight because Kayla and Timmy were there. I wasn't going to be home until the next day, so Kayla offered to help watch Kadin and Kazem. Sahir complained that he whacked his side on the corner of his pigeon coupe and that he had a hard time moving. Kayla told him not to worry because she was going to help out. I had such guilt knowing that Kayla would have so much responsibility placed on her. All I kept thinking about was how fast I would try to come home. I knew the Turkish way of females waiting hand and foot on all males. Sahir had reinforced that rule every day, and I didn't want Kayla to be treated like a slave.

I slept for quite a while after the surgery. The hospital gave me pretty heavy doses of painkillers, which made me extremely tired. The nurse kept telling me that I was sleeping too much, but I couldn't seem to stay awake no matter how hard I tried.

When I finally attempted to sit up, I became dizzy from the morphine they gave me. I felt like I was going to be sick, so I laid my head down while in a sitting position and fell back asleep. The nurse then tried to get me to walk around to get the anesthesia out of my system. I had difficulty breathing due to chest pains. There was a lot of air trapped in my chest from the surgery, so it was difficult to walk. Regardless of how bad I felt, I knew I had to get back on my feet for my children, so I kept pushing myself.

The doctor had me on a liquid diet. All I was allowed to eat was Jell-O and Italian ices. The thought of eating something sweet made me feel sick, so I ate nothing. I craved something solid and salty, but the doctor felt it was too soon to have anything other than liquids. The lady in the bed next to me was happy because I kept giving her all my Jell-O and Italian ices. She enjoyed them quite a bit.

The next day I still didn't feel well, but I knew I had to hurry home. My children needed me, so I was going to do anything to leave the hospital that day. I still craved a piece of bread or anything solid. I hadn't eaten in two days, and I was starving. After many requests, the nurse finally sent in some real food late in the afternoon. Eating something solid gave me a bit of strength, so I felt it was time to go home.

The nurse was unable to find my doctor and couldn't release me without her consent. I insisted I was feeling better and that I had to get home. She went out of her way to find a doctor on call, who could examine me and sign the consent form so I could leave. Physically I wasn't ready to leave. If the circumstances were different I would have preferred to stay in the hospital one more day, but I just had to get home for my kids. For some reason I had an uneasy feeling.

When I arrived home poor Kayla was exasperated and almost in tears. When Sahir went outside to smoke a cigarette, Kayla and I had a chat. She said that the entire time she ran around waiting on everyone, Sahir did nothing but lie on the couch. Omer ordered her around like she was his servant. I felt bad for her having to go through all that. I gave her a big hug and thanked her for all her help. She said she was happy to do it for me and that she was just upset about the way Sahir and Omer treated her.

A few hours later my mother drove Kayla and Timmy back to their father's house. I was glad Kayla could get some rest because I knew she was tired from all the running around. She was probably also happy to get away from Sahir and Omer ordering her around.

The next morning I felt nauseous and had a difficult time breathing. By afternoon I developed a high fever and I felt sick. My difficulty with breathing got so bad that I started to panic because I felt like I couldn't get enough air. Deb drove me to emergency, and when I got there the nurse took me in to get x-rays. The doctor wanted to make sure that I didn't develop pneumonia from the anesthesia. The x-ray came back normal, and they couldn't find anything wrong with me other than the fact that I had a fever. The doctor said that if I wanted to I could stay the night in the hospital. I knew I had to get home for the kids, and I didn't see any point in staying if there wasn't anything he could do for me, so I went home.

When I arrived home Sahir said he would stay with me to make sure I was okay. I was relieved that he offered to stay because I still couldn't breathe right. Just as I was thinking about how nice it was that he cared about me, Sahir suddenly started asking me when I was going to go to sleep. He asked it in such a way as if he was rushing me. The minute after I lay down to try to close my eyes, Sahir headed right for the door and said he was going to see his brothers. He stayed with me not more than ten minutes before he was gone. I managed to block out all the bad feelings I had that night, and I finally fell asleep.

A few days after my surgery, my brother Corey and I had a sixtieth birthday party for my mom. We had planned it long in advance, so even though I still didn't totally recover, we decided to go on with the party. I was excited about surprising my mother, and I was also looking forward to spending time with the family. My children and I always loved getting together with everyone. Sahir refused to go to the party, and I was happy about him not coming. Not having him there meant that I could enjoy myself without having to watch everything I said.

My children and all my relatives also looked a lot more relaxed without Sahir being there. They, too, didn't have to watch their every move. We all had a great time, and I kept thinking about how I wished my life were always that relaxing. Feeling free was something I hadn't felt in a long time. I almost forgot what it was like to be able to make my own choices without getting yelled at or beat up for it. It made me realize just how much I longed to have my freedom back.

About a week or two later I spotted an ad in the newspaper for a Huey Lewis concert at Westbury Music Fair. He was one of my favorite singers, and when I saw that he was performing, I thought about how much I would love to see his concert. The last time I

113

saw him perform was more than ten years earlier. I just had to go!

I thought of a plan to ask Sahir using a begging type approach. It was obviously going to be difficult because Huey Lewis is a guy, and I knew that Sahir would be jealous of him. If he said yes, I thought it would be great if my Aunt Bernice and Uncle Jake could come. They came with me to Huey's concert the last time, and I knew that they, too, loved his music. Sahir had always liked Bernice and Jake, and for some reason he never had any jealousy toward them, so I knew that me asking them to come wouldn't be a problem. I had to plan my approach carefully before I made any moves to ask Sahir.

After much pondering, I finally had the courage to ask. There weren't too many things I'd dare to ask him, but this was one of the few, and I was nervous. He actually didn't get angry when I asked him about the concert, but I could tell he wasn't impressed. He said he was planning to go to Turkey with Sarim to visit his family and didn't know if he could go. (He didn't want me to go without him). He said he had to talk to Sarim as to when they would leave, then he'd give me an answer. I would have preferred to go without Sahir, but if it was the only way I could go, I'd jump at the chance.

By the next day Sahir told me Sarim wanted to go to Turkey the same week as the concert. It was so convenient that it just happened to be the same time. It was as though Sahir had planned it that way just so I couldn't go. I begged him to let me go and promised to take Timmy with me. To my surprise, he actually felt secure enough to let me go. He probably figured that no one would flirt with me because I had a child with me. I don't know what his thinking was, but it didn't matter because I was allowed to go, and he wasn't going to be there. I was elated over the thought! The only two things left to do were to ask Bernice and Jake and buy the tickets. I was praying everything would work out.

When I called Bernice and Jake about going to the concert, they were delighted. They said that they'd love to go and appreciated me asking them. I was so excited when they told me they'd go. I told them I'd pick up the tickets right after I got off the phone with them. Immediately after hanging up, I rushed down to Ticketmaster where I was able to purchase four great tickets. We were going to be only seven rows back! Things went so well that day that I thought I must have been dreaming because it was too good to be true.

When I got home and told Sahir about the tickets, rather than being happy for me, he gave me a look of disappointment. It was evident that he had hoped I was unable to get tickets. I quickly changed the subject and spoke no more about the concert. I was hoping his preparation for the trip to Turkey would help occupy his mind. This way he wouldn't spend all his time thinking about how I was going out somewhere without him.

A couple of weeks before his trip to Turkey, Sahir planned another family trip to Lake George, New York. He decided to take Omer on the trip because Timmy was coming with us. Sahir would frequently invite Omer to our house and on family outings, not because he wanted to see him so much, but rather because he was always jealous that I have two kids from a previous marriage. He did love Omer, but sadly he used him as a tool to get back at me. Sahir would always show how jealous he was over the fact that he wasn't the father of Kayla and Timmy. He would blurt out hurtful nonsense such as, "The Irish mother fucker has two free kids (referring to Kayla and Timmy's father). You left your two kids (referring to my divorce). You're a hooker."

Sahir wouldn't even celebrate Mother's Day until Kadin was born. He used to get so angry if he heard someone wish me a Happy Mother's Day. Upon hearing those words, he would say to me, "What's this Mother's Day thing? Do you think I'm going to wish you a Happy Mother's Day?"

More and more Sahir would say those horrible things in front of Kayla and Timmy. He would upset Kayla to the point where she began resenting him. The cruel things he said would make her so angry. She's the oldest of my four children, and probably the most perceptive about his behavior. It was evident that she wanted to tell him off, but she kept quiet out of fear of what he might do.

Kayla was unable to go with us to Lake George because during that time she went to China with my mom. I was so happy she could go on such a wonderful trip. She could spend quality time with my mother and learn about her heritage. China is a beautiful place to visit, and many people would jump at the chance to have a three-week vacation there.

I missed Kayla a lot when she didn't come with us, but I knew she was better off with my mom. She could get away from Sahir's controlling personality and actually enjoy her surroundings. If she went on our trip, she would spend most of her time tip-toeing around as usual. At that time, a good family trip meant everyone succeeded in keeping Sahir's temper at bay. I was so sad I could never offer my children the kind of life they deserved. Would God ever answer my prayers and help free us from Sahir's grasp? I never totally gave up. Deep in my heart I kept holding on to the small hope that there would be a way out of the hell I was in.

Just before Sahir was to leave for Turkey, Bernice called and said that she and Jake wouldn't be able to come to the concert. My Cousins Lara and Jacob, their daughter and son, would be returning home from China that day. They wanted to be there when Lara and Jacob returned. They felt bad about not being able to go, so they kept apologizing. I was disappointed, but I completely understood their situation.

When I told Sahir that Bernice and Jake couldn't go, he replied by telling me I was no longer allowed to go. I quickly came up with an alternate solution by suggesting that Kadin go with us. Kadin was old enough to sit still during the concert, and I knew he would probably enjoy going with us. I figured that maybe my parents wouldn't mind watching Kazem until we got home. I hated to ask my mom since she would be returning from a long trip the same day. At least Kayla could help her since she would be at my parents' house.

Lucky for me, Sahir agreed to my proposal. I could tell he still wished I couldn't go, but he didn't forbid me probably because he knew Kadin would be there. Having another child there made him feel more confident that no men would talk to me. He probably also had it in his mind that Kadin would tell him if anyone talked to me.

Bernice offered to have me, Timmy and Kadin sleep over after the concert because Westbury Music Fair is located near her house. She figured this way I wouldn't have to drive home so late. When I presented the idea to Sahir, he became jealous and insisted I drive right home after the concert. I didn't want to push my luck, so I didn't press the issue. The only thing left to do was to ask my mother, but I had to wait until she came home. I kept my fingers crossed.

I was so happy when Sahir finally left for his trip and also lucky that he didn't force me to go with him. The pain and stiffness in my knee I still suffered from gave me a good excuse not to go. Sahir also knew that Kadin and Kazem couldn't sit for that long a period of time. Dealing with their fussing was something he would never have the patience to do. I was so thankful because I didn't want to go back to Turkey.

I also didn't want Kazem and Kadin to go there. Sahir kept telling me how he wanted to make them into Turkish citizens, and that was something I definitely didn't want! He had threatened so many times to take them to Turkey, and getting a Turkish citizenship would make it easier for him to do just that. I feared the day when Kadin and Kazem got a little older and Sahir insisted they go to Turkey. I just had to keep them safe, but how?

Things became quiet and relaxing at home without Sahir there. I felt like a human being again now that I had space to breathe. I kept wishing he would stay there and never come back. He would be gone a month, so I was in my glory. The kids even seemed more relaxed since he left. Sahir's presence always put tension in the atmosphere. Even Colin and Lea next door picked up on Sahir's controlling behavior. They appeared to be fearful of him, so they always kept their distance.

Several days after Sahir left, the builders began framing our new home. The kids and I were so excited that we would drive by every day to see the house being built. It was a nice new neighborhood, and my children would have their own yard to play in. They would also have their own room and bathroom.

Moving into the new home would be the perfect time to transition Kadin and Kazem into sleeping in their own beds. It would also be the perfect opportunity to get them to bed earlier. Sahir got them in the habit of staying up until 12 or 1 o'clock in the morning. He would play with them and get them all hyper late at night. It was definitely time for a change. Kadin would be starting school in the fall, so he needed to learn to get to bed at a descent time.

The day finally came when my mom and Kayla arrived home from their trip. I had missed them so much so I was happy to see them. I kept feeling guilty that I had to ask them to watch Kazem because I knew they were going to be tired.

As it turned out, my dad had already asked my mom by the time I got to their house. I felt awkward about the situation, so I was happy that I didn't have to be the one to ask. Knowing just how much the concert meant to me, my mom agreed to watch Kazem even though she was so tired. She knew I never got out and that it was one of the few opportunities where I could actually enjoy myself. A huge smile appeared on my face because I was so happy I could go. Timmy and Kadin were looking forward to the concert as well. It was the first time the three of us could go on an outing together without a care in the world.

Huey Lewis put on an excellent concert that night. We had a great time singing and dancing to his music. There was no one watching our every move, and we could enjoy ourselves for a change. If Sahir were there, I would never be able to sing and dance, and I know for a fact he would spend the entire time being jealous and angry. I had almost forgotten what it was like to have such a good time.

The time Sahir was away seemed to go by so fast. Before I knew it, he was back home again. I missed having the freedom that I enjoyed while he was gone. It was back to the caged life I was living. I remember one morning when I was sitting at the breakfast table alone. I stared at Sahir's birdcage in the corner of the room and realized I was no different than those birds. I felt like a canary in a cage, and all I could think about was how much I longed to be free.

During the next couple of months my knee began improving. I was walking much better, and the pain lessened quite a bit. I was pleased with the doctor whom I was seeing. He kept his promise and did everything he could to help my knee problem. It was the best my knee had felt since the accident. I wasn't totally pain free, but it was a big improvement from before. I was grateful to him for being so kind and helpful.

My stomach on the other hand wasn't doing well. I had hoped that the gallbladder surgery was the cure for my ailing stomach, but it wasn't. The doctor continued sending me for different types of tests to rule out other problems. She sent me for a catscan and a colonoscopy, which came out normal. She suspected it was indeed her first thought, which was Irritable Bowel Syndrome, but she wanted to do one more test.

After thinking about it a while I decided not to have the final test. I figured I went through enough and I was pretty confident that she was right about her first diagnosis. It all made sense when the doctor had told me that stress causes IBS. Sahir had caused me a lot of stress for years. I'd been taking so much from him and holding it all inside. The only thing the doctor could do for me was to prescribe a stomach tranquilizer. I knew the stress wasn't going to disappear, so all I could do was try the medicine and hope it would at least help.

CHAPTER 13
The Life Changing Incident

In the fall of 1999, Kadin started going to school. He had difficulty sitting still and concentrating on his schoolwork. When his class began learning how to write, Kadin struggled and became frustrated. I had to sit with him every day and consistently have him practice so he could get the hang of it. After much effort, he finally learned how to write his name. In time he learned how to write more and more, although he continued to have problems sitting still.

After one month of being in school, Kadin began rocking back and forth in class. His teacher became concerned and called me to set up a conference so we could discuss Kadin's problem. When I met with her she told me she felt that Kadin had anxiety about something. When she showed me how he was rocking, I told her I felt that it was just a habit he had when he couldn't sit still. Kadin was always a bit hyper when he was little, and I guess I was used to seeing him move about. The teacher agreed that maybe he was just a bit antsy.

After I went home, I got to thinking about what his teacher had told me about Kadin's rocking. Was it possible that he was anxious? His father's temper had been slowly building, and perhaps Kadin sensed something was going to happen. I, too, was full of anxiety. Things had been quiet for a while, and I felt Sahir could blow at any time. I hoped Kadin wasn't stressed. He was a small child who should be having fun and living like a child is supposed to.

Toward the end of October, Sahir finally blew his fuse. He was angry that I had a different opinion about something. He grabbed me by the throat and dragged me into the bedroom. He closed the door because all four of my children were present. He began punching me hard in the head. I started to scream and cry because he was hitting me so hard. I tried to get away and run out the door, but Sahir threw me to the floor just as I was opening the door. Sahir grabbed me by my ankles and started dragging me into the kitchen.

Horrified by what they saw, Kayla and Timmy begged him not to hurt me. I felt so bad that they had to see him beating me up. Sahir quickly calmed down upon realizing that the kids were watching and getting upset. He then went outside to smoke. While he was outside I quickly took my children into the spare bedroom and closed the door. I put on some music to get their minds off the incident. We were all extremely upset so we huddled together and tried to listen to the soothing music. During that time I was afraid Sahir would come into the room and start again, but luckily he stayed away.

The next day, after Sahir went to work, I sat on the end of the bed crying. I couldn't take anymore of Sahir's abuse. I didn't want my children to see another episode like the one they witnessed the night before. Desperate for help, I talked to my deceased grandmother and asked her to please say prayers for my children and me. I asked her that if she was listening and could reach out and help us, to please do whatever she could.

Feeling helpless, I picked up a stuffed bear that my mom gave me a while back. She gave it to me because she knew I was under a tremendous amount of stress. She told me to shake the bear anytime I was sad (the bear had a rattle inside). At that moment I gave the bear a shake, and I began crying uncontrollably. How was I ever going to get away from this monster? I spent the entire day pondering that question, and I still had no answers.

November 6, 1999 was the day my whole life changed. It started out as a typical day until Sahir returned home from work that evening. Shortly after dinner, a chain of events began that turned my life upside down. Kadin and Kazem were watching TV and listening to one of their favorite songs. I heard "Mambo #5" playing on the TV, and from the corner of my eye I saw them dancing to the music. I then overheard Sahir telling them the song was no good. In a nice tone of voice I told Sahir there was nothing wrong with the song, and that Kadin and Kazem always liked to bop around when they heard it. He got into an instant rage and said, "There's a bad video!"

The video only showed some women dancing with short skirts. It wasn't so terrible, but I apologized anyway and told him I didn't see that there was a bad video. He then yelled at me, "Well, you should have seen!"

Before I knew it, Sahir's face was about two inches from mine. Afraid he was going to attack, I told him to get away from me. The next thing I knew, he grabbed me by my neck. I screamed and asked him to leave me alone. He dragged me into the bedroom and threw me on the bed. He began punching me in the head so hard that my skull felt like it was cracking.

Kadin picked up one of his toy trucks and began hitting Sahir in the head frantically, trying to stop him from hitting me. Kayla and Timmy pleaded with Sahir not to hurt me. Sahir turned in Timmy's direction and started to head toward him. I was so afraid that Sahir was now going after him, so I held Sahir's arm and tried to hold him back. Sahir screamed at Timmy to get in the room.

I banged on the wall and screamed for help, hoping that Lea and Colin would hear my cries. I then tried to reach the phone to call the police. This was the first time that I thought my children were in danger, and I was going to stop at nothing to get the police to the house. Kayla saw Sahir approaching, so she lay across my body and begged him not to hurt me. First he grabbed the phone from my hands and threw it across the room, almost hitting Kayla in the head. The phone broke into pieces when it struck a brick wall. He then grabbed Kayla by the arm and threw her to the floor. Kayla was lying on the floor crying that her arm hurt.

While Sahir was distracted I tried to run into the living room to grab the other phone. Just as I was about to pick up the phone, Sahir smashed it against the wall. Frantically, I made a run for the door, but before I could make it, he grabbed my hair and threw me on the ground. He then dragged me by the hair into the living room. He proceeded to kick me in the back and stomach. I was in such agony from the pain that I could barely breathe. His rage was so out of control that I feared for my life. Just as my body was about to give way, Sahir grabbed me again and threw my head into the wood of the couch. I hit my head so hard that I collapsed on the floor and began gasping for air.

Sahir began throwing water on me to revive me, then realized Timmy was gone. While I lay there on the floor crying and feeling half dead, Kazem laid his body over me crying in sheer terror.

Sahir was now panicked because Timmy was nowhere to be found. I'm sure Sahir feared that Timmy ran away to get help. Just then, there was a knock at the door. When Sahir answered and saw the police standing there, he turned white. He tried to look like nothing happened and that he was a concerned parent looking for one of his missing stepchildren. He asked the police if they knew where Timmy was. Looking puzzled, the police asked him who Timmy was. Sahir now tried to speak softly and politely because he didn't want to get in trouble. He was always good at putting on an act when he had to.

Already knowing just what had been going on, the police took me outside and asked me what happened. I was extremely frightened, but I told the police everything. I knew my children were in danger, and I was going to protect them. They asked if I wanted to press charges, and fear once again paralyzed me. I had such a look of fright in my eyes that the police didn't make me answer. They told me they didn't like the looks of things and that they were going to arrest Sahir. I was so relieved they didn't make me say anything else and that they were going to arrest him.

Sahir was totally shocked when the police came back into the house and arrested him. He probably figured I would be too afraid to tell the police the truth. Suddenly this raging tyrant turned into a frightened child. Sahir was good at beating up and scar-

126

ing those who were weaker than he was, but when someone with authority finally stepped in, he changed into a totally different person. I was glad the police finally put a stop to his abuse.

After they arrested Sahir and took him to jail, my mother and Kayla's stepmother came to my apartment. Timmy then returned to the house. When I asked where he went, he said that he had jumped out the bathroom window and went to a neighbor's house for help. I was so proud of him for being so brave. I was also sad my children had to witness such a horrible incident and that Kayla hurt her arm trying to protect me.

Physically and emotionally drained, I felt like I was just run over by a car. My body ached from all the beatings, and my head was dizzy from hitting it on the couch. I was so full of confusion and mixed emotions. I felt as if it was the beginning of the end of my life.

An ambulance took Kayla and me to the hospital. A police officer took pictures of the large bump on my forehead. I can't even describe how I felt at the time the photos were taken. I just wanted to be somewhere else. The officer was sympathetic to my feelings and apologized for having to put me through any more than I had been already. Kayla and I were then examined to determine if we had any serious injuries. I was so thankful that Kayla's arm wasn't broken. She had risked her life for me, and I'll always feel guilty about it. I was so glad she wasn't seriously injured. She had some bruising and a sprain, but her arm was going to be okay. The doctor advised my mom to keep watching over me during the night to make sure I didn't have a concussion. After a few hours in the hospital my mom took me to her house, and Kayla went home with her step mom.

By the time I got to my parents' house, it was late. My head was pounding from hitting my head and crying so much. Kadin, Kazem and I tried to huddle together to get some sleep. I had a hearing to go to first thing in the morning, so I needed to get some rest. Even though I was extremely exhausted, I was much too upset to fall asleep. My head throbbed the entire night and flashbacks of the incident constantly filled my brain. I knew I wasn't going to get any sleep.

When it was time to get up in the morning, the only thing I was capable of doing was to continue crying. I had cried the entire night and still was unable to stop. My mother tried to get me to function, but the only thing I was able to do was get in the car to head down to the courthouse. By the time I arrived, I looked like the walking dead. My eyes were swollen from crying so much, and I had no make-up on. The only clothes I had were those I wore the night before. I had on a tee shirt and sweat pants (something I would never wear to court under normal circumstances). My forehead had a huge bump on it, and I looked tattered and torn.

My mother and I, along with Kadin and Kazem, sat in the lobby of the courthouse. Almost immediately after, Sahir's defense attorney approached us. He tried to tell me that Sahir still loved me in hope of getting me to drop the charges. I began crying even harder because I was so confused. My mom told him straight out that he shouldn't be talking to me and that he should go away. I'm glad she's strong and wise. She helped protect me at that time when I was weak and vulnerable. Had I been alone, it probably would have been easy for Sahir's lawyer to take advantage of me.

While I sat there waiting to be called into the

courtroom I stared out the window feeling all alone. I was glad I would be able to go home and not have to answer to anyone, but wished I had a loving spouse who treated me with respect. Why did I have to go through this torture? I felt like I had died and gone to hell.

Just before I was supposed to enter the courtroom, a lady approached me. She was an advocate from the Women's Coalition Against Domestic Violence. She was a sweet lady who offered a lot of support. She helped me file an Order Of Protection for my children and me against Sahir. She also supported me during the hearing and spoke out on my behalf.

Sahir was charged with third degree assault and the judge gave me a temporary Order Of Protection. Sahir was to have no contact with Kayla, Timmy, Kadin, Kazem and me by any means. He was scheduled for a hearing at a later date to determine whether or not he was found guilty of the charges against him.

Before I left the courthouse, the advocate gave me the number of VIBS (Victim Information Bureau). She told me they offer counseling for battered women. I took the phone number and thanked her for everything she had done for me. I was in need of support and looked forward to speaking with someone from that organization.

After the hearing was over, we headed back to my apartment. I dreaded going back there because it was a terrible reminder of the incident that had occurred the previous night. I also had so many bad memories in that apartment, and I wanted nothing more than to move out. When we arrived home, Colin from next door asked if I was okay. He said he was going to come over with a gun that previous night, but Lea stopped him. I wished he would have called the police instead, but I guess in the end he chose not to get involved. Maybe he was afraid. I don't what his reasons were for not helping.

The next morning, after Kadin left for school, I called his teacher and requested a meeting. My mom offered to watch Kadin and Kazem so I could talk to the teacher after school. When I met with the teacher I told her all about the incident with Sahir and his previous abuse. Tears poured down my face as I told her everything. Knowing what a terrible ordeal I had just been through, she comforted me while she listened.

After I was done speaking she offered her support and told me I could call her anytime. She said that she would watch over Kadin and call me if he had any problems. She also sent me to the school social worker to talk to him and arrange for Kadin to meet with him on a regular basis. He could provide counseling for Kadin to help him get through the trauma he experienced. I was grateful for all the help she offered me.

Right after leaving the teacher's room, I headed down to the social worker's office. When I met with him, I was pleased. He was a nice man with a heart of gold. He sat and listened while I told my story. I once again began crying as I spoke. He was kind and showed a lot of support, which I was in dire need of. He agreed to meet with Kadin once a week and told me to call anytime I needed to talk. He set up an immediate crisis appointment for Kadin because he knew Kadin was probably holding a lot inside. When I left his office I felt a great sense of relief. I, too, had been holding in so much. It felt good to let it out and talk to people who cared.

After talking to Kadin's teacher and the social worker, I called Kayla and Timmy's school. I set up an appointment with the social worker to speak with her about the incident. When I met with her she was also nice. She agreed to meet with Kayla and Timmy once a week. When I spoke to Kayla about the counseling, she welcomed the idea because she felt she needed to talk to someone about what happened. Timmy on the other hand didn't want anything to do with it. He said he didn't like telling other people about his problems. I think it's harder for guys to open up about their feelings. I didn't want to pressure Timmy about it, so I just asked him to give it a try.

The next thing I needed to take care of was my own psychological well being. I called VIBS to make an appointment to speak with someone. They put me on a waiting list because so many people wanted to go there for counseling. They promised to call when they had an opening. They then would set me up for an orientation. An orientation consisted of three meetings, which were mandatory to come for counseling there. I was hoping a space would open up soon because I needed someone to talk to.

CHAPTER 14
CPS Gets Involved

When I returned home I was exhausted from lack of sleep and emotional and physical stress. I felt like I could barely stand. I was in the door only a few minutes when there was a knock at the door. When I opened the door there was a lady standing there. She introduced herself as an emergency caseworker from Child Protective Services, also known as CPS. I was totally oblivious to what their job was. I figured they were there to help.

My mom and I sat at the table with the caseworker telling her everything that had happened the night before. I spilled my guts out about what transpired over the years with Sahir. I told her about the mental and physical abuse I had endured. Every detail, including all the threats that Sahir had made to scare me, was told. I told her about the Order Of Protection I had obtained for my children and myself. It felt like a great weight had been lifted off my shoulders because I was finally able to tell someone about the abuse. Just as I was about to take a deep breath of relief, I got my first blow of being victimized all over again.

The caseworker blurted out, "My, don't we have an ego problem?"

I was shocked, to say the least, and I began to wonder what kind of people this organization had. How could a person be so cruel to someone who had just been through so much? I broke down in tears and felt like the little self-esteem I had left just withered away.

After about an hour to an hour and a half of questions and filling out paper work, the CPS caseworker left. She said someone from CPS would contact me soon. At that point, even with the caseworker's crude remark, I still felt CPS would help keep my children safe and would also give us the mental support we so desperately needed.

I spent the rest of the day trying to clean up the house. It was torn apart by Sahir the night before. Things were thrown about from his anger. The furniture was knocked all out of place from him dragging and throwing me into things.

I tried to pull myself together so I could be there for my children. Gosh, I could only imagine what they were going through. I always wanted the best for them, and this life was definitely not what I had in mind. Kazem, even though he was still only two, was even stressed and confused. All I could do at that point was give them a hug and tell them how much I love them. They had many questions such as, "Why did Baba get so mad, and why did he have to go to jail?" (Baba means father in Turkish and that's what Kadin and Kazem used to call Sahir).

It was always hard knowing how much to tell them and what the right answer was. Whenever they had a question about their father I always told the truth, but I made it as simple as possible. I tried to avoid getting into detail to prevent them from getting upset. Usually attempting to change the subject was the best thing.

I never said anything negative about their father regardless of what happened. It's a hard thing to do when someone has done so much to hurt you and your children.

Sometime during the day, April stopped by. When I opened the door and saw her standing there, I started to cry again. She could be cruel, and she was always jealous of me, but I was so run down that seeing anyone at that moment was a shoulder to cry on.

At first she comforted me and said not to worry and that things would get better. Then, within minutes, her true nature came out. She handed me a Nextel phone and told me that Sahir wanted me to have the phone so he could call me without CPS or the police knowing. I told her I didn't want to break the Order Of Protection because if CPS found out, they could take Kadin and Kazem away from me and put them in a foster home. This was true, and what I didn't have the courage to tell her was that I didn't want to talk to him. I was so angry with him and what he did to our children. She just kept saying that CPS and the police would never find out because there was no phone record with that phone. I grudgingly accepted the phone. She even had the nerve to call Sahir before handing me the phone. I made the call as short as possible. My heart felt like it was going to burst out of my chest. The anxiety was more than I could bear.

I just kept wondering when April was going to leave. Her presence was now getting on my nerves. I tried to think of something to say to politely ask her to leave. Before I had time to think, she said something so cruel and unbelievable that I'll never forget it. To this day her words continue to run through my head. April blurted out, "Remember when we were sitting in court this morning? I saw Sahir sitting up there with all the criminals. He just didn't belong there. I just wanted to grab you and shake you for what you did to him!"

Was she serious? I couldn't believe she stooped that low to say something as cruel and untrue as that. I was so outraged! I'm glad that at least I had the courage to tell her she was wrong, and that he did deserve to be where he was. I could no longer speak to her, and even though she had said something so wrong, I still politely asked to be alone. Thank God she finally left.

After she left, Sahir called again. He was desperately trying to convince me to let him come over so he could see me. He kept telling me he loved me and that he was sorry. Luckily, I could tell him that CPS would take our children away if he were to come over, (which really was what CPS had told me). I didn't want him over because I was so angry with him, and I didn't feel safe around him. He kept crying and begging me to let him come home. When I felt I couldn't take it anymore, I told him I had to go, and I begged him to let me get off the phone. I didn't have the nerve to just hang up. He still had that control over me, and I hated it. He finally agreed to hang up, but it was only the first of many calls he made that day.

Within a short period of time I received a call from a lady who claimed to be a friend of Sahir's. She said she had been a customer of Sahir's for a long time and she worked for a company that does the alcohol testing for the courts.

Sahir obviously didn't tell her the whole story of everything that happened the night before, because she kept telling me that CPS wouldn't take our children away if he came home. She also said that everything would be fine. I asked if she realized that he abused me in front of my children, and that my daughter's arm was injured because of him. I also told her about the abuse from the past. Her response was that she was unaware of anything else. By her tone of voice she sounded shocked, so I can only imagine the story that Sahir must have told her.

I can't remember just how many times Sahir called that day, but I'll always remember the last call, and I'm filled with disgust every time I think about it. It was late at night and I was playing "Silent Hill" on Play-station. I always play scary games to relieve stress. It has always been a strange outlet for me. Sahir called to request a sexual satisfaction for himself via tele-phone. I was so angry thinking about his self-centeredness. How dare he ask such a thing after all he did! I couldn't bring myself to tell him no. Words could never express how awful I felt during that time. Why did I allow myself to be controlled like that? I look back now and wish I would have hung up on him and told him to get lost. It took a long time to learn the "hang up the phone" technique.

After that awful task of fulfilling an undeserving man, I told Sahir I had to go because it was getting late. I was so exhausted from everything that went on that day. As nightmarish as the past thirty hours had been, it was only the beginning.

CHAPTER 15

More Shocking News

A couple of days passed, and each of those days was spent trying to hold myself together. I was filled with mixed emotions. I was feeling lonely and sad, but at the same time angry. Sometimes I wished that horrible incident never happened, but deep inside I knew it happened for a reason. At that time I wasn't sure why. Even though I was so lonely, I felt I could breathe again, and I didn't have to tip-toe around anymore. For once in my life I wasn't afraid that I'd get beaten up if I said the wrong thing.

Just as I was feeling a sense of relief, I received a letter in the mail from CPS. It stated that I was another person named in a report of suspected child abuse or maltreatment. It informed me of an ongoing investigation to determine whether or not I was a subject of the report. After reading the letter I suddenly felt ill. I was the victim, not the perpetrator! It was unbelievable that they were actually blaming me for what happened! I was now starting to see that CPS's involvement wasn't a positive thing.

By the end of the month I got even worse news. One afternoon there was a knock at the door. I thought it might be my mom stopping by to see if I was okay. When I opened the door I was totally shocked to see the sheriff standing there. I remember his words like it was yesterday. He said that he was there to serve me some papers. I was puzzled as to what kind of papers he was serving me. When I glanced at the papers my stomach dropped. I was being served with child neglect papers and a mandated court appearance!

I told the sheriff that there must be some mistake. Sahir was the one who went out of control. The Sheriff apologized and told me that he had nothing to do with it. He also said that he was only there to serve the papers. I felt my legs buckling underneath me and a real sick feeling overcame my stomach. This was the first time in my life that I was so upset I almost threw up. As I read the papers I felt victimized all over again.

Hysterically crying, I called my mom. When I told her what had happened, she, too, was shocked. She said she would be right over. I then called April. I don't know if I called her out of hysteria or more to prove to her just how much trouble Sahir had caused. Fears started running through my head. Was I going to lose my children? I began sobbing uncontrollably. At that moment I just wanted to die. I felt helpless and didn't know which way to turn. All I ever tried to do was keep my children safe and happy. When someone constantly threatens to take your children to another country or to kill you if you leave, it's enough to scare you into staying. I don't think the victim should be held accountable.

I don't remember who showed up first, my mom or April, but April looked at this as another opportunity to call Sahir and put me on the phone. I knew it was going to be another day with a million of his phone calls. Luckily, my mom was there to support me, and she told April straight out that Sahir shouldn't be calling.

After a short time April left. My mom told me that I needed to get a lawyer. She had a list of phone numbers she obtained while we were in court the morning after the incident. She knew how delicate my state of mind was, so she made sure that she kept all the court papers organized. I owe her a lot because she was there for me during the whole ordeal. Without her, I don't think I would have made it through all that. I thank God that she's so strong and that she's a loving mom. All my strength was pretty much drained, and I was ready to have a nervous breakdown. My mom just kept telling me that I had to be strong for the sake of my children. This helped me dig deep within to find the strength I didn't know I still had. I loved my children so much. They were my life, and they meant the world to me.

We contacted the advocate from the Women's Coalition Of Domestic Violence, since she was so helpful and supportive in court. She told us about some VIBS lawyers that charged much less per hour than a normal lawyer. Having little money, I needed a lawyer who specialized in neglect cases. I was lucky to find one because they're so over-booked. I didn't realize just how many women were in the same situation. The name of the lawyer I found was Rachael and she gave me an appointment for the next day. My mom helped me organize all the papers so we would be ready for the lawyer in the morning.

The next morning my mom and I went down to Rachael's office. I was a bundle of nerves wondering what Rachael was going say about the case. All I kept wishing was that it all was a nightmare and that I would soon wake up from it.

Rachael asked a bunch of questions and looked

over the paper work. She told me that I had a chance of having my children taken away! I told her I didn't do anything wrong and that it was Sahir's fault. I showed her the Order Of Protection I had obtained against Sahir, and informed her about my refusal to let him in the house. I couldn't believe this was happening! Once again I broke out in tears.

Rachael seemed pretty cold and unsympathetic to the whole situation, but in time I came to realize that she had to be straightforward about the serious nature of the situation. She seemed to have much knowledge and experience in that field, so I put our family's life in her hands. After she took down all the information about my case and had me sign a retainer, she promised to call when all the paper work was typed up. As I left her office, I felt like I was on the verge of collapsing.

Sometime later in the month I received a phone call from VIBS. They called to inform me that they had an opening. They scheduled me to start orientation on December 7th. I was happy that I now would have someone to talk to. Even though my family was always there for me, it is sometimes necessary to talk to someone on the outside. There are always certain things you can't discuss with family members.

The first family court hearing took place on December 6, 1999. My mother and brother came with me to court that morning. When I arrived, I became nervous. I was still in total disbelief that such a thing was happening. I had always tried my best to be a good parent. God knows just how much I love my children and that I would never deliberately put them in harm's way. Before the November 6th incident, I never felt that my children's safety was at risk. The only risk I saw was that if I left Sahir, Kazem and Kadin would be taken away from me. In my mind their chance of disappearing outweighed everything else. There was no way of knowing that things would turn out the way they did.

Tim and Betty also showed up at the court. When they arrived, my mother and brother shook Tim's hand. When Sahir saw how friendly my family was to Tim, he became jealous. He glared in their direction and displayed his total disapproval. He angrily muttered some words under his breath and never took his eyes off of everyone. I hated that look of Sahir's, as I became all too familiar with those angry glaring eyes. It was like the look of death. It was the eyes he usually gave me right before a severe beating. Waiting for the hearing seemed like a lifetime, and I couldn't wait until it was all over.

When we finally went inside the courtroom I was shaking like a leaf. CPS as well as the Law Guardian Bureau was there. After both attorneys spoke, one on my behalf and one on Sahir's, the judge issued a temporary Order Of Protection for my children and me. He also ordered that Sahir could only visit Kadin and Kazem supervised by the court-appointed supervised visitation program (EAC).

The court was adjourned to a later date, so CPS could finish their investigation. They planned to make visits to our home and inspect every aspect of our living to make sure the kids were safe. They were also going to make visits to Sahir's house to check on him. I was mandated to go to VIBS counseling, which I was already enrolled in. The next court date was set for January 12, 2000.

The hearing was another nerve-shattering experience. It was bad enough being treated like a horrible parent, but to have to put up with Sahir's evil stares the entire time made it even worse. By the time I got back home I was completely exasperated. Having my mom and brother there helped me get through it all. My brother also had a locksmith change all the locks on my doors, which helped me feel a bit safer. Sahir was unpredictable, so having new locks further protected us from him trying to pop in.

The next day I attended the first of three group orientation sessions at VIBS. The room was filled with other women in similar situations. I was sad to see that other women had to go through the same thing, but at the same time I felt like I wasn't alone. It was an informative meeting, and I looked forward to the other meetings and group counseling.

A couple of days before Christmas Eve the house was finished, and I was able to close on it. Right after the closing, Timmy and I started to move all the boxes over to our new home. Kayla watched Kadin and Kazem so we could get more done. By Christmas Eve we finished moving everything except the furniture. We planned to rent a U-haul right after Christmas. My children and I were so happy to move into the house. We could leave all our bad memories that took place in our old apartment behind and make a new start. It was so refreshing to be in a new environment where we could make new memories and feel totally relaxed. There was no more yelling, hitting or tip-toeing around.

The day after Christmas I rented the truck as planned. My mom, dad and two cousins helped us move all the furniture. The truck had to be back that day before closing, and since it was Sunday, that meant 6:00 pm. We had limited time to get everything moved. Everyone's hustling and hard work paid off because we finished just in time. I was so thankful for my family's help. I never would have finished in time if it weren't for them.

Once we were settled into the new house, I had to start concentrating on the neglect charge. The next hearing date was rapidly approaching, and I wasn't looking forward to going. I felt as though I was treated like a criminal rather than the victim. I was accused of participating in domestic violence. I didn't choose to be beaten up, and I certainly didn't provoke Sahir in any way.

Sahir was so strong that I couldn't even protect myself. He made me so frightened from his threats of taking Kadin and Kazem to Turkey that I felt they would be safe if I kept quiet. How could I be blamed for that? What about his threats on my life and on my mother and brother? I felt I made the best decision I could at that time and definitely under those circumstances. Had I known things were going to turn out the way they did, I wouldn't have made the same decisions.

I also had to arrange for supervised visitation for Kadin and Kazem. At the beginning of January I went to CASA, the place where supervised visits are held. After filling out some paper work, a lady scheduled Sahir a one-hour supervised visit once a week with Kadin and Kazem. This meant I'd have to drive down there and wait in the waiting room until the kids' visit was over. CASA was about a thirty to forty minute drive from where we lived, so the visits would take up a good portion of the day by the time we got home.

January 12th soon arrived, and I dreaded going back to court. My attorney wound up being late, so we weren't called until the afternoon.

The judge gave me a one-year order of protection against Sahir. He wasn't allowed to contact me in any way except written communication. He couldn't contact Kayla and Timmy by any means until their eighteenth birthday. The visits with Kadin and Kazem would remain supervised until he completed the batterers program. He could then apply for modification of the order.

The judge adjourned the proceedings for one year and granted me a contemplation of dismissal (ACOD). If I continued with VIBS counseling, which I already had planned to, and there was no domestic violence in the house, Which there wouldn't be because Sahir was not there, then he would dismiss the neglect charge within my family. The downside was that if CPS found me guilty of neglect after they finished their investigation, it would remain on record with the state. That means if I ever went for a child care position, a neglect charge against me would show up.

I was upset about the neglect charge, but decided to wait to hear from CPS instead of dwelling on it then. By the time we left the courthouse it was nearly time for dinner. We had spent the entire day there just because Rachael had to be late. My mom and I were drained from all the stress.

On January 20, 2000, I received a letter in the mail from CPS. They found me guilty of neglect! I was hysterical after reading the letter. I immediately called CPS and asked to speak to the supervisor. After a lengthy conversation with the supervisor, she agreed to look over the case. If she concluded that I wasn't guilty, she would amend the finding to "Unfounded" versus "Indicated."

At the end of January I met the new CPS caseworker assigned to our case. Her name was Madie. She seemed friendly, which was a relief because I feared she would be cold like the intake caseworker who came to the house the day after the incident. Even though she appeared to be nice, I reserved judgment due to past negative experiences with CPS.

Shortly after meeting with Madie, I received a phone call from her supervisor. She said that after reviewing all the information, she felt that CPS had made the right decision concerning the neglect case against me. She also told me that I could request a fair hearing to try to amend the decision. I was extremely upset after our conversation, and I was determined to request the fair hearing. I strongly felt that I was unjustly convicted of child neglect.

In February 2000 I had my attorney write a letter to the Department of Social Services Child Abuse and Maltreatment Register. I had her request to amend the report to "unfounded" and also send a copy of the CPS investigation report. Waiting for their reply seemed like forever. It was bad enough having my children and myself go through this nightmare that Sahir caused, but being unjustly accused of child neglect was totally draining the last bit of energy I had left. I was filled with so much anxiety. I had flashbacks and nightmares of Sahir's abuse. I was trying to help my children recover from the trauma they went through and keep a nice home to provide comfort for them. On top of all these things, I was fighting for justice.

Toward the end of the month I received a response from CPS. They sent the information my attorney requested and stated that I could request an administrative review to possibly amend or modify the indicated record. If my request was denied, I would have to ask for a fair hearing. My next move was to write the letter requesting the administrative review and wait once again. After writing the letter, I decided to try not to spend too much energy thinking about the situation with CPS. I'd focus my attention on getting my children and myself better. We needed to recover from the trauma we had been through.

CHAPTER 16
The Road To Recovery

In addition to seeing the school social worker, Kadin was now seeing a psychologist outside of the school. I felt the additional therapy would give him more time to speak about things he had on his mind. He was also struggling with school because of the emotional stress he was under. I found the psychologist through my insurance company. Her name was Bernice, and although she usually didn't have children as patients, she agreed to see Kadin. She saw him once a week, and he seemed comfortable speaking with her.

Kayla and Timmy were still seeing the school social worker. Kayla enjoyed opening up and discussing her feelings during the sessions. Timmy on the other hand refused to speak. He was so uncomfortable about opening up that he actually got sarcastic when the social worker tried to talk to him. He told her she was wasting her time and that he wasn't going to say anything. I repeatedly tried to talk to Timmy in hope that he would change his attitude about therapy, but it was of no use.

VIBS was going well for me. The counseling consisted of group sessions that took place once a week. I met a new friend named Baylee. She approached me the first day I went there and we hit it off right from the start. I'll never forget what she did for me the second time she saw me. What seems like such a small gesture meant a lot to me. She brought me a banana to eat because she said that she was worried about me. I was only 108 lbs., and she was afraid I wasn't eating. I thought it was so nice of her to care about me like that. We spent time in the waiting room talking to each other about the abuse we went through and we exchanged phone numbers so we could keep in touch. I was so happy to find such a great friend.

I was also so fortunate to have a wonderful counselor named Sage. She was the sweetest person, and I felt comfortable talking to her. She helped me release all the hurt and anger I had toward Sahir. Her caring ways and good advice helped me become stronger. Sahir had stripped me of any self-esteem I had, and Sage slowly helped me build it back up.

There were other women in the group who had also been abused. Everyone had her turn to speak while others listened. They all had different situations, and my heart cried out for every one of them. I felt so sorry for them knowing what they were going through. The sessions were emotional, and I often had tears in my eyes.

Baylee said something funny to me after one of the therapy sessions. She said, "I noticed that every time I see you at VIBS, your shorts get shorter and shorter." Upon hearing that, I just had to laugh. It was true that my shorts did get shorter. I guess it was therapeutic for me because Sahir always forbid me to wear shorts. With him no longer there to tell me what to do, I was not only going to wear them, but also wear them as short as I liked.

Baylee told me she was proud of me and that she saw a positive change in me since we first met. I was beginning to feel better about myself. Words can't describe just how good it felt to be free again. I could wear anything I wanted and talk to whoever I chose to talk to. It was like coming back to life after being dead for so long. You take certain little freedoms you have for granted until you lose them. I grew so tired of wearing long pants in 97-degree weather. It felt great wearing shorts once again!

Kadin and Kazem were happier, too. They made new friends in our neighborhood and no longer had to live in a tense atmosphere. When the weather got a little warmer Kadin and Kazem began spending more and more time outside. The next door neighbor had four children who came to our house and introduced themselves. They were polite and well behaved. Kadin and Kazem made friends with them, and I went over to their parents to say hello. I was pleased to have such a wonderful family living next door to us.

Kadin and Kazem's new-found friends helped them take their minds off of their problems, but occasionally they would still talk about the incident and how upset they were. I would always try to get their minds off of it by distracting them with something else.

Visitation was becoming a real problem. Sahir would always try to approach me in the parking lot even though I would ask him to stay away. I still had the Order Of Protection, but he would constantly violate it. I chose not to call the police because I didn't want to upset the kids. I did, however, give him a warning numerous times. I even told authorities at the visitation place and asked them to hold Sahir until I left so he wouldn't approach me after the visit.

Another problem that made me uneasy was Sarim and April's constant checking up on me. They tried to make it look like they were visiting (unannounced, of course), but what they were obviously doing was spying on me. Sahir would constantly call (another order violation) and tell me that he thought I was going to find someone else. I believe he kept sending Sarim and April over to see if another man was there.

On one of Sarim and April's visits, Sarim held Kadin on his lap. Kadin opened Sarim's jacket and to my horrible surprise, Sarim had a gun in a holster! Still in shock, I asked Sarim to put it in the basement until he left. I wondered if Sarim had done that to scare me.

I grew tired of their visits and began thinking of a way to put a stop to them. I was tired of them badgering me about Sahir. Sarim also kept pressuring me about dropping the criminal charges against Sahir. I didn't want to drop them, but I was becoming more and more fearful of Sarim. I was afraid of what he and Sahir would do to me if I didn't drop the charges. I knew their tempers well, and I wished I didn't have to hear or see anyone in their family ever again. Life should be that easy!

I spent a lot of time thinking about my situation. Thoughts of how Sahir was to soon start the batterers program entered my mind. It was only a matter of time that the court might allow him to be near me again once the program was completed. The idea caused me to be panic-stricken. I was happy about living free and not having to walk on eggshells.

Sahir was never going to change, and I definitely didn't want to go back to the hell I was once in. He had the capability of convincing people he changed. He even tried to convince me on the phone, but I proved him wrong. During one conversation I tested him by asking if he realized I now wore shorts and that I would wear whatever I pleased. He replied by saying he didn't know if he could take that. I also told him I was going to my twentieth high school reunion. In a jealous tone he asked, "What kind of mother goes to her high school reunion?"

I didn't have to prove to myself that he would never change because I already knew he wouldn't. I guess I just needed to reinforce that fact about him. Hearing his true nature once again was just what I needed.

One afternoon, when Kadin was at therapy, Kazem and I were sitting in the waiting room. Kazem was asleep on my lap, and I sat there relaxing. Thoughts about the last conversation with Sahir entered my mind once again. At that moment I made up my mind that I wanted a divorce. I didn't have a single doubt about my decision, and I knew I would have to call him and tell him the minute I got home. I didn't want to wait a second longer because time would make way to fear. Some courage came from deep within me, and I didn't want to lose it.

Just as I planned, I called Sahir the minute after I walked in the door to our house. When I told him about the divorce, he was totally shocked. He began crying and pleading with me in hope of changing my mind. I didn't give in to his act and told him I wasn't going to change my mind. I then hung up the phone.

A short time after he called back and pleaded with me once again. He then attempted to be manipulative by telling me he tried to kill himself with a knife, but Omer stopped him. I told Sahir that I wasn't going to allow him to manipulate me, and that I didn't want Sarim and April coming to the house anymore. I then hung up. He kept trying to call back, but I refused to answer the phone.

Later in the evening Sarim and April came to the house and tried to change my mind. I told them I wasn't going to change my mind, and I handed Sarim the Nextel phone back. I told him I no longer wanted the phone and to tell Sahir not to call anymore. After Sarim left I thought about how proud I was of myself. I was shaking from fright, but I felt good inside. For once I stood up for myself. I felt a huge load come off of my shoulders.

I was successful about telling Sahir I wanted the divorce, but the situation involving Sahir's visitation with Kadin and Kazem became worse. Every time I arrived in the parking lot, Sahir and Sarim approached me. They both tried to convince me that Sahir changed, and to give him another chance. I would constantly ask them to please leave me alone. There was never any security in the parking lot, so I always feared being there.

The phone calls from Sahir became more frequent, and he stopped sending support money for Kadin and Kazem. Previous to telling him about the divorce, Sahir was sending me about $1500 per month as child support. He probably figured when I ran out of money, I would need him. I wasn't able to work because I was home with Kadin and Kazem, so it appeared as though his plan was to make me destitute.

After many failed attempts to get me to change my mind about the divorce, Sahir came up with another plan. He knew that the CPS caseworker was a religious and family-orientated lady. He tried to make himself look like a nice man who loved his family and that he only made a little mistake. He gave her this sob story about how crushed he was losing me, and

152

he made her feel sorry for him. It almost seemed as though he also enticed her with his good looks. I found out about this when Madie came for a visit. She said Sahir was devastated over the divorce, and I should "consider seeking professional advice before making a rash decision and that CPS's sole purpose was to reunite families."

I was totally blown away by her remark. I couldn't believe she was trying to get me to go back into the hands of an abuser. This was like a real kick in the face for me. This man almost killed me so many times and hurt my children physically and emotionally. I felt like telling her off, but I knew I was at CPS's mercy, so the only response I gave her was that I made up my mind.

I was definitely not going back with Sahir no matter who tried to convince me or how bad my money situation got. I had to find a way to get a job. After speaking with my mother about the situation, she offered to watch Kadin and Kazem so I could work. She said she would give up a year of her life to help me. I knew it was only a temporary solution, but I had to take one day at a time. What I was going to do after that remained a mystery. It was too much to think about at the moment.

Now that I had a babysitter, another problem stood in my way. Sahir had made me so isolated over the years that I was extremely shy. I was scared to death to go to work, so I had to push myself and remember that it was something I had to do. I found a help wanted ad in the newspaper from a nearby banquet hall. They were looking for catering waiters and waitresses. I had driven by the banquet hall many times, and it looked like it was a pleasant place to work. They had many beautiful weddings and

153

other big celebrations there. It would also be a job where I could meet many new people.

When I went to apply for the job I was extremely nervous. The moment after I walked into the door I was greeted with a big smile by the lady behind the desk. She was friendly and introduced herself as Karla. She had me fill out an application, then had me speak to a man named Rich. I told Rich about my situation with Sahir and about how I desperately needed the job. He was kind and sympathetic. He immediately gave me the job and promised I'd always be safe from Sahir while I was working there. I was looking forward to starting my new job because everyone seemed so nice. They made me feel welcome there from the moment I stepped into the place. I was excited about getting the job, and I couldn't wait until I started.

I started working the following weekend. It was a Saturday night, and the party was a wedding reception. I was so nervous because I had never waited on tables before, and it was a fancy wedding. It was someone's special day so I didn't want to make any mistakes.

When they assigned me two tables to take care of, I almost had a heart attack. Lucky for me I met two waiters who helped whenever I had questions. One of them came to be a close friend of mine. His name was Earl. Earl was a sweet guy who always cared about everyone. He always listened when I needed to talk about my problems and helped me any time I asked. He was a hard worker who always put a lot of pride into his work. Everyone loved him, and in my opinion, he was the best waiter I had ever seen.

Two other people I became close with were

mai'tre Ds Joann and Francine. I was going through a tough time when I met them, and often they would see me with tears in my eyes. They were so busy at work, but never was there a time that they didn't stop what they were doing to listen to me. They would ask what was wrong, and they tried to cheer me up. I'll always love them both, and remember everything they did for me.

That first night I did a good job, considering it was my first time. I liked my job and felt good about meeting so many nice people. The only bad thing was that I would have to work every weekend, and I also would have to work around Kadin and Kazem's visitation with their father. I was fortunate that my employer was flexible with the hours I worked. Every week they made my schedule according to my availability. I was limited to the amount of hours I could work, so I knew the money wouldn't be enough to live on. I was lucky to have a little money left from my accident, so I had something to fall back on for a while.

My mom knew I had been under tremendous stress for a long time. She felt it was time I had a break from it all, so she asked Kayla to baby-sit one evening so she could take me out to a movie. I liked the idea of getting out and spending some quality time with my mom.

We both enjoyed the time together that evening, but the enjoyment was ruined when we returned home. Kayla was all shaken up from a phone call she received from Sahir. He questioned Kayla about where I was and whom I was with. He asked if I was with another man. Kayla was extremely upset that he had harassed her. I was so angry at what he had done to Kayla, so I called him and told him never to bother her again. I then put my mom on the phone, and she politely told him he had to stop calling. He kept apologizing and saying he knew he had to stop calling. He may have told my mom that, but we all knew he wasn't going to stop.

Another family court hearing was held in the middle of May. Sahir wanted to modify the court order so he could visit Kadin and Kazem supervised by Sarim and April rather than EAC. I wasn't thrilled about the idea, but was willing to give it a try. It was only a one-hour visit once or twice a week. I still had an uneasy feeling, though, because of Sahir's past threats, but I knew the court would never deny the visits based on fear and past threats. I agreed to drop off Kadin and Kazem for these visits at Sarim's house because I didn't want Sarim and April coming to ours.

Sahir's criminal hearing was rapidly approaching. Two days before the hearing, Sarim called in a final effort to get me to drop the criminal charges against Sahir. He kept telling me it wasn't good for Kadin and Kazem if Sahir had a permanent record. He almost convinced me until after I thought about it for a while. I eventually realized that Sarim just used the kids to try to get to me. Immediately after I gave it some thought, I called the DA and asked him to give Sahir the maximum conviction that he could. I told him everything Sahir had done to my children and me. Sahir was lucky that he only got caught this one time. He got off much too easy.

On the day of the hearing, the DA said hello to me with a big smile and complimented me for the way I was dressed for court. I could see Sahir glaring at the DA out of jealousy. He didn't like the fact I was talking to a man, and when he saw the DA's hand on my shoulder, the look in his eyes became even worse. I knew exactly what Sahir was thinking because I learned how to read him like a book.

The hearing didn't take long, and shortly after all the facts had been presented to the judge, a decision was made. Sahir was convicted of third degree assault. He had a three-year probation and I was granted a three-year Order Of Protection.

In July I finally retained a divorce attorney. His fee was reasonable, and I knew he was honest because he handled my first divorce. My parents and I have known his family since I was a kid. Kayla's father actually recommended the lawyer because he remembered how aggressive the lawyer was during our divorce. I was surprised that Tim offered that information, but I was appreciative of his help.

Sahir and Sarim stooped even lower once they found out I hired a divorce lawyer. They canceled the health insurance that they had for Kadin, Kazem and me. I didn't care that they canceled mine, but to cancel Kadin and Kazem's was unspeakable. How could a father cancel his own children's health insurance out of spitefulness? Sahir and Sarim had done many horrible things before, but this just topped the cake.

I desperately needed to get health insurance for Kadin and Kazem, but I knew I couldn't afford to pay for it. Thanks to one of the women at VIBS I found out about Family Health Plus, a government insurance that was free to those with little or no income. It took a while before I was able to get the coverage because every time I'd call, someone who didn't know much about the insurance would answer the phone. I kept getting the run around until I finally talked to somebody competent.

Since Sahir and Sarim canceled the health insurance, Kadin's therapist was no longer covered. I wasn't impressed with the therapist anyway. It was evident she didn't have much patience with children because on one occasion she actually ended one of the sessions early. She felt she wasn't getting through to Kadin. I don't believe it was the reason. It was more likely she just didn't have the patience.

I decided to find another therapist once we were covered by Family Health Plus. Besides, Kadin was still seeing the school social worker and that was doing wonders for him. The social worker was patient, and Kadin had no problems opening up to him about his feelings. I would meet with the social worker from time to time and call him regularly to discuss issues that Kadin had.

The visitation supervised by Sarim and April started having negative effects on Kadin and Kazem. Sahir began using the visitation time to badger the kids about me. He would constantly question them about what I was doing and whom I was with. He would lie and tell them I broke up our marriage and that he paid for our house. Sarim and April were also making negative remarks about me in front of them.

I would always hear about all the badgering going on when Kadin and Kazem would blurt it out. They would be relaxing and having their tub when suddenly they would mention it to me out of the blue. I told them the next time anyone said something negative about me or questioned them to tell that person that they shouldn't put them in the middle. I also advised Sahir he should spend quality time with his children and that he shouldn't be badgering them. (Sahir was still calling me and he would approach me when I dropped the kids off and picked them up).

I, too, was suffering from the visitation arrangement. Sahir was not only approaching me every time I went there, but he was also blocking my vehicle and preventing me from leaving. He would keep pleading with me to go back with him. I would constantly remind him that he wasn't allowed to go near me. I even warned him that I would call the police if he didn't stop. As it turned out, I never did call because Kadin and Kazem would always ask me not to. They were still sad that Sahir went to jail the night of the incident. I didn't want to upset them any more than they already were. I was beginning to get anxious every time there was a visit because I knew he was going to bother me.

The visitations weren't the only times when Sahir approached me. He somehow found out where I worked, and on several occasions he waited by the entrance until I got there. I would tell him to leave and to stop bothering me.

Many people I worked with were customers of Sahir. He would even have the nerve to question them about me. I had to explain the situation to them and ask them not to say anything to him concerning me.

I also caught Sahir stalking me in the grocery store. I turned around and spotted him hiding behind the cheese case. He was spying on me, and when I attempted to walk away he approached my children and me. When I asked him to go away, he followed me into the parking lot and stood behind my car so I couldn't leave. After many failed attempts to get him to leave me alone, I threatened to call the police. He finally moved out of the way so I could leave.

In September I began dating a bartender at my work. His name was Paul and he had a ten-year-old daughter named Geri. Paul was a bit on the hyper side, but overall seemed like a nice guy. In addition to working as a bartender, he also worked a full-time job as a heavy equipment operator.

I knew Kadin and Kazem would eventually tell Sahir about Paul, and I feared what Sahir would do. Sahir was capable of anything, and he had no conscience. His jealousy was so strong that he would try anything to break up my new relationship. I tried to explain to Kadin and Kazem how it was better to not tell their father about Paul. They both agreed with me that telling him would just fuel his jealousy. I also told them that even if their father pressured them into answering questions about me to just tell their father that they didn't want to talk about their mother.

As time went on, Sahir continued to pressure Kadin and Kazem into telling him if I had met anyone. After being questioned repeatedly, Kadin and Kazem gave in and told Sahir about Paul. At the beginning Of October Sahir called me in a jealous frenzy. He kept asking about Paul, and when I told him to leave me alone because it was none of his business, he became angry.

I hung up the phone and within seconds he called me right back. I once again told him to leave me alone and that I wouldn't answer the phone if he called again. His calling and constant harassment was getting on my nerves.

After hanging up for the second time, he called back almost instantly. The phone rang until my answering machine picked up. Sahir must have finally realized that I meant it when I said I wouldn't answer the phone if he called again. He didn't make any more attempts to call me.

I was so upset about Sahir bothering me that I had trouble falling asleep. I decided to watch TV so I could get my mind off of things. At midnight the doorbell rang. I became frightened, and I wondered who would possibly come to the door so late at night. Sitting there petrified, I didn't dare make a sound. Whoever was out there eventually went away because I didn't answer the door. Now that I was freaked out about someone being out there, I had even more trouble falling asleep.

The next evening Paul stopped over for a visit. Immediately after he left, Sahir called. He started questioning me once again about Paul. He said that he sent his brother over the night before to give me money (in actuality he was spying on me) and his brother saw Paul's car there. I was furious that Sahir had not only invaded my privacy again, but that he also had scared me half to death. I told Sahir it was none of his business and to stop having his family spy on me. I also told him not to call anymore, and I then hung up.

Sahir rang the phone the entire night, and each and every time I refused to pick up. He called a total of fifty-three times! The next morning I was exhausted from the lack of sleep, and I had a sickening knot in my stomach from all the phone calls.

Paul stopped by on his way to work, and shortly after he left I received a phone call from him. He told me that someone was following him. When I asked him to describe the car, it fit the description of Sahir's brother's car.

Immediately after my phone conversation with Paul, Sahir called. I asked if he sent his brother over to follow Paul. Sahir answered yes, then began questioning me about Paul again. He once again told me that it was his brother who rang the doorbell at midnight two nights before. He claimed that he sent his brother over to give me money for a computer for

Kadin and Kazem. I told Sahir he wasn't being truthful about sending his brother over to give me money, and that I had enough of his stalking me. I then told him I was going to call the police. Sahir had been violating the Order Of Protection long enough, and this was the last straw.

When the police arrived I showed them the caller ID which showed Sahir's phone number fifty-three times in a row. They then called the number, and when Sahir answered, they asked who it was. Sahir told them his name. The police then went to Sahir's house and arrested him for breaking the court order.

A hearing took place the next morning. The judge set another hearing for a later date. He ordered Sahir to stay away from me and released him thereafter.

In December the family court judge increased the visitations to two four-to-eight hour visits. During the hearing I attempted to keep the visitation schedule as it was for two reasons. One was because of my work schedule, and the other was that Kadin was still struggling with school and his homework. I knew that no one at Sarim's house would help Kadin or was even capable of helping him with his homework. Regardless of anything I said, Sahir was still granted the extended visits. I was now starting to see cracks in the justice system.

CHAPTER 17
More Rocky Road Ahead

As Kadin and Kazem's visits with Sahir increased, so did the mental badgering. Every time my children would return home from a visit, they would be totally stressed out. They would be extremely upset about the negative remarks Sahir and April would say about me. Sahir would tell Kadin and Kazem I was a hooker and that I took all of his money. He'd become angry if they told him that they loved me. They were not allowed to call me while they were visiting their father and couldn't show affection toward me when I dropped them off for a visit. Sahir would constantly threaten to go back to Turkey and never see them again if he saw them hug and kiss me. It broke my heart to see Kadin and Kazem in such a fearful state.

Things were getting so bad that I knew something had to be done. I called the Law Guardian and explained the situation. I told her all about Sahir's mental abuse and how Kadin and Kazem were affected by it. She felt bad that her hands were tied. She told me that unfortunately the abuse would probably get worse and that, unless there was some physical proof of abuse, nothing could be done about it. I couldn't believe nothing could stop Sahir. He was mentally destroying my children. I began thinking about how sad it was that the law put the father's rights over the children's. Sahir could be as abusive as he pleased, and Kadin and Kazem couldn't be protected.

Knowing there was nothing I could do about the situation, I contacted the school social worker. I told him about Sahir's mental abuse and asked if he could talk to Kadin to at least help him deal with his feelings.

In mid-January 2001, another family court hearing took place. The judge granted me a dismissal on the neglect charge filed against me, however, it would still remain in the state register. I was still waiting to hear from the administrative review as to whether or not they would amend their findings. By this time, I was so tired of going to court. I couldn't believe one person could cause so much trouble within a family. It wasn't so much about what he did to me, but more about what he did to my four children. He knew that he could no longer hurt me, but could get to me by hurting my children and anyone else I loved.

As bad as things were with Kadin and Kazem's visits, they increased regardless. On April 10th another hearing was held. Sahir wanted to modify the court order again so he could have overnight visits. I tried everything I could to prevent him from being granted the overnights. When I told the judge all about the mental badgering of the kids, the only thing that came out of it was a warning. Sahir was told that he's not to say negative things about me to Kadin and Kazem. Sahir, of course, told the judge that he would never say anything bad about me to the kids. He was good at telling people exactly what they wanted to hear even though he never meant anything he said.

When the judge granted Sahir the overnights, I got a heart-wrenching pain inside. I feared not only for the mental safety of my children, but the physical as well. I knew just how bad Sahir's temper was. Kadin was becoming more and more mentally disturbed, and his temper was becoming volatile. I had visions of Kadin and Sahir butting heads, and I became scared that Sahir would get angry with Kadin and hurt him.

Sahir used to tell me stories about how his father took a two-by-four and hit him and his brothers in the back of the legs when they misbehaved. When I remarked about how horrible that was, Sahir would tell me it was good his father disciplined him that way. He also told me that when Kadin and Kazem were older, he wouldn't think twice about smacking them if they misbehaved. I became ill as those thoughts ran through my mind.

Toward the end of the month Sahir had his criminal court hearing for violating the Order Of Protection. When I was told that I didn't have to be there I was relieved because I was so afraid of Sahir and Sarim. I hated their glaring eyes every time I would run into them in court. As it turned out, it probably would have been better if I had gone. Sahir was granted a dismissal under the condition that he didn't violate his parole. He once again got off too easy. I kicked myself for not going to the hearing.

Even though Sahir was arrested for violating the Order Of Protection, he still continued to call. His phone calls would range from pleading with me to come back, to jealous rages over Paul. He and his family continued to approach me when I dropped off and picked up Kadin and Kazem for visitation. Even Sahir's mother would attempt to change my mind by speaking to me in simple Turkish terms that I understood. I felt uncomfortable with their constant badgering.

The overnight visits were a nightmare. Sahir would

bring Kadin and Kazem to his store and keep them there late at night. Sometimes they would stay as late as four o'clock in the morning. Sahir used the extra time to question Kadin and Kazem about Paul and me. He would tell them that Paul was going to jail, and that I was a hooker. He would also constantly make anti-American remarks and say how much he hated this country.

By the time Kadin and Kazem would come home from their visits, they were extremely tired and irritable. It would take a few days to return to their normal selves. Kadin's temper slowly began to escalate with each visit. When Kadin would have an outburst, he would say many horrible things, such as, "Americans are stupid! I hate this country!" and "You're a hooker, mom!"

After Kadin would calm down, he would tearfully apologize and say that he heard those things from his father. Kadin's schoolwork also deteriorated. He began lying about his homework and was unable to focus in school. Kadin's teacher and I talked on the phone, and we agreed to keep in touch so I could make sure that Kadin would bring his homework home. I spent every day helping him with the homework and discussing his behavior. I tried to help him release his anger in a constructive manner. There were days when it helped, and other times Kadin would put up a wall and couldn't be reached. I decided it was time to get more outside help for him.

In May 2002, Kadin began seeing a psychologist who specialized in helping children with attention span problems. Kadin was definitely displaying signs of ADHD (Attention Deficit Hyperactivity Disorder), so I was hoping the psychologist could help him. The insurance company highly recommended the psychologist, so I figured I'd give him a try. I had nothing to lose because Kadin's level of frustration was at an all-time high. His temper was getting so bad that he started to get physical when he was angry. He would shove me at times and even swing at me on certain occasions. It broke my heart to see Kadin the way he was. Deep inside he was a sweet loving child, but the mental abuse from his father was causing confusion and rage in him. I was going to try anything to help my child.

When I first met with the psychologist I told him everything that had transpired over the years. He told me that he had a lot of experience dealing with children with similar problems. After speaking with him I felt confident that he could help Kadin. He left a good impression on me, and I looked forward to Kadin's sessions with him.

Kadin began meeting with the psychologist once a week, and he took to him right from the start. He felt comfortable speaking with him and opened up about his problems immediately. I think Kadin needed to vent all his pent-up feelings. Having an additional person on the outside to speak to was positive. The more Kadin spoke of his problems, the better he felt. He would let out a deep sigh after a session and say, "Ahh, I feel better mom." It didn't make Kadin's problems disappear, but it helped him deal with them.

In June 2002, I received a letter from the Bureau of Special Hearings. They informed me that my request for an administrative review to amend the neglect charge was denied. I now had to request a special hearing. This would be my last hope in amending the neglect charge. I was so down when I read the letter, but despite how I felt, I decided not to give up hope.

I wrote the letter requesting the special hearing. I

was then filled with so much anxiety. I hated the thought of having to stand up in front of people to state my case. I was always scared to death of speaking in front of people, and I also feared being victimized again. If my request was denied, I knew I'd fall apart. I almost wished I hadn't requested the hearing because I went through so much already. My strength was too depleted for me to be put through further torment.

In addition to all the other stress in my life, I also had problems in my relationship with Paul. He was an insecure person who, like Sahir, was jealous. He wasn't explosive like Sahir, but his increasing jealousy started giving me red flags about him.

He started questioning me constantly about the people I worked with and eventually began following me around work. It got so bad that I asked my boss to put us on opposite work schedules. We were unable to work together because he would put on such a scene, and customers started to notice. Before the parties began, I had to actually hide under tables at work just to get away from him. Even if he was bartending a different party, he'd leave his bar to check on me in a different room.

Changing work schedules didn't totally resolve the problem. He resented the fact that we were on opposite schedules, and the minute I got off work he would call to question me. He would come to the house and continue badgering me until I couldn't take it anymore. I would then refuse to talk about it any further. Paul became so consumed with jealousy that he spent most of our time together dwelling on my work environment. Having dinners at restaurants became a waste of money because I no longer enjoyed them. I would spend the majority of the dinner date staring off into space in an effort to block out his interrogations.

In addition to Paul's jealousy, my divorce proceedings put a further strain on our relationship. Sahir's jealousy toward Paul became so bad that he falsely accused Paul of physically disciplining Kadin and Kazem. Sahir alleged that Paul was spanking them and that he threw Kazem into his car seat.

Paul was always good to Kadin and Kazem. He would never even raise his voice to them. Sahir made up the car seat story from a time when I had trouble getting Kazem into his car seat. One evening Kazem was having a temper tantrum when I tried to get him into his seat. Paul tried to help me by holding Kazem in while I lowered the bar to lock the seat. As I lowered the bar Kazem became angry and attempted to push himself out of the seat. He then said that I hurt his neck (he only said it because he was angry). Kazem must have told Sahir, so Sahir used the story and twisted it around to make Paul look bad in the eyes of the court.

As a result of Sahir's false accusations against Paul, a Law Guardian was assigned to the case. Sahir was ordered to pay for the costs, and from what I remember, the judge chose the Law Guardian. The one the judge chose wasn't the same as the one we had during the neglect proceedings, so she was new to our case.

She set up an appointment to first speak with Sahir and my two children, then with me along with my two children. I wanted to be first to speak with her so I could inform her of all the mental badgering Sahir had done to Kadin and Kazem, and to also discuss how Sahir used scare tactics to get them to say whatever he wanted. Kadin and Kazem told me that during one of their visits, their father threatened to go back to Turkey if they didn't say that Paul was hitting them.

For some strange reason the Law Guardian refused to let me go first. Sahir even canceled his first appointment, which should have allowed me to meet with her before Sahir, but instead she rescheduled my appointment. I felt frustrated that she seemed indifferent to anything I told her on the phone. Even though I told her about all the concerns I had, she acted like it was nothing. I was truly worried for my children's well being, and she seemed to not care at all.

After Kadin and Kazem went with Sahir to speak to the Law Guardian, they were disturbed. They told me their father made them lie about Paul, and that they were scared. Sahir made them believe he'd go to Turkey and never see them again if they didn't cooperate with him. I was flabbergasted when they told me how the meeting went. I was torn between feeling sorry for Kadin and Kazem, knowing what they had been through, and feeling angry that Sahir had once again stooped so low. I dreaded speaking with the Law Guardian knowing what I was up against.

When I first met the Law Guardian, she seemed nice, but my opinion of her quickly changed after speaking with her a while. Despite everything I told her, she told me that Sahir seemed to be a nice man and that she felt I was hiding something. I was so shocked that he fooled someone who was supposed to be an expert in that field. My mouth nearly dropped when I heard her say those things. I felt like screaming and crying, but I knew I had to remain calm and composed. Like the CPS caseworker, she appeared to be enticed by Sahir. I thought, is she for real? Where do they find these people?

I couldn't believe she could be so blind to everything. Unlike Sahir, I refrained from questioning the kids about what they talked about with the Law Guardian. The judge had warned Sahir and me about how we should refrain from discussing the situation with our children. I knew it would be better if I could talk things over with them because Sahir was scaring them, but I listened to the judge. Sahir on the other hand constantly went against everything the judge told him and took advantage of the fact that I said nothing. The only thing I told Kadin and Kazem was to tell the truth. Unfortunately, Sahir made it impossible for them.

By the beginning of fall, my relationship with Paul completely fell apart. The stress caused by his constant jealousy and the pressure of Sahir's false accusations completely melted down what little bond was left between Paul and me.

I decided I wanted to break up with Paul, and the only thing that made my decision extremely difficult was my relationship with Paul's daughter Geri. We became close, and I felt like she was one of my own children. I'll always love her like one of my own. I knew in my heart I'd have to let her go because Paul was another person who would put his child in the middle. I didn't want him to use his daughter as a way to get to me. Her mom was a nice person, and she definitely would have let me visit her daughter, but I didn't want Geri to go through the same thing that Kadin and Kazem were going through. She didn't need anymore stress in her life. Geri was already being questioned by her father about things concerning her mother. I felt such a hurtful loss knowing I'd never be able to see or hear from her again, but I knew it was for her own good.

When I told Paul our relationship was over, he took it hard. He kept pleading with me and telling me he would change. Like Sahir, the endless phone calls began. He also constantly came knocking at my door in a desperate attempt to try to get me to take him back. He even had his mother and sister call me to change my mind.

The persistent phone calling started getting on my nerves. The more Paul and his family called, the more I started to resent Paul. Neighbors began staring every time Paul made a scene in front of my house. Sometimes he would show up while I was outside, and when I'd ask him to leave, he would refuse. I would try to get away from him, and he would follow me to the point that we'd be circling around my mini van. I could only imagine what was going through the neighbors' minds. The show that Paul would put on was quite embarrassing.

One of my neighbors actually called me one evening asking me if I was okay. They saw Paul knock on my door late one night and they became concern. I explained the situation to them and said I was fine. They told me I could call them anytime if I needed help. It meant a lot to me that I had neighbors who cared. I felt a lot more secure knowing that someone was watching over me. Not only was I dealing with Paul's erratic behavior, but also I was always afraid of Sahir and his family and what they might do to me.

This was definitely one of the lowest points in my life. I was lonely, overwhelmed, and I pretty much felt that all men were horrible. I began losing weight again, not because I had anorexia as I did before, but rather because I had no appetite. The thought of never having a man in my life who truly loved me made me sad. I longed for that special someone who would care about me more than himself. In addition to that, I also wished my children had a better life and that they didn't have to deal with Sahir's evildoings. I was always thankful for having four wonderful children, but felt so guilty that I couldn't give them the life they deserved.

I needed to talk to someone outside the family to take my mind off of my problems. Other than the people I worked with, I had no friends. Even though they listened in the past, I didn't want to keep unloading all my problems on them.

After thinking about it long enough, I decided to find a chat room on the computer just to talk to someone. I didn't care what we talked about as long as it took my mind off of my stressful situation. I actually got the idea from Paul. When I broke up with him he was afraid I would meet someone in a chat room. The thought never even crossed my mind since I had never visited a chat room, but his idea made me think it would be a great way just to shoot the breeze with someone. I didn't intend to meet anyone, but rather just wanted to talk to someone who would listen. Little did I know that my decision would be one of the best decisions I ever made. It would be the beginning of a whole new life for me filled with much love and happiness.

CHAPTER 18

The Sunshine In My Life

The first time I logged into a chat room I was totally puzzled. The only thing I saw was many conversations going on at one time on a single screen. I thought, my gosh, how can anyone carry on a conversation with so much going on at once?

As I stared at the screen I became dizzy, and I was thinking that the chat room wasn't something cut out for me. It wasn't long after those thoughts ran through my mind that I discovered anyone could have a personal chat if they so desired. The original screen I saw was a public chat where everyone spoke his or her mind. The way that I found out about the personal chat was when someone clicked on my screen name and invited me to have a one-on-one conversation. It was much better than trying to keep up with the many conversations going on at once in the public chat.

For the next two weeks I chatted with about a dozen different people. The majority ended almost immediately after the conversation started. They were people trying to get a sexual thrill online. I became so disgusted with the type of people that were out there. I wanted nothing more than to have an intelligent conversation with a decent person. I was beginning to think that no one in this world cared about anyone but himself or herself.

There was only one guy I spoke to who seemed normal. I was actually able to carry on a conversation with him. He was a 22-year-old guy from Finland who had a career in programming computers. We enjoyed talking from time to time, but our friendship had its limits because of his inability to respect my feelings. He had at one time asked me a question about the computer I was using. It was my first computer and I only had it for a short period of time, so my knowledge about it was limited. When I didn't know the answer to his question, he became impatient and made me feel embarrassed. We didn't talk much after that conversation.

I started to feel like a zombie sitting in front of the computer. I was growing increasingly weak from working so hard and losing weight. Friends at my work became concerned because I was becoming so thin. My friend Joann would constantly make me milk shakes at work in hope of getting me to gain a few pounds. I actually did drink them because I was always so dehydrated at work from running around so much.

In addition to my waiting on tables, I became a bridal captain. The job entailed a lot of heavy lifting, running up and down stairs and going non-stop for the entire evening. I enjoyed my job, but I was totally exhausted from it. Despite how late at night I got home and how tired I was, I still went on the computer at night in hope of finding someone nice to talk to. I was beginning to think that such a person didn't exist.

Just as my hopes were totally diminished, a miracle happened. On October 18, 2002 I logged into a support chat room for divorced people. On the list of names there was a *Nice But Shy Guy*. I liked his screen name, and a little voice in my head told me to click on him. I didn't expect much because of my negative past experiences with chat rooms.

To my surprise he was a charming 47-year-old from Arizona named Beni. When I asked what his occupation was, he told me that he managed a RV park. I wondered what a RV park was since it wasn't common where I lived. I can't remember how he explained it to me, but I do remember him mentioning something about hitching trailers. It didn't matter to me what he did for a living. I only asked so I could get to know him a little better.

Beni was kind to me from the moment we began chatting, and he was sympathetic to my situation. The only thing I was disappointed about was the fact that he lived all the way in Arizona. Why couldn't he live in New York? Nonetheless, I was happy to finally speak to someone who was so sweet and caring.

Beni was also going through a tough time in his life. He was separated due to an unhappy marriage. His ex-wife never appreciated anything he did, and she constantly criticized him. We both knew what it was like to walk on eggshells every day because of an irrational person in our lives. He told me his stories concerning his ex-wife. Like me, he wondered what each day had in store for him. Was it going to be a good day or bad day? Beni would try to start the day on a positive note. He would get out of bed in the morning and with a big smile say, "The sun is shining. The birds are singing. The tap water is running."

The only response Beni would get from his ex-wife was a disgruntled, "Don't be so positive!"

She was extremely bi-polar, and most of the time

she had negative mood swings. Beni tried for so many years to make his marriage work, but after eighteen years, realized there was no hope. I felt so sorry for Beni that he had to go through so much. We were both fortunate to find each other. I couldn't believe we were lucky enough to be logged into that chat room at the same moment. Beni was also new to that chat room and, like me, he had only been chatting online about two weeks. I felt that God had led me to him, and I was extremely thankful.

Every night after Kadin and Kazem were in bed, we would talk to each other. Even on nights that I worked late, I would still talk to him. We decided to talk on instant messenger through MSN rather than the chat room. It was much more private since other people couldn't click in during our conversations. Beni started sending me beautiful cards in my e-mail. He wrote those cards from his heart, and they always brought tears to my eyes. I never knew such a wonderful man existed. I had to pinch myself because it felt like a dream. When I told Joann and Francine at work about Beni, they were happy for me. They said my face was glowing, and that they had never seen me so happy before.

Beni and I were anxious to see what the other looked like. I asked Beni to send me a picture of himself via e-mail. When I received his photo I was impressed. He was a gorgeous man with a beautiful smile. In the photo he was wearing sunglasses so I couldn't see his eyes. When I asked if he could send another one so I could see them, he promised to take more pictures and send one later that day.

Beni put quite a bit of effort into making the perfect photo. In the evening I was so excited to see e-mail from him containing the picture. When I opened the e-mail, I melted in my seat. Beni had the most gorgeous blue green eyes I had ever seen. I stared at the picture for quite some time and wished that I could see him face to face.

Beni also asked if I could send a photo of myself. I didn't have any photos on the computer, and I didn't own a scanner, so I decided to go out the next day and buy one. I purchased one almost immediately, but still being a novice at computers, I had no idea how to set it up and use it.

After spending that afternoon reading all the instructions, I was finally able to set it up. Using the scanner was easier than I thought, and I was so excited that I could send Beni a picture of myself. I had to wait until that night to send it, though, because I had to go to work. I couldn't wait until I got home that night.

When I arrived home from work that night, I quickly searched for a photo to scan so I could send it to Beni. The only recent photo I could find where I was nicely dressed was one that was taken at my dad's birthday party. It was a nice photo except for the fact that I had a black eye. It wasn't the black eye that I received from Sahir, but rather the one I got as a result of getting hit by a tray at work. A waiter was carrying a tray full of heavy plates and, as he turned toward me, he accidentally hit me right in the eye with the tray, knocking me on my butt. Boy, did that hurt! Anyway, I decided to send Beni the photo even if my eye was a little purple.

Beni and I were chatting on the computer as I sent him the photo. We stopped our conversation a moment so Beni could open the e-mail and look at the picture. As I waited, the moment of silence made me nervous. What if he didn't like the picture and thought

I was ugly? That moment seemed like forever while I was waiting in silence. Just then Beni resumed our conversation. His first words were, "Laurie, I've got to tell you that you're a beautiful woman. Your ex-husband was a real jerk."

Upon hearing him say that, I was relieved that he liked my picture, and I was also flattered. We were both happy that we now could visualize each other as we talked. In addition to our emotional attraction toward each other, there was a physical one as well.

Talking on the computer was great, but after a while we both longed to hear each other's voice. Beni politely asked for my phone number, but reassured me that he wasn't pressuring me. He told me that if I wasn't comfortable giving it to him that he would understand. Just by talking to him every day, I developed a sense of trust in him, so I agreed to give him my phone number. Beni told me he had a Swiss accent and he hoped that I liked his voice. I was fond of accents, so I was excited to hear him speak.

He immediately called, and when I saw his RV Park's name on my caller ID, I became both excited and nervous. I was always phone shy, so I was afraid that I wouldn't know what to say. As I answered the phone, my heart began pounding like it was going to explode. The nerves quickly dissipated when I heard Beni's voice. My heart quickly calmed down and simply melted. He had a soft voice with the most beautiful accent that I ever heard. I fell in love with his voice the moment I heard him speak. Talking to him on the phone was like being in heaven.

We spent several hours on the phone enjoying each other's company. I felt so guilty knowing that his phone bill was going to be expensive because we were talking so long. Beni told me not to worry about how much it cost because hearing my voice was worth every penny.

During the next couple of weeks, Beni and I began talking more and more. We shared all our inner thoughts and emotions, and we started to realize that we were falling in love. We had never seen each other in person, but from talking every day, a strong bond developed between us. We were both filled with so much love and passion toward each other. It was a feeling that both of us had never felt before. I longed to see him in person and feel his warm embrace. My heart, body and soul wanted to become one with him. Feeling his touch and making love to him was something I yearned for. Beni shared those same feelings and knew that he just had to make a trip to New York.

About a week or so before Thanksgiving, Beni booked a flight to New York. I was so happy that I would finally get to meet him in person. He went out of his way so we could be together. He knew I had concerns about the distance between us, so he reassured me that anything is possible if you put your mind to it. He told me he actually owned the RV Park and that his friend Jerri would manage it while he was gone. He even let me talk to her as kind of a reference for him. He didn't want me to be afraid to meet him. I never had any doubts about Beni because his true nature always showed during our conversations. My heart could feel the type of person he was, and unlike any other relationship I had, there were never any red flags concerning Beni. He was always open about everything, and he never had any problem answering questions.

Beni's planned trip to New York made me open my eyes to how sickly skinny I had become. I was a mere 100 lbs. and I didn't want Beni to see such a walking skeleton when he met me. I became self-conscious, so I tried desperately to put on a few pounds before he arrived. Unfortunately I had little time to put on the pounds, and I could only eat so much because my stomach had shrunk from not eating.

A few days before Beni's trip, I found a dozen red roses at my doorstep. The note read, *Soon I will be there.* Beni was so romantic in every way. It was already the second time he sent me red roses. He was spoiling me with his cards, love letters and red roses. No one ever thought of me as much as Beni did. Never in my life did I shed so many tears of joy. I was truly blessed, and once again I had to pinch myself to make sure that it wasn't just a dream.

I didn't tell my parents or anyone else in my family about Beni coming to New york. My parents had been through so much because of Sahir, and as a result of it, they were protective of me. I knew they would worry, so I kept it secret. The only family members I told were Kayla and Timmy. I made them promise that they wouldn't tell anyone about Beni. Somehow my mom figured it out anyway. It might have been that she read the note that came with my flowers. I don't know, but two days before he was to come, my mom looked me straight in the eyes and said in an extremely upset tone, "Let me look at your face one last time because I may never see you again."

I knew exactly what she was referring to, but I didn't know how she found out. I raised my eyes and thought that her worrying was a little ridiculous, and I was annoyed that she had no trust in my judgment. As upset as I was, I couldn't be angry with her because I knew that she loved me and, if I were in her shoes, I would worry, too. After dealing with someone like Sahir, you lose your trust in people. God knows that there are a lot of crazy people out there.

People at work were supportive about me meeting Beni. My good friend Butch told me not to worry about what others thought. His exact words were, "Nothing ventured, nothing gained." I was glad to have his support. I needed to hear that someone had confidence in me. Unfortunately I was always the type of person who needed the approval of others, and that type of personality leads to much disappointment in life. I found out the hard way that no matter how hard you try, you'll never please everyone. It's a hard truth that I've worked on dealing with my whole life. Every day I try to change my thinking and do what I think is right and not worry what everyone else thinks. It's a constant struggle trying to block out those feelings of hurt that result from the disapproval of others. Having Butch as an ally definitely helped me get through that period of self-doubt.

When the day of Beni's trip finally arrived I was extremely excited. I couldn't wait until the moment that I could see him and hold him in my arms. I envisioned the warmth of his body as we embraced and the softness of his lips as we kissed. I was still only 100 lbs., but I didn't dwell too much on my weight because I was too happy about Beni coming to see me.

My enjoying the beautiful thoughts about Beni quickly came to a screeching halt when I received a phone call from him. When I answered the phone Beni sounded so shocked and disappointed. When he went to check in at the airport, he was told that his flight was canceled. The airline had gone out of business just two days prior to his flight. Our hearts sank, as our hopes for meeting that day seemed to fade away. Finding another flight for that same day was tough. I was so disappointed that I was on the verge of tears. Beni cheered me up and told me he would do everything he could to find another flight. He said he would call me back when he had some information.

I anxiously awaited his phone call and prayed that he could still come. We both had our hearts set on seeing each other so we were both nervous. Not long after his first call, Beni called back. He had wonderful news. He was able to get a flight with another airline. The down side of it was that this flight cost over $700 versus the $375 that the original flight cost. I felt so bad that he had to pay so much more money just so he could still come. Beni told me he didn't care how much it cost because I was worth more to him than anything. He was so sweet to say that, but still I couldn't help feeling guilty that he paid so much.

The new flight wasn't going to depart until about midnight, so Beni had time to kill in Las Vegas. He decided to play the slots in the Tropicana, and lucky for him that he did. He won a $1200 jackpot on one of the machines! I was so happy for him when he told me the great news. Beni had gone so much out of his way for me, and I couldn't think of a more deserving person to win that jackpot.

Falling asleep that night was difficult because I was too excited about seeing Beni the next day. When morning finally arrived, Beni called me early and told me that he landed safely in Newark, New Jersey. He had to rent a car, and we agreed to meet in the parking lot of a nearby 711 store. He was going to call me when he was about five minutes from our meeting place. I couldn't believe that he was finally almost here. It was one of the happiest days in my life.

Beni called a little before lunchtime to tell me that he was close. Kayla agreed to watch Kadin and Kazem for me so I could leave for a while. As I pulled the car out of the driveway, reality kicked in and I thought, wow, Beni is really here! I suddenly became so nervous and shy. I was still extremely happy, but I knew that I would be so nervous when I met him that I would start shaking. I was wondering what I would say to him and whether or not he would like what he saw when he laid eyes on me. I hoped I would make a good impression.

It only took a few minutes to reach our meeting place, and the minute I pulled into the parking lot I spotted Beni. I had no idea what kind of car he had, but I saw a gorgeous man who resembled his photo leaning on the back of a car. I couldn't see his eyes because he was wearing sunglasses, but I just knew in my heart it was he. When I got out of my car, I walked over to him and gave him a great big hug. It was the warm embrace that I had envisioned in the past, and it was every bit as wonderful as I had imagined. He got into my van and took off his sunglasses so I could see his beautiful eyes. We hugged and kissed as the imaginary fireworks went off around us. Words can't describe just how good we both felt at that moment. We hit it off right from the start and realized that the physical and emotional attraction was even stronger now that we met face to face.

We decided to go out for lunch so we could talk and get to know each other even better. It was the first time in both of our lives that we fell in love before we even physically met. It was so great that we already knew so much about each other and that we had so much in common. I was still so nervous and shy, but Beni's soothing personality helped me relax. He was always such a soft-spoken man with a heart of gold. He had a lot of patience and always listened when anyone had something to say. I was one of the luckiest women in the world to have met such a wonderful man.

After lunch I drove Beni to the house to meet my children. He was warm and friendly to them, and they in return were comfortable and outspoken. Kadin began showing Beni his Yugioh card collection. My children had looked forward to meeting Beni because I had told them so much about him. They were impressed with his personality and looked forward to getting to know him better. After a few hours Beni had to go back to his motel because I had to work that evening. He was extremely exhausted from his trip because he didn't sleep all night. His "redeye" flight kept him up all night, and he was so excited about meeting me that he couldn't even sleep on the plane. I think he welcomed the chance to get some shuteye.

I spent the entire time at work thinking about Beni and about how happy I was that he was in New York visiting me. I had a tough time concentrating on my work that night. I couldn't wait to see Beni again and wrap my arms around him. I dreamed about his warm touch all over my body and his gorgeous eyes gazing into mine. Many of my co-workers caught me staring off into space, and they wondered what I was thinking about. If only they knew! I decided that I just had to stop by to see Beni on my way home from work. Waiting until the next day would just be too long.

Kayla and Timmy were home watching Kadin and Kazem, so I headed straight over to see Beni after work. Beni was so happy to see me when he answered the door. We gave each other a big hug and as our bodies met, we were both filled with such a strong desire for each other. We made passionate love, and I felt like I had never felt before. For the first time in my life I felt so much love. It wasn't only a physical satisfaction, but an emotional one as well. I never thought I could feel as good as I felt that night, and it was only the beginning of wonderful days to come. I didn't want to leave that night, but I knew I had to get back home. After I left, I felt like I was floating on a cloud.

Beni could only stay for one week because he had to go back and take care of his business. We spent every day together and enjoyed each other's company. With each passing moment our love for each other grew stronger. Never in my life had I met such a wonderful man. He was a real gentleman and showed me more love than I had seen in a lifetime. He took care of me and treated me with respect, unlike Sahir, who probably didn't even know what that word meant. As the days went by, I became sad because I knew that Beni would have to leave. I wished he could stay longer, but I understood that he had obligations to fulfill.

Before the day came that Beni had to leave he made it a point to call my mom. He knew how worried she was, so he wanted to reassure her that I was in good hands with him. He called her on my cellphone so she could get to know him. After a short conversation, he promised her to take good care of me. My mom was polite on the phone, but she spoke cautiously. Beni understood her position and told me he realized that he would have to earn my parents' trust. Knowing what they had been through with Sahir, he had no problem with the fact that he would have to prove himself over time.

On the day that Beni had to leave, Kayla once again offered to stay with Kadin and Kazem so I could see him off. I decided to drive with Beni to the Newark airport and take the train back home. I wanted to spend every moment I could with him before he had to go. He, too, was happy to have the extra time with me.

When the time came to say goodbye, tears began to run down my face. I sobbed uncontrollably because I didn't want him to leave. Beni looked back as he walked through security, and his heart broke as he saw me standing there looking so sad. His heart was also aching knowing that we had to part. Seeing him leave was one of the hardest things I had to do. I was already missing him even though he had just left. As sad as I felt, I was still thankful that I got to meet Beni in person. It was one of the best weeks of my entire life.

CHAPTER 19

The Mental Badgering Continues And Kadin's Temper Escalates

he train ride home was quiet and lonely. I kept wishing I'd turn around and see that Beni had changed his mind about going back to Arizona. No matter how many times I looked back, Beni never did appear. The week we were together just seemed to fly by because we had so much fun. I hoped Beni could come back soon.

It was strange chatting on the computer for the first time after Beni left. I got so used to hearing his voice that it seemed so empty just seeing his words appear on a screen. Tears started running down my face as I thought about how much I missed him. Thank God for telephones. When Beni called me I felt much better. At least I could hear the sound of his voice, although I longed to have him in my arms. Beni told me that he was also sad not having me near him. He decided to get a cellphone so we could talk more often. I was pleased to hear him say that.

I was so fortunate to find the man of my dreams, but at the same time I was extremely scared. What if Sahir found out about Beni? I feared that Sahir would try to harm Beni or falsely accuse him just like he did to Paul. The thought of Sahir hurting Beni was unbearable. I loved Beni too much to let something like that happen. I prayed that Sahir would never find out, but deep inside I knew it was only a matter of time before Sahir would pressure Kadin and Kadin into telling him.

Kadin and Kazem's visitations with their father turned more into mental brain washing sessions rather than quality family time together. Sahir continued to question the kids about who I was with and what I was doing. The negative remarks that Sahir, Sarim and April made about my family and me increased with time. As a result of these badgering sessions, Kadin's temper escalated even more. There were times that I actually had to call the psychologist because Kadin's rage got out of control. He was getting more physical, and he was so strong that I sometimes would fall on the ground when I tried to restrain him. I was so sad to see my child in such a bad state of mind.

Kazem was also suffering from all this. He couldn't stand Kadin's loud screaming, and he would get upset about Kadin's behavior. The staying up late at their father's house made both children moody and reluctant to obey the rules at home. The psychologist recommended putting Kadin on a medicine for children with ADHD. It was a brain stimulant, which was supposed to help children with that condition concentrate better. It was also known to curb temper tantrums. I was always against putting children on medication, but I tried everything else, and I didn't know what else to do. I decided to give it a try. Unlike other medicines, Kadin wouldn't have to be weaned off of it if I didn't like the results. It was also non-addictive, which was important for me. I still didn't like the idea, but I didn't have any other answers.

Two days before Christmas Eve, Beni surprised me by booking a flight. I was so happy that he was going to fly in Christmas Eve and spend the holiday with my family and me. It was the best Christmas gift I had ever received.

When Beni arrived, my parents invited Beni to their house with a warm welcome and treated him like family. It meant a lot to me that they opened their house to him. All my relatives enjoyed talking to Beni. They admired his warm personality, and they saw how loving he was toward my children and me. For the first time, my family saw me having so much fun and in a relaxed state of mind. They got so used to seeing me uptight every time Sahir was around, so it was like a breath of fresh air when they finally got to see me enjoy myself. My family also saw how well my children got along with Beni and just how relaxed they also were.

I could honestly say that it was the best Christmas I ever had. It will always be a wonderful memory in my mind. Just a couple of months before, I was so lonely and sad. I owe my life to Beni because he gave me so much love and joy. He picked me up when my spirits were down, and I'll be forever grateful. My children spent more time bonding with Beni. Even Kayla, who was hard to get approval from because of what Sahir did to her, liked Beni. She saw how kind he was to everyone, and she felt comfortable talking to him.

On February 14, 2003, after three grueling years of dragged out divorce proceedings, Sahir finally signed the papers. I had tried everything to prove that Sahir was hiding his income, but he and Sarim hid it so well that I had no way of proving it. I was only going to receive $286 per month for child support.

During the proceedings, Sharif's girlfriend Deb had offered to be a witness to the fact that Sahir was a co-owner of the business that Sarim ran, but she was scared off by Sahir and Sarim during the examination.

She was my last hope, so when that fell through I decided to do whatever it took to get the divorce papers signed. I didn't care about the money. I just wanted the divorce over with so I could go on with my life. It was the last ball and chain that Sahir had on me, so it was a relief to be finally rid of him.

A few weeks earlier, Beni had booked a flight for me to visit him in Arizona on that same day. Kadin and Kazem were visiting their father during that week because they were off from school. I dreaded having them visit for a full week, but there was nothing I could do about it. I worried knowing that Sahir was going to brainwash them for an entire week. All I could do was help them deal with the situation when they returned. Aside from the concerns I had, that Valentine's Day was the best I ever had. I was ecstatic! My divorce papers were actually signed, and I was on my way to see the man I loved so dearly. I had never been to Las Vegas or Arizona, so I was excited.

I finished with the lawyer only twenty minutes before I had to leave for the airport, so I was pressed for time. I had to drop off Kadin and Kazem at their father's house. It was the last time I would have to drive them because we agreed in the divorce papers that Sarim and April would do the dropping off and picking up.

Sahir, of course, once again blocked my vehicle so I couldn't leave. He made another attempt to try to change my mind about him. It upset me that he always made a scene in front of Kadin and Kazem. I reminded him that he was breaking the court order again and that he shouldn't be putting the kids in the middle. He didn't care about anything I said, and it took a lot of pleading with him before he finally let me leave. I was so glad it was the last time he was going to have the opportunity to put me in that uncomfortable situation. After Sahir finally moved out of my way, I quickly drove home and got back just in time for the taxi to take me to the airport.

I arrived at the airport about 1 1/2 hours before departure time. When I walked in the entrance I almost fainted! There was a long line that almost went out the door! At that moment I thought I would never make it. I started to panic and almost began to cry because I feared that I wouldn't be able to get on the plane in time. Thanks to Southwest Airlines, the lines went fast. They were professional about the way they handled things. They were organized and even took people who were running late ahead of others. I actually checked in earlier than I expected, and boy, was I relieved. Thank you, Southwest!

I have to laugh when I think back to that day when I stood in the check in line. It was one of the few times I traveled by plane, and I had so much luggage. It was a one-week trip, and I had two large duffle bags and two carry-ons. It was enough luggage for three people. Moving all four bags by myself was difficult, and it was probably pretty funny watching it from the outside.

When I finally boarded the plane, I let out a huge sigh of relief. I thought, yes, I made it! I was so thrilled to be on my way to see my sweetheart. It was strange how everything worked out so well that day because a few weeks earlier I had a fortune cookie that said good news was on the way. I had told Beni that maybe the cookie meant my divorce papers would be signed and that I could come to Arizona to visit. I only said it as wishful thinking. We were both skeptical that we could be that lucky, so when it really did happen, we were extremely surprised. I'm so glad that things turned out the way they did.

When I arrived in Las Vegas, it was about 9:00 pm. The strip was full of many different kinds of buildings and beautiful lights. I had never seen so many casinos before. It was such a great sight to see and never in my life would I have imagined that I would actually get the chance to go there. I couldn't wait until the next day so I could see the mountains. Long Island is flat, so mountains are non-existent there. I've only seen movies and pictures of the desert and mountains, and I always thought they were so beautiful. To actually see them with my own eyes would be a first for me, so I looked forward to it.

As I came down the escalator that led to the luggage area, I immediately spotted Beni waiting there for me. I ran up to him and gave him the biggest hug and kiss ever. It felt so good to be in each other's arms again. Being away from each other was tough, so you can imagine just how good it felt to be together again.

Beni had a good laugh when we picked up my luggage. He was an experienced traveler who always packed light. He was shocked when he saw my two large duffle bags. The look on his face was priceless. To this day we both look back and have a good laugh. After picking up the luggage, we headed for Beni's RV Park. He owned a two-bedroom house in his park, which was also the main office. I looked forward to seeing his park because he told me so much about it. It looked nice from the photos he showed me. It was located on the Colorado River just across the casinos that were in Laughlin, Nevada.

When we arrived in Arizona, the first one I had the pleasure of meeting was Rusty. He was Beni's beautiful Sheltie. He was the cutest dog I had ever seen, and he was extremely smart and obedient. He welcomed me the minute I walked in the door. We became friends right after we met, and he has been my faithful companion ever since. It was late when we got to Beni's house, and we were both exhausted from the trip, so we only stayed up for about an hour, then we crashed. I got to sleep in Beni's arms, and it was the most wonderful place in the world. I don't think I ever slept so soundly in my life as I did that night. All the bad things I had gone through in the past seemed to disappear, and all my worries faded away. As my eyes closed, I felt like I was floating on a cloud.

When I woke up the next morning Beni already began spoiling me. He served me breakfast in bed, and I can honestly say that it was the first time in my life anyone ever did that for me. He always treated me like a princess. He was a real gentleman in every way. I was impressed the way he opened the car door for me every time I went to get in. He was like my knight in shining armor who had rescued me from an evil ex-husband. Beni was pampering me so much that I actually felt guilty. I was used to having a life similar to Cinderella's, except for the fact that it was an evil ex-husband versus the evil stepmother and stepsisters like in the story. I have to admit that even though I felt guilty, I still enjoyed being treated like a princess. I thought about how Beni's ex-wife was a fool to not appreciate him.

Beni spent the first day of my visit showing me around his RV Park. It was well kept and had a beautiful river view. The mountains were even more beautiful than I had imagined, so I couldn't take my eyes off of them. No wonder Beni loved Arizona so much. I fell in love with the place the first day I was there. I wished my children and I could move there and live with Beni, but I knew that life could never be that easy.

Beni also introduced me to his friend Jerri. She was a friendly person who gave me a warm welcome the first time we met. I told her how grateful I was that she watched the park so Beni could come to New York. I also told her how I appreciated the fact that she supported Beni when he first met me. Jerri knew that our long distance relationship was out of the ordinary, but always told Beni to follow his heart. She never discouraged him from pursuing our relationship. It was thanks to her that Beni was able to go back and forth to New York. Without her, we would never have been able to spend time together.

During my visit, Beni took me to see many beautiful places that I had never seen before. I enjoyed walking in the desert looking for creatures that inhabited it. I've always been terrified of any kind of bug, especially Scorpions, Black Widows and Tarantulas, but I still searched for them anyway. I don't mind studying them from a distance in the desert. I just don't want them in my house or crawling on me. I also searched for Rattlesnakes, (from a distance, of course). During my travels I didn't come across a single creature. It was probably because February is too cold for them. They usually don't come out until May when it's hot. Oh, well, it was fun exploring the desert anyway.

Seeing the desert for the first time was amazing! After observing all the pointy cactuses I thought just how much I would hate to run through it at night. Boy, that could be painful! I could only imagine the type of creatures that lurked during those summer nights ...

yuk! Definitely not for me!

Beni also took me to Lake Havasu to see the London Bridge. It was cool to see the real London Bridge that was disassembled in England and rebuilt in Arizona.

He also booked a hotel room at the Tropicana in Las Vegas so he could show me around the strip. I was like a child on Christmas morning as I walked down the strip. I never realized just how long it was and how beautiful the lights looked at night. We only had enough time to see less than a quarter of it because it was so big. To see everything, you'd probably need a week or two. Even though we only had one night, I had a wonderful time and it was a romantic evening. Beni made sure that the room had a jacuzzi in it. It even had mirrored ceilings over the bed. I'll leave the rest to your imagination. Yes, it was a night to remember.

I was enjoying my stay in Arizona so much that the days went by so quickly. I missed my children, but dreaded going back to New York. There were so many bad memories that I so desperately wanted to leave behind. I still wished that my children and I could move to Arizona and make a new start. Kadin and Kazem would love Arizona because they both loved animals, and I knew they would love to catch lizards and other creatures. They were fond of the outdoors and if they saw the Colorado River, they would love to swim in it. I decided that I would have to bring them there one day for a vacation. The sunsets were also incredible. They were filled with beautiful colors that were simply breathtaking.

During my visit to Arizona, New York was hit with a pretty severe snowstorm. I didn't look forward to shoveling all that snow when I got home. All the problems I had put aside were slowly returning to my mind. When I got home I was going to have to deal with all the mental damage that Sahir did to Kadin and Kazem. Why couldn't he love his children enough to not do such a terrible thing? I didn't care what he thought about me, but why did he have to subject his own children to such cruelty? It hurt me so much to see Kadin and Kazem go through that time and time again. How was I ever going to stop Sahir's mental abuse?

Saying goodbye to Beni once again was extremely difficult. Tears filled my eyes as I hugged him before I went through security. I clung to him so tightly and found it hard to let go. I loved him so much, and I prayed that one day we would no longer have to part. It took forty years to finally find my soul mate, and being apart from him made me feel so empty inside. As I waved goodbye I continued whimpering.

We slowly lost sight of each other, and sadness quickly set in. I was so upset that I had to try to think of something else. I didn't want the whole airport to see me crying. It was extremely difficult, though, for me to put my mind elsewhere, so it took a long time to compose myself. By the time I boarded the plane, I had exhausted myself from crying so much. I spent most of the flight sleeping because I knew I had my work cut out for me when I got home.

When I arrived home it was late, and when I stepped out of the taxi, I just stared at the driveway. It was totally covered by deep snow. I had the difficult task of carrying many heavy bags up the driveway through the snow that totally blocked my path. I didn't receive any assistance from the taxi driver, so it was a real challenge. After much struggling, I finally made it into the house. Kadin and Kazem weren't coming home until the next evening, so the house seemed empty. I missed Beni and my children so much that I began to cry. I looked forward to seeing my kids because I hadn't seen them for a whole week. I didn't know when Beni would make another trip to New York, but I prayed it would be soon.

The next morning I went out to shovel the driveway and dig out a path to the mailbox. I couldn't remember the last time New York had so much snow. Shoveling snow was actually something I liked to do, but the amount of snow that I had to shovel was a bit too much for one petite lady like myself to handle.

While I was shoveling, I was quite surprised to see one of my neighbors drive by with his snowplow and do nothing but wave to me. He had helped other neighbors clear their driveways with his plow, but even though he saw me killing myself trying to clear my driveway, he never offered a helping hand. I was pretty shocked by his indifference to my situation, but nevertheless, after many hours of hard work, I completed the job. I was so sore by the time I finished that I could barely move.

When Kadin and Kazem came home that evening, I was so happy to see them. They looked extremely exhausted, and when I asked them both why they looked so tired, they told me that their father kept them at the store until 4:00 a.m. They claimed that Sahir had to "close the shift." I told Kadin and Kazem they needed their sleep and that they shouldn't stay up late. I also told them that staying at the store in the middle of the night wasn't safe. Gas stations and convenience stores had been held up at gunpoint in the past, and I didn't want my children's safety at risk.

I decided to give April a call to inform Sahir about

my concerns. When I called her, I received the response that I expected. Even though she agreed to tell Sahir, her tone of voice gave the impression that she didn't care and that she was annoyed I bothered her. Even if she actually gave Sahir the message, chances were more in favor that he would completely ignore everything I said. At least I tried, and I still hoped it would help.

During the week that I was in Arizona, I had called Kadin and Kazem to see how they were doing. I never once received a phone call from them. When I asked them why they never called, they said their father forbid them to call me. They claimed he was so jealous that he would get angry if they even mentioned my name. I felt so bad for both of them.

The situation was getting so out of hand that I decided to start writing a log of all of their visitations and behaviors. It included times and dates as well as any problems that occurred each day. I also began secretly videotaping Kadin and Kazem when they returned home from their father's house. I did this so I had proof that the mental badgering was going on. I figured that if one day the courts would listen to me about how bad the situation was becoming, I would have something to back up what I was saying. The log was also a way of reminding me about behavior problems that needed to be discussed with the psychologist. So many negative things were happening at once that it was hard to keep track of them all. I knew that if I was going to be able to help my children, I would have to be organized and keep on top of everything.

I hated that our family had to live this way. I wished that my children could have a normal life and didn't have to walk on eggshells. It upset me to think that I would probably have to write this log every day until Kazem was eighteen. I was so mentally and physically exhausted, but my love for my children kept me going.

Sahir's probation ended in the spring, and immediately he took a trip to Turkey. Kadin and Kazem were upset that he decided to go for a whole month. I, on the other hand, was relieved that they would be away from his mental manipulation for a while. I felt bad that they were so sad, but I knew that the time would give them the peace and quiet they needed. It would also give me a chance to help Kadin catch up on his studies. He was falling so far behind, and the visits were cutting into his homework. He never received any help from Sahir and his family during visitation, so during the week we had to rush his homework. I always had to help him the best I could before he was picked up.

The month Sahir was away was probably one of the most peaceful months that we ever had. Kadin's behavior improved, and he did much better in school. Even the teacher told me that he seemed a lot less distracted. I was happy with his progress, but at the same time sad knowing it probably wouldn't last because Sahir would start bothering the kids when he returned. That month seemed to fly by, and before I knew it Sahir was back again. I'm sad to say that in my heart I wished he would never come back. Regardless of how I felt, I never displayed any negative feelings about Sahir in front of Kadin and Kazem. I kept everything bottled up inside because he was still their father, and I didn't want to hurt them.

It wasn't long after Sahir returned that Kadin's behavior took a turn for the worst. His temper once again reached an all-time high. I remember one of his severe temper tantrums that started over a video game. He got mad because he was having trouble with the game. I was on the phone and couldn't help him. That infuriated Kadin even more. He was screaming so loud that when I hung up the phone I shut the game off and told him he could no longer play because of his bad behavior. He began shouting horrible things such as, "I hate you mom! You are a stupid American mom! I hope America gets into another war and more Americans die!"

I was so thrown back by his words. It was upsetting to hear him say such horrible things. I realized that I'd have to let him calm down before even attempting to talk to him. I told him that the things he said were terrible, and that I wanted him to calm down and think about what he just said. After leaving him in the room alone for about ten minutes, Kadin finally composed himself. I had a talk with him, and he apologized and said that his father kept telling him those things. He also said his father made him so angry all the time. I tried to explain to Kadin the seriousness of the things that came out of his mouth and how he had to work hard at controlling his temper.

The psychologist and school social worker also talked with Kadin about these issues. They were both so good with Kadin, and I would always see a positive change in his attitude after his sessions with them. I was glad to have two nice counselors for Kadin, who made a real difference in his life. It was evident they cared about Kadin and that they truly tried to help him.

CHAPTER 20
Beni Moves To New York

Having a long distance relationship was becoming extremely difficult. Beni and I were too empty inside when we were apart, so Beni decided to make a change. He planned to talk to Jerri and see if she wanted to become his business partner. If she agreed, Beni would move to New York and live with my children and me. Jerri would manage the park while Beni was away, and Beni would do business over the phone and Internet. He would still have to go back and forth between New York and Arizona to do projects and maintenance at the RV Park, but he would be able to stay in New York for longer periods of time.

After discussing the plan with Jerri, Beni was happy to tell me the great news that she accepted the business proposition. She liked the idea of owning a part of the company and also receiving a salary. It was beneficial for everyone involved. My children and I were pleased to hear the wonderful news. Beni planned to bring Rusty with him on the plane, so we were also looking forward to his arrival as well.

Beni arrived in New York in May 2003. Everyone was so excited to have Beni living with us. I could now sleep in his arms every night and feel his warm touch.

Having him next to me was a dream come true. We could spend quality time together as a family.

I was even more fearful now that Sahir would find out about Beni. Even if the kids didn't tell Sahir, April or Sarim might see Beni when they picked up the kids for visitation. I decided to try not to think about it. I wasn't going to tip-toe around anymore, and I wasn't going to hide the fact that Beni was now a part of our lives. Letting my fears get in the way of our happiness was something that I refused to do. All I could do was pray and keep documenting our daily lives.

Despite my worries, Beni's arrival was a memorable day. Rusty also liked his new home. He spent the first day exploring all the new rooms in the house. He, too, was excited about being a part of our family.

Now that Beni was living with us, my parents no longer had to baby-sit while I was at work. Only during the times that Beni would return to Arizona would I have to call on them. I think Kayla and Timmy were glad that they could also get a break from watching Kadin and Kazem. They had helped many times in the past, especially when I worked late. They made it possible for my parents to leave earlier rather than staying until I got home.

Beni enjoyed taking care of the kids and loved doing activities with them. He would take walks with them, ride bikes and take them places. He would read to them every night before bed and always listened when they had something to say. Beni was patient with them no matter how busy he was. He would always stop what he was doing if they needed him. Kadin and Kazem developed a close bond with Beni and they told him just how much they loved him. The stable and loving environment that Beni provided for them had a positive effect on Kadin and Kazem.

Kadin began doing better in school and they both seemed much happier.

Enjoying the comfort of their environment at home didn't last long, thanks to Sahir and his family. April saw Beni outside the house when she came to pick up Kadin and Kazem for one of their visits with their father. In sheer panic, I told Beni that April was definitely going to report Beni's presence to Sahir, and that I was afraid of what Sahir would do. Beni told me not to worry about it and that we would deal with it when the problem arose. We agreed that we couldn't tiptoe around for the rest of our lives. I still couldn't help worrying because I knew just how angry and vengeful Sahir could get.

When Kadin and Kazem arrived home from their visit, they were once again agitated. They told me their father found out about Beni and he kept questioning them about him. Sahir instructed them not to show affection toward Beni and me and threatened to go back to Turkey if he ever found out that they did. April reinforced that threat by saying she would watch them every time she dropped them off and picked them up. She swore that if she ever saw them hug or kiss us, she would tell Sahir. I explained to them that it was just a scare tactic and that their father would never leave. Unfortunately, no matter how many times I reassured them, their fear never subsided.

From that day forward, every time April came to pick them up, Kazem would close the door so he could hug and kiss me goodbye. When I asked why he did that, he would tell me that April would see him and tell his father. He reminded me that he wasn't allowed to hug or kiss me. Seeing my seven-year-old son filled with so much fear simply broke my heart.

Sahir was trying to alienate Kadin and Kazem from Beni and me, and I had no way of stopping him. Nothing I said helped my children overcome the fear that Sahir and his family instilled in them. The only thing I was able to do was talk to them and have the psychologists help them deal with the bad situation.

With each visitation, the mental badgering increased. Sahir's jealousy was once again at an all-time high. He began telling the kids that Beni was going to jail. Sahir constantly forbid them to love Beni and spoke only negatively about him. Kadin and Kazem kept telling me how they wished that their father would stop acting the way he did.

After every visitation, Beni and I would have to do what we called *Damage Control*. We would sit down with Kadin and Kazem and have a nice soothing talk with them. We'd reassure them that everything was going to be fine and that Sahir's threats were just a way of scaring them so he could get his way. It would take a couple of days just to get them back to their normal selves. The worst part was that just when they finally calmed down, it was time for another visit.

We always felt that we were constantly back at square one. It was an endless cycle, and we were getting nowhere. Beni and I wanted to help Kadin and Kazem because we loved them so much. It hurt us knowing that we were so limited as to what we could do for them. Why couldn't Sahir just love his kids the way he should? Why couldn't Kadin and Kazem have a normal happy childhood? I kept praying for a solution.

The summer was slowly approaching, and I dreaded it because Kadin and Kazem would be spending three long weeks with their father. This meant that he would have more time to fill their heads with negative thoughts. I was worried about their physical and mental safety. With Sahir's temper on the rise, God only knew what he was capable of doing.

By the beginning of June I was still in the dark about when Sahir wanted Kadin and Kazem to visit. I had asked April numerous times to ask Sahir when he wanted to have them. It was the first summer that they would spend three weeks with their father. Beni and I decided to make plans for the summer since Sahir was taking his time answering our question concerning the kids' visit. He was just going to have to visit Kadin and Kazem around our schedule. We figured that we had waited long enough for an answer.

About one week later, I called April in a final attempt to find out if and when Sahir wanted Kadin and Kazem to visit. I told her we went ahead and made plans for the summer because we never got an answer from Sahir. I informed her of the times that the kids were free. Her reply was given in a nasty tone. She told me that Sahir wanted the kids the first three weeks after school let out. It wasn't possible for Kadin and Kazem to go at that time, and when I let her know that, she snapped at me and said, "Sahir told me that if he can't have them those three weeks, then he's not taking them at all!"

I once again repeated my answer that it wasn't possible, and I asked her to give Sahir that very message. When I got off the phone with her I decided to write Sahir a letter. The letter stated that Kadin and Kazem could only visit at a certain time or not at all. If he chose to have them over the summer, he would have to let me know right away. I was so tired of Sahir's game-playing, and summer vacations are something that should be worked out months in advance rather than a couple of weeks before. I put the letter in a sealed envelope and asked the kids to give it to their father when they went for their next visit.

Kadin and Kazem gave the letter to their father as we instructed. When they returned home from their visitation they seemed uneasy and upset. They said that their father was angry about the letter. They also told me he wasn't going to take them during the summer and that he planned to go to Turkey. After hearing how angry Sahir was and how upset Kadin and Kazem were, I got a knot in my stomach. I felt so sad for Kadin and Kazem, and I also feared that Sahir would retaliate because he didn't get his way. Knowing Sahir's violent capabilities, I kept wondering what he would do. I hated feeling that way, and it was a feeling I knew all too well.

My fears turned to reality when I went outside the next morning. Two of Beni's car windows were smashed. I knew in my heart that Sahir and Sarim were behind the vandalism. Sahir had bragged in the past about smashing the windows on cars that were owned by certain people he had grudges against. It was evident that the incident was a personal attack. I talked to several other neighbors to see if anyone else on the block had vandalism done to their car. Beni's car was the only one vandalized, and the persons who did it went up the driveway between my van and Beni's car to get to one of his windows. They also went around to the other side of his car to smash the second window. In my opinion, someone who was getting his or her kicks out of smashing windows would have quickly ridden by, targeting cars in the road rather than singling out a car parked on a driveway.

I called the police about the incident and when the officer arrived, I told her everything that happened. Even though I knew who did it, it was of no use because I didn't actually see the person responsible. I tried to obtain a new Order Of Protection against Sahir since my old one expired, but I was told that since he didn't directly threaten me, I was unable to obtain one. I found that to be such an injustice considering everything Sahir had done to me in the past and everything that he was still doing to my family and me.

There are many holes in the justice system that need to be fixed. Abusers easily find these holes and take advantage of the situation. I think victims of abuse should have the right to keep former abusers away from them whether or not they continue to directly threaten them. Many times victims don't get protection until it's too late. Something bad has to happen before anything is done. An Order Of Protection may be only a piece of paper, but it's better than nothing. In some cases it successfully acts as a deterrent for abusers to contact the victim, and those who violate it get arrested.

Over the years the laws have improved to protect victims of domestic violence, but I believe there's still room for improvement. There should be stricter punishments for those perpetrators of domestic violence.

The police officer did everything she could and wished that she could do more. After she left I once again felt that Sahir had gotten away with his evil doings. I felt so guilty that Beni had to suffer because I had an ex-husband who would do anything to hurt me. In addition to that, I also felt sorry for Kadin and Kazem because they, too, were upset over the vandalism done to Beni's car. When they first saw the broken windows, they asked if their father had done it. I answered by saying that I didn't know. I didn't want to upset them, so I didn't tell them how I really felt. It was something they didn't need to know. Deep inside you could tell they had a real sense that their father did indeed do the crime. They had that look in their eyes, and they displayed a feeling of uneasiness.

A couple of days after the incident Sahir conveniently called concerning the next visitation with Kadin and Kazem. Most of the time I spoke to April, so it was strange he called that particular time. It was almost as if he was calling to see if I would mention the car incident. Well, I in fact did mention the car, and I pretended that a neighbor saw who did it. I told him that the person responsible was going to be in big trouble because I reported it to the police. I said it in such a way as to imply it was he without actually accusing him just to see how he would react. He became defensive and blatantly denied having anything to do with it.

I don't know what I thought I would accomplish by bringing it up because even though I was certain it was he, I had no proof. Being so angered by what he did, I guess that I needed to vent my feelings. I was also hoping that by telling him my neighbors were watching the house, he would think twice about trying anything else.

My efforts to keep the car-smashing incident quiet for the sake of my children was futile. During a visit with their father, Kadin and Kazem were bombarded with April's negative comments concerning my last phone conversation with Sahir. She told them that I accused their father of smashing Beni's windows. April always made a habit of saying bad things about me, and it appeared as though she would get satisfaction out of upsetting Kadin and Kazem. The kids constantly complained about how much they disliked her comments. On several occasions I confronted her about the situation, but it seemed to go in one ear and out the other.

My children were becoming increasingly stressed over Sahir and his family's attempts to alienate them from Beni and me. Kadin's behavior became more erratic, and his temper tantrums became more frequent. I continued video taping the kids before and after their visitations and also during Kadin's outbursts. I kept hoping that one day I'd be given a chance to show the judge proof of how serious the situation was. Every time the mental badgering increased, Kadin's progress in school deteriorated.

Sahir left for Turkey at the beginning of July, and upon leaving he promised Kadin and Kazem that he would return one month later. They were extremely upset, not only because he left, but also because they remembered how he said that he wasn't going to visit them during the summer. Kazem cried for hours that evening and kept asking why his father left him. He was so heartbroken, and my heart just died seeing him so hurt. All I could do was hug him and tell him that his father would return soon. Sahir's constant threats to the kids about leaving and never coming back instilled such a fear in Kazem. He actually believed he would never see his father again. I had to keep reassuring him that his father would indeed return.

After a couple of days Kadin and Kazem were back to their normal selves. They were finally convinced that their father's trip was just a vacation and that he would be back. As the days passed, their behavior became much better and Kadin's attention span improved significantly. I was able to carry on a normal conversation with him without constantly redirecting his attention. Normally Kadin would constantly look the other way or seem like he was somewhere else while I was talking to him.

There were no visits with their father, therefore they were free from any mental badgering. They had a stable environment free from all the worries that they normally had, and they seemed to thrive once again. It was a long time since I had seen them so relaxed, and I was so happy for them. I wished they could always live that carefree. It was the kind of life that children should be living. I prayed that one day things could always be that way for them.

Kadin's behavior during that month improved so much that Beni and I decided to stop giving him the medicine for his ADHD. We never liked giving it to him in the first place because of its bad side effects, such as headaches and stomach pains. He would also have trouble falling asleep at night, and on top of all that, we didn't want him to take medication for the rest of his life. We only tried the medication because everything else failed. We came to realize that most of Kadin's ADHD was circumstantial. It all resulted from the mental abuse inflicted by Sahir and his family.

We had a long talk with Kadin, and we complimented him for his excellent progress. He agreed that he could control his temper and do well in school all on his own. We told him how proud of him we were.

Beni and I kept encouraging Kadin every day. We always praised Kadin and Kazem every time they had good behavior, but we began exaggerating the praise, especially for Kadin, to help boost his confidence. At times when Kadin had an outburst, I tried a different approach. Rather than try to reason with him while he was exploding, which never worked because he wouldn't hear a word I said, I would give him a hug and tell him that I loved him. I would then tell him to calm down and that I would talk to him when he was ready.

Usually about ten minutes later Kadin would be ready to talk. I would calmly tell him what he did wrong and ask him why he was so angry. Even though Kadin would get a consequence, he wouldn't blow up, and he would actually admit that he was wrong. Kadin seemed to respond much better to this approach. It was refreshing to see that I could finally get through to him. In the past, trying to confront Kadin about his bad behavior was like being in a shouting match in which I always lost and wound up frazzled.

Our consistency and patience, along with the help of the psychologist and school social worker, finally seemed to pay off. I was happy we succeeded, but in the back of my mind I wondered if Sahir would undermine everything we had accomplished when he returned from his trip.

On the day that Sahir was due back from his trip, April called. She said that Sahir decided to stay another month in Turkey. I was relieved to find out that things would be quiet for another month, but on the other hand, I felt bad knowing the kids would be heartbroken from the news. How would I break it to them? They were both doing so well, and they were happy that their father was coming home. It wasn't going to be easy, but I knew I'd have to tell them right away.

When the moment was right we sat down with the kids to discuss Sahir's extension on his trip. Upon hearing the news, Kadin went into a crying rage. He began screaming that he hated his father, and he proceeded to call him a liar. He began swearing as he paced back and forth in his room. Kazem didn't lose his temper, but sobbed uncontrollably and cried out that his father was a liar. I gave them both a hug and tried to explain that their father probably had things to do, and that he would return when he was finished. I reassured them that he did love them and that something probably came up.

Luckily, after a short while they both calmed down. Kadin and Kazem needed to let out their disappointment, and to my surprise, it wasn't long before they forgot how upset they were. It seemed as if they were more upset about being lied to than anything. Deep inside, their sense of security while Sahir was away appeared to outweigh their missing him.

At the beginning of September the new school year began. During the first week Kadin had a lot of anxiety. Almost every day I received a phone call from the school notifying me that Kadin had a stomach ache. The school agreed with me that Kadin's nerves were the cause of his stomach ailments. They worked with me trying to calm him down by letting him lie down in the nurse's office a while, then sending him back to class. Kadin always had problems adjusting to change. Whenever something changed from his normal routine, he would have anxiety, especially when it was the start of a new school year. After a week or so went by, Kadin finally adapted and the stomach aches subsided.

I arranged a meeting with Kadin's teacher to let her know about his ADHD and also give her a background on things. By understanding his problems she was able to work with him, and she knew where his limitations were. She was a wonderful teacher who quickly learned what he should and shouldn't get away with. She always kept in contact with me so we could work together to help him succeed academically. Kadin would conveniently forget his homework or lie and say that he didn't have any. This started to happen frequently, so the teacher and I kept on top of him. It became impossible for him to get away with it anymore.

The only downside to having that particular teacher was the fact that she was pregnant. She had to go on maternity leave during that school year. At that time I had no idea how good the substitute would be, and once again it would be another change Kadin would have to adjust to. I decided to face that problem when the time came.

Before I knew it, the time for Sahir to return arrived again. Kadin and Kazem became excited that they would finally see their father. Once again the phone rang, and when I heard the sound of April's voice on the other end I had a strange feeling that Sahir still didn't return. As it turned out, it was just as I had expected. Sahir didn't come back from Turkey. I couldn't believe he would disappoint the kids again. It was bad enough that he broke his promise the first time, but again? Kadin went into another of his screaming outbursts. At the top of his lungs he began shouting, "My father lied again! I hate him, and I don't want him as a father anymore! He never keeps his promises!"

Kazem kept his composure, but with teary eyes he also mumbled how upset he was because his father lied. I was stuck for words because I knew they had a right to be upset. The only thing I could tell them was that I was sure their father would return soon. I desperately tried to put their minds elsewhere. Kadin quickly quieted down, and fortunately they both put

214

their attention toward other things.

Seeing them go through such a disappointment made me sad. April claimed Sahir would be back within a week, but did he really mean it this time? I told Kadin and Kazem that while I was sure their father would return soon, I didn't know exactly when. This way they wouldn't expect him at a specific day. I didn't have the heart to see them disappointed a third time.

Four days later Sahir finally called to tell me that he came back from his trip. We arranged a visitation for the following day. I was never comfortable talking to Sahir on the phone because he had harassed me so many times in the past about taking him back. I agreed to talk to him if he promised only to discuss things concerning Kadin and Kazem. I warned him that if he ever broke that promise and began harassing me again, I would only speak to April on the phone. I was doubtful he would actually keep that promise, but I was willing to give it a try.

I hated playing messenger via April because she was unreliable, and she loved to make trouble. Every time I gave her a message, I could never be sure that she would give it to Sahir or relay it exactly as I told her.

The next day, when Kadin and Kazem were ready to leave for their visit with their father, they were in a good mood. They were looking forward to seeing their father, and they were forgiving about Sahir's lack of keeping his promise.

While they seemed in good spirits, they still displayed their usual anxiety when April arrived to pick them up. Kazem once again closed the door so he could hug me and kiss me goodbye. He again reminded me he couldn't let April see him show any affection toward me or his father would find out and get angry. Kadin agreed with Kazem and also added that his father would leave for Turkey and never come back. My heart again cried out in pain as I saw my two innocent children victimized all over again by Sahir and his family.

When my children returned home from the visit, they were both hysterically crying. Seeing them in such a state gave me such a scare. I had already been worried about their safety just as I always was because of Sahir's unpredictability. He was such a ticking time bomb all the time, and one could never predict just when he would blow up. I quickly asked Kadin and Kazem what was wrong, and thankfully it wasn't as bad as I had imagined. They said their father brought back a lady named Serin. He claimed she was a girlfriend whom he met in Turkey. While playing at their cousin's house, their Cousin Omer told them that Serin was actually his wife.

After Kadin and Kazem confronted their father about the lie, he admitted that he got married while he was in Turkey. Kadin and Kazem were extremely upset not only because there father lied about the marriage, but also because he broke his promise that there would never be anyone else.

I tried to explain to them that they should be happy for him. I agreed that Sahir should have been honest, but at the same time I tried to explain that he probably didn't want to upset them. It wasn't hard for me to understand why they both were so upset. Sahir had always badgered them about how I broke the marriage and how he was so distraught over losing me. He constantly told them that he would never be with anyone else. He also promised the kids that they would always be the center of attention. The kids al-

216

ways told me how he tried to make me look bad because I found someone else.

Even though Kadin and Kazem had a right to be upset, I still tried to convince them both that as long as Serin was nice to them, they should be happy for their father. I told them she was now their stepmother and that they had to treat her with love and respect. Nothing I said seemed to help, so I decided to direct their attention elsewhere so they could calm down. They needed time to take in the change in their lives and adjust to it.

I was glad Sahir had found someone else because I figured he would no longer bother me. It concerned me, though, that likely he would eventually abuse Serin and further put my children at risk. I also felt bad another woman to have to go through the same thing that I went through with Sahir.

CHAPTER 21
Talks Of Relocation And Sahir's Threats

Kadin's behavior had become increasingly worse after his father came back from Turkey. All the progress that Beni and I had made concerning Kadin's behavior and academics seemed to disappear with the blink of an eye. Kadin was fixated on the fact that his father had lied to him about Serin. Jealousy over her consumed his mind to the point that he couldn't control his temper. He would have an outburst nearly every day, which would escalate so much that he began throwing objects and banging walls and furniture in his room. When I tried to intervene, he would get physical by shoving or swatting at me. During the times that he had a disagreement with Kazem, he would push or hit him so hard, that I was afraid he would seriously injure him. I would always have to jump in the middle and sometimes get hurt in the process.

During this time, Beni and I talked about the possibility of the kids and me relocating to Arizona. I was struggling financially, and also it was extremely difficult for Beni to run his business from New York. Sahir had left me with disabilities from all the beatings. The vertigo from the head smashing constantly came back, and I was left with stomach problems from all the stress and the kicks that I received in the stomach. Waitressing at times became difficult because I carried many heavy trays with glassware, and getting a dizzy spell while holding one was risky. I was also limited to the number of hours I could work because Kadin needed so much attention due to his problems.

The fact that everything in New York was expensive further added to my financial struggles. The yearly taxes on my house alone went up to a whopping $8000! I was only making a mere $11,000-$12,000 a year. Sahir was only giving me $286 per month for child support. Beni willingly helped support my children, but going back and forth between New York and Arizona was difficult and expensive. It was also hard on everyone emotionally because our family had to be split up so much. Beni was willing to sell his business if we were unable to relocate, but it would be in the children's best interest if we could move. Arizona's cost of living was much lower than New York, and it had many business opportunities. Beni had a nice RV Park, so selling it would not have been a good move.

The down side to the relocation was that Kayla and Timmy wouldn't be able to come. They were almost finished with high school, and I would never want to pull them out so close to the end. They were happy living with their father, and I planned to visit and call them frequently.

I knew Sahir definitely wouldn't agree to the relocation, and that it was hard to be granted one in New York. It was definitely in my children's best interest, but Beni and I had the burden of proving it to the judge. I also greatly feared what Sahir would do once I actually filed. I knew he would do something to retaliate, but what exactly it was I had no idea. I had a bad feeling about it.

I decided to give Sahir a call concerning Kadin's feelings about Serin and the lies that he told him. I wanted to discuss how Kadin was affected by it and just how bad his behavior had become. I decided that while I was on the phone I would also mention the relocation just to feel him out. I wanted to see his reaction to the whole idea.

I started the conversation off by saying, "Kadin and Kazem were upset that you were gone so long and that you didn't return at the time you promised. They were also upset about the fact that you lied to them about Serin. I tried to explain to them that they should be happy for you. I'm happy for you that you finally went on with your life and that you're happy."

Sahir replied in a disappointed voice, "I don't like that you said that you're happy for me. I still love you, and I'll wait forever for you. You're the best woman."

I tried to change the subject immediately by mentioning my financial situation and the relocation. I started the topic off with, "You pay little child support. You hide your true income, and I have no way of proving it. You know that you could do the right thing and pay more child support. I want to relocate to Arizona because I can't afford New York. I'm not trying to take the kids from you. I'd make sure that they visit and contact you often."

Upon hearing that, Sahir blew up. He yelled, "They are the only reason that I'm in this country. If you can't handle them, why don't you give them to me!"

I replied, "I love them and just because I'm struggling financially doesn't mean that I can't handle them."

I could tell that Sahir was furious. I was beginning

to shake with fear as the tone of his voice was filled with rage. He then said, "I don't want my money going to cans!"

Totally confused by his answer, I asked what he meant. He then replied, "You know that Beni drinks a lot! He also burned Kazem with a cigarette!"

I was so upset about Sahir making up those lies about Beni. I knew it was only a matter of time before he did such a rotten thing. He had done it to Paul in the past. I was certainly not going to let him do it to Beni. Beni was always so wonderful to all of my children, and he barely ever drank. He and I only had an occasional glass of wine, and usually it was only on a special occasion. We were both not drinkers, and he definitely would never hurt any of my children. He had a lot of patience and a heart of gold.

I snapped back at Sahir by saying, "Beni is a wonderful man, and if you make up lies like you did with Paul, I'll sue you for defamation of character! You also have to stop badgering the kids. You should use your time in a constructive manner. From now on I only want to speak with April concerning the kids."

I was extremely upset by Sahir's lies. When I got off the phone I broke out in tears. I never wanted to speak to him again. Beni gave me a hug and told me not to worry. I knew that Sahir was beginning to scheme something evil. He was going to try his hardest to make Beni look bad. Beni tried to calm me down and told me to take things as they come. I had so much fear of Sahir and his family that it was impossible not to worry.

Beni and I tried to increase our family outings to help Kadin and Kazem get their minds off of their troubles. On one of our outings we took the kids to get ice cream. When we arrived home Kadin went into a rage which started over a Cyclone (ice cream) that we bought him. He began shouting, "This Cyclone stinks! The people who made it are assholes! I hate this country! You ruined my life because you broke up the marriage! You used to say Sahir, this, Sahir, that when you were married."

It was obvious that Kadin repeated all those things after hearing his father say it during the visitation. The mental badgering built up so much that he had to let it out. I knew deep down that Kadin didn't mean any of the things he said, but it was still hurtful. It was even more so seeing just how much pain Kadin was subjected to by his father. If the badgering continued, it was only a matter of time before irreparable damage was done to Kadin mentally. Something had to be done.

After Kadin calmed down, he apologized for everything he said. He told me he couldn't help it because his father kept telling him things. I told Kadin he needed to discuss things with the therapist. I explained that the therapist was there to help and that he could talk about anything on his mind. The good thing about Kadin was that he was never afraid to speak his mind. He was always open about his feelings. This made it easier to help him resolve any issues he had. Timmy on the other hand held everything inside, which always made it difficult to help him.

I contacted the psychologist to update him on everything. I told him about the phone conversation with Sahir and about Kadin's outbursts. He told me that he would work on Kadin's behavior issues next time he met with him. Speaking with the psychologist helped me deal with the situation a lot better. When I ran out of solutions on how to cope with everything, the psychologist offered good advice. I was usually pretty stressed out, so I welcomed the advice given to me.

I had often wondered why Kadin had lashed out at me so much. I asked Kadin if he ever acted that way when he visited his father, and he told me that he didn't. It all made sense to me when the therapist explained that Kadin felt safe around me, therefore he let out his frustrations at home. He advised me to keep disciplining him when he misbehaved, which Beni and I were already doing. He also added that every time Kadin refuses to comply, I should compound the punishment. We would take a privilege away, and if that didn't work, we would take something else away until he finally listened. This seemed to be effective, but it usually took a while, and Kadin most of the time lost several privileges at a time.

With every visit that took place, Kadin's behavior became even worse. Both children were extremely tired when they returned from their weekend visits, and they complained how they didn't go to bed before one or two in the morning. Kadin got into his rages over the smallest things. He also began making anti-American remarks, and he became even more physical. I remember one of his temper tantrums that started when Kazem and he knocked over a cup of coffee because they were fooling around. Beni sent both of them to their rooms, and Kadin became fresh. He shouted, "All mom cares about is her stupid rug!"

Beni immediately told Kadin not to ever speak to me that way and punished him by taking away his TV. Kadin got into an instant rage and started screaming, "They were right in shooting Abraham Lincoln! I hate America! I hate you all! I hate the schools and all the kids! My father will get you for that! I hate you, mom! You stole the house from my father!"

I made the mistake of trying to stop his rage by trying to yell at him for saying such horrible things. We began yelling back and forth, and Kadin became so enraged that he shoved me. When I tried to restrain him, I wound up tumbling over the bed and hurting myself. He was much heavier than I was, and I couldn't hold him back. Beni felt so helpless because his hands were tied. We both knew he couldn't intervene and restrain Kadin out of the fact that Sahir would blow it out of proportion and try to use it against him. Sahir had already made false accusations and threats against Beni, so we were careful not to give him anymore opportunities to lie about Beni. Things were getting bad, and I knew we needed help, so I decided to call the school social worker and arrange for Beni and me to meet with him.

The school social worker set up an emergency meeting with Beni and me. We explained how out of control Kadin was becoming due to Sahir's constant attempts to alienate Kadin and Kazem from Beni and me. We also told him about Sahir's lies and threats against Beni. The social worker agreed that I needed help restraining Kadin when he got physical. When we mentioned our concerns about Beni helping me, he suggested that we give CPS a call and try to stay proactive with them. We thought his idea was good, so we decided to give them a call when we got home. The social worker also promised to meet with Kadin to see what was going on inside his head.

I immediately gave CPS a call the minute I walked into the house. I explained the situation and asked how I could become proactive with CPS. The CPS worker told me there was no such thing as being proactive with CPS and that the only way they would even speak to me was if I had a case. I was disappointed about the answer I received and realized that CPS wouldn't offer any help for my children. They seemed quick at pointing the finger at the wrong people and did nothing to stop those who posed a danger to a child.

Unfortunately I had heard many others with bad stories concerning CPS. When I used to sit at CASA waiting for Kadin and Kazem to finish the supervised visitation with their father, I overheard many sad stories. One father who was sitting in the waiting area told how he was slapped with a neglect charge because his wife tried to suffocate his child. He had no idea she would do such a horrible thing. He was blamed for something he had no control over. I don't know any details about his case other than what I heard, but I know that I didn't have a positive experience with CPS. There was also another lady I met who claimed she had physical evidence that her daughter was being molested by her father. He was still granted overnight visits with his daughter. I was shocked to hear that.

I can't totally blame CPS for every bad thing that happens. I know their intentions are good, and I'm sure there are also positive stories out there, too, but if you're unfortunate enough to get a bad caseworker, the children wind up suffering for it. There are definitely times when some parents should be held liable for the actions of their spouse, but other times such as in my case, they shouldn't. I guess there are many holes in the system and I just happened to be one of the cases that fell in one. I'm not bitter about it, and in the end things turned out okay, (which I'll discuss in a later chapter), but while I was going through the whole ordeal, my children and I went through hell. It was something I would never wish another family to go through.

I realized I was at another dead end. I ran out of options, and all I could do was keep in contact with the therapist and the school social worker. I constantly tried to sit down with Kadin to discuss his behavior. While he was calm he was always reasonable. He would apologize for his bad behavior and even cry and tell me how much he wanted to stop acting the way he did. His father's constant manipulation was always his excuse for the outbursts. Kadin would talk about his father's anti-American remarks and the terrible things that were said about me. I was shocked to hear that Sahir even told Kadin I was a hooker and that I used men for sex and money. I knew Kadin was being truthful about his father saying those things because Sahir used to say those terrible things to my face when he was angry.

Kadin also made a strange comment about Serin during one of our discussions. He told me that Serin said she sees the devil, and that she's scared all the time. He also claimed that Serin cries all the time and that she's crazy. I didn't know what to make of the comments he made concerning Serin. I can't remember what Kazem said when he heard Kadin say that, but I do remember him agreeing with Kadin about Serin crying all the time. I kept wondering if Sahir was beating her, too. I felt sorry for her and hoped that my instincts were wrong. It was unlikely, though, that he hadn't already laid his hands on her.

My worries increased as the kids' Christmas vacation arrived. It was Sahir's turn to spend their vacation with them. I always had a knot in my stomach every time the kids had a lengthy visit. It was impossible not to worry about them. I decided that worrying wasn't going to change anything, so Beni and I flew to Arizona for some relaxation. We also planned to look for a lot so we could build a house if I was granted a relocation one day. Even if I wasn't permitted to leave New York, Beni could keep the land as an investment. We also decided to look at the pre-manufactured homes, which were beautiful and much less expensive than stick-built houses.

During our trip, we discovered a large lot located in a court of a nice neighborhood. We were fortunate because nice lots were hard to find. Most were already taken. We only stumbled upon it because we saw a sign for a different piece of land that was already sold. When we called the number, the lady informed us of a lot that was next door to her. The owner was supposed to build a home on it, but she and her husband split up. We just happened to be in the right place at the right time. They hadn't even listed the lot on the market yet, and it was lucky for us because lots went quickly once they were listed.

When we went to see the lot it was love at first sight. I let out a sigh as I saw the beautiful desert mountains and the view of the Colorado River. While I was happy about the land, I also had feelings of sadness. What if I wasn't allowed to move? That was a good possibility. I tried to remain positive, but my fears of Sahir also began filling my head. Thoughts of Sahir retaliating once we filed made my heart start to pound. I felt a drop in my stomach as the fear consumed my entire body. Beni calmed my nerves and told me to think positively. He gave me a hug and told me he would be right there by my side. Beni was always supportive, and he got me through a lot of trying moments. I felt that he was an angel sent down from heaven to look after me. I'll never forget how truly blessed I am.

Beni contacted the owner of the property and immediately made arrangements to purchase the land. Lucky for us the lot was already cleared of any brush and was pretty level. If we did indeed build a house one day, we wouldn't have much land work to do. That would save us a lot of money. Having found the perfect lot, we decided to look at the pre-manufactured homes. I was surprised how spacious and beautiful the homes were for a fraction of the cost. The square footage was double that of what we had in New York, and the houses were built solidly. I was truly amazed when we walked through some of them. I once again had a feeling of sadness as the thought of not being allowed to move once again entered my mind. This time I took Beni's advice and quickly changed to positive thinking.

During the vacation I made sure that I called the kids to see how they were doing. I missed them so much, and I knew Sahir wouldn't allow them to call me. He had no right to forbid them, but there was no way I could change that. I was relieved to hear that they were okay, but I still had concerns because I knew they wouldn't tell me even if there was a problem. They were fearful of their father and would never say anything as long as he was around. At least I knew they were physically safe for the time being.

When the vacation was over and Kadin and Kazem returned home, they were extremely tired, as usual. As I feared, Kadin gained more weight because his father let him eat anything he wanted. Both children came home with several open bags of cookies and assorted junk food that was half eaten.

Every time Kadin spent time with his father, he

would put on pounds at an alarming rate. I had discussed the matter in the past with Sahir, but he refused to do anything about it. Kadin was overweight, and every time I would get him to eat healthy and lose a few pounds, Sahir would feed him tons of junk food again. Kadin was starting to have difficulty breathing because his stomach got so big. He was also self-conscious about the way he looked, but he lacked the will power to say no to the junk that his father offered him.

In April 2004 Kadin and Kazem had a spring break, and once again it was Sahir's turn to have them. He planned to take them to Disney World in Florida. The thought of them going on a plane made me nervous because of Sahir's many threats in the past about taking them to Turkey. I made Sahir promise he'd call me the moment they landed in Florida. I let the kids know that Sahir agreed to call and told them to remind their father.

Beni and I decided to take another trip to Arizona except this time we planned to drive cross-country. Beni had to be there at the end of the month because there was a special event going on across the river in Laughlin, Nevada called The River Run. It takes place the same time every year, and thousands of Harley Davidson riders from all parts of the U.S. attend the event. Beni's RV Park was always full at that time, so Beni had to be there. The kid's vacation was only about ten days long, so I would have to fly back by myself. While I was happy to be on vacation with Beni, I was also sad thinking about the lonely flight home and how I would miss him while we were apart. After the River Run, Beni had to take care of some projects at the RV Park before he could return to New York.

The kids soon left for their trip, and my worries immediately began. When the time came that the kids were to arrive in Florida I nervously awaited their call. It was no surprise that Sahir never did call. I decided to give him a call, and when Sahir answered he seemed agitated. He sounded annoyed that I called. When I asked to speak to Kadin and Kazem he grudgingly gave them the phone. I asked if they were both okay, and I also double-checked that they were in Florida where they were supposed to be. They answered yes, then Sahir grabbed the phone. He rushed me off the phone in an angry manner, which made me worry even more.

During the vacation I didn't receive any phone calls from Kadin and Kazem which was what I had anticipated. I gave them another call to see how things were going. They weren't talkative, and I figured it was because Sahir was jealous I had called them. It was evident they were afraid to show affection toward me on the phone. It was the same tenseness they displayed when leaving for visitation. I could feel just what they were feeling at that moment. I had lived with that feeling for more than eight years, and it pained me that they, too, had to feel that way.

The flight home was lonely. I cried because I already missed Beni so much. Being apart for a couple of weeks was going to be tough. When the kids arrived home I was so glad, and at the same time relieved. They seemed to have a good time on their trip, but Kadin said he needed to talk. He said that during the trip his father got angry with him about something and grabbed his face. This alarmed me because that was what Sahir used to do to my neck just before he lost control. Grabbing me would eventually lead to the physical abuse he subjected me to.

I was afraid that in time Kadin would be his next victim. I was aware that Sahir grabbing Kadin's face wasn't enough to get a case started against him, so I just had to be on guard.

Kadin and Kazem both apologized for not calling me and for being so quiet on the phone when I called. They said their father wouldn't let them call, and that he was mad when I called. I told them they didn't have to apologize because they did nothing wrong, and that I knew they were under pressure. They both seemed like they wanted to tell me something, but were afraid. I didn't want to pry and upset them, so I left them alone. I knew they would tell me when they were ready. They were tired and also sad that Beni was away. We all agreed to cheer each other up until Beni got back.

The next couple of weeks seemed to go by slow because Beni was away, and we were all so sad. When he finally did come back all of us were extremely happy. Since the kids were behaved while Beni was away, we decided to take them to the movies. No sooner than we complemented their good behavior, Kadin started an attitude. He was angry that we were only buying popcorn, and that we wouldn't buy candy at the movies.

During the car ride home after the movie, Kadin continued on about how mad he was about the candy. When we told him to stop complaining and change his attitude, he told us that he couldn't because he was mad at his father. He said his father claimed to love animals, but he always sent them away or let them die. When I asked what he meant, he said his father sent his dogs to Turkey and that he let his lizard die. As I explained to him that lizards die easily and I was sure it wasn't his father's fault, Kadin then blurted that his father was also back to his old self. I had a bad feeling when I heard Kadin say that, so I asked him to explain what he meant. Kadin said, "When we were in the hotel in Florida, my father got angry with Serin. He made us wait out in the hall, and he closed the door. He then began pushing her and hitting her."

I asked Kazem if he saw it, too, and he said yes. I asked them both how they saw it if the door was closed. They both told me that the door was opened a crack so they peeked in. While they were looking in they saw him push her into the other room. They couldn't actually see him hit her, but they heard banging noises and Serin crying.

In addition to that incident, they also said their father drank a lot of beer in Florida. My gut feeling was right. Sahir was now abusing Serin and once again putting Kadin and Kazem at risk. The kids made me promise not to tell Sahir because they knew he'd get angry at them for telling. Horrified by the news, I knew I had to do something. I couldn't call CPS because the kids were too afraid to talk, and reporting it was useless unless Kadin and Kazem were willing to tell everything that happened. I didn't want Sahir to find out they told me unless CPS would take action because God knows what Sahir would subject the kids to. I decided to call the school social worker and arrange another meeting.

I was able to get an immediate appointment with the social worker. Beni and I sat down with him and told everything the kids had said concerning the alleged abuse. We explained our concerns about reporting it to CPS, and the social worker agreed to meet with Kadin and Kazem before we took any further action. Kadin and Kazem were both comfortable with the idea of speaking with him. I assured them that he was only there to help, and that he wasn't going to tell their father what they spoke about.

After meeting with the kids, the social worker called me. The kids were open with him about what happened. He agreed with me that CPS probably wouldn't start a case because they didn't actually see him hit Serin. Even though the evidence pointed to it actually happening, it wasn't enough. Also they were fearful of their father finding out they told, so it was likely that they wouldn't talk to CPS. The social worker told me he'd keep meeting with them on a regular basis to keep the line of communication open. My next step was to inform the psychologist of what happened. Even if nothing could be done, at least it was documented. Kadin was also going to need extra help in dealing with the bad situation.

As another school year was near its end, Kadin and Kazem began looking forward to the summer. This time their father set a date to have them during that time. He was going away to Turkey for a month, so he decided to take them the last three weeks in August. Now that I knew for sure Sahir was abusing Serin, I dreaded them going there for three weeks. I once again felt helpless being unable to prevent them from going. Sahir posed a definite risk to them, and there wasn't a single thing I could legally do about it.

At the end of June we took Kadin and Kazem to Arizona for a three-week vacation. Their father was away, so it wouldn't interfere with their visitation. They had always wished they could go there, so it was like a dream come true, and they were excited about the trip. They couldn't wait until they could explore the desert and look for lizards and snakes.

While they were so elated about the trip, a scary

thought entered their minds. What if their father called from Turkey and asked where they were? He would be so jealous and angry. The chilling thought made both of them quiver with fear. I told them he had no right to be angry, and that they didn't have to tell him if he didn't ask. I didn't see any point in telling him because I knew they were right about him getting angry. I felt they should be able to enjoy their vacation without him pressuring them and making them feel guilty.

I, too, had worries he would call, but I didn't let on that I was scared. He never called them when he was away in the past, so I figured chances were that he wouldn't call this time. Even though that was true, I couldn't help but ask myself, what if? Regardless of how worried I was, I refused to let it spoil our trip.

Kadin and Kazem loved Arizona from day one. They enjoyed helping Beni in the RV Park and swimming in the Colorado River every day. Exploring the desert was even more fun than they imagined. We went on desert hikes where they found many different lizards and cacti. Kadin made the mistake of touching a cactus that didn't appear to be pointy. To his disappointment, it had fine pricks that stuck into his hand. It was painful and irritating. He quickly learned a valuable lesson about how you should never touch a cactus.

On the fourth of July we were invited to a neighbor's barbeque. The neighbor had a house right on the river located next to Beni's RV Park. He invited everyone from the neighborhood, and it was the biggest party I had ever seen. Kadin and Kazem made some new friends, and we all had a wonderful time. We finished the celebration with a great fireworks show put on by the casinos across the river. We had the perfect view since we were on the river's edge. It was truly amazing!

The kids loved Arizona so much that they kept asking to move there. At the time they asked, I found it to be the perfect moment to see if they would be happy moving there. I mentioned our plans to file for relocation and asked them how they felt about it. They both said they would miss their father, but that they could visit him. They said they would love to move to Arizona. We showed them the lot Beni purchased and some of the houses we looked at. Their faces had the biggest smile as they begged us to please move there. I explained that the process would be long and hard. Their only concern was that they feared their father would be angry. They were also scared of what he might do when he found out. I couldn't agree more, but I kept that thought to myself. I assured them everything would be all right and that they didn't have to worry.

During one of our outings I received a phone call on my cellphone. My caller ID displayed a long phone number. My heart stopped as I realized it must be Sahir. During the few seconds that passed before I answered it, nervous thoughts ran through my mind. What if he asked the kids where they were? How are we going to avoid telling him? My body started to shake as I answered the phone. Sahir started his conversation with his typical "I want you back" tone of voice. I quickly cut the conversation short and asked if he wanted to speak to the kids. When Kadin and Kazem got on the phone, they both appeared nervous. They avoided telling Sahir where they were and just told him that they were going for a drive with us, which was the truth.

When they got off the phone, they both claimed that their father was suspiciously questioning them, but never asked where they were. He only asked what they were doing. They were relieved when they got off the phone. I hated seeing them so stressed out all the time. I was sad they couldn't enjoy their childhood the way they should. Despite the nerve-racking phone call, we quickly forgot how tense we were, and we enjoyed our outing.

The vacation went by much too fast. We had a wonderful time in Arizona. The trip was so relaxing because none of us had to fear Sahir since he was so far away. I wished our lives could be like that all the time. The kids could be themselves and not have to live in fear every day. Sad to say, it could never be that way, and Sahir was soon to return. The kids would be spending three weeks with him, and my worrying would soon begin. I wouldn't be able to re-lax until the kids safely returned from their three-week visit with their father.

Beni's divorce hearing was scheduled in the Yukon during the same time the kids were visiting their father. I planned to go with him and offer him some support during the hearing. Beni's ex wouldn't agree to Beni's fair offers, so they had to go to court to settle the matter. She was being unreasonable, as she always was in the past. Poor Beni had to suffer for it.

We spent the first two weeks enjoying ourselves. Beni had a beautiful house that he built on Jackson Lake. It was a peaceful place where you could hear all the different sounds of nature. It was simply breath taking. I could see why Beni loved his place so much.

It was my first trip to the Yukon and I was excited to be there. We enjoyed sitting on the porch listening to the sound of the loons and other animals. When it was raining you could hear the tranquil sound of the raindrops falling. On top of all that beauty, I had the most wonderful man in the world right next to me. Being in such a peaceful place was something Beni and I needed. We were both under tremendous stress for so long. I wished Beni didn't have to go through the headache of dealing with the divorce. At least he would have a couple of weeks to enjoy his surroundings.

Beni introduced me to all of his friends who lived there. Everyone was friendly, and they all made me feel welcome. Beni had always told me all about the good friends he had in the Yukon.

One of Beni's closest friends was a man named Horst and his wife Alicia. They had three beautiful girls. I had spoken to them on the phone and seen many pictures of them, but I never had a chance to meet them until that trip. I was so glad to finally meet them in person. They were one of the nicest families I had ever met. They were warm, friendly and giving. They are the type of people who would give the shirts off of their backs. Their three daughters were beautiful and extremely smart. I enjoyed spending time with them while I was there.

I also got to meet a couple of other close friends, Ralph and Jodi. They owned a beautiful house on Emerald Lake and had many dogs that they gave a lot of love to. They invited us to their house and took us for a ride on their boat. Ralph had a pawnshop that I loved to visit while we were there. He had a lot of cool things to look at. Ralph and Jodi were also kind to me, and I had a wonderful time being with them.

It was refreshing to see neighbors act so warm and friendly toward each other. Everyone stopped by for a visit, and sometimes they would even stay for dinner. When we stopped by their places, they, too, greeted us with a warm welcome. That was the first time I was surrounded by so many friendly neighbors. I lived in my house in New York for nearly six years and only knew a couple of neighbors. It was pretty lonely most of the time because everyone was usually busy. I guess I, too, was also busy working or helping the kids with school so I never made any attempts to socialize. I have to admit it felt good meeting so many wonderful people.

Most of the people we ran into were friendly, but it's a fact of life that you also run into the not so nice people. Beni knew many people from one of the churches in town. He and his ex used to attend the church together before they separated. His ex still attends the masses and talks to all the people. She blamed Beni entirely for their failed marriage and made everyone feel sorry for her. It's unfortunate that people involve themselves in family matters they know nothing about. Needless to say, a select few took her side and gave Beni the cold shoulder. Even though Beni didn't show just how hurt he was, I knew that deep inside he was sad. I always tried to stay neutral concerning the marital problems of others. Only the people involved know what's really going on.

The first two weeks of our vacation were relaxing, and we had such a great time. As usual the time just seemed to fly by. Before we knew it the court date had arrived. Three days were set aside to hear the divorce case and to try to come to a settlement. Out of respect to Beni's ex, I chose to stay out of the courtroom. I didn't want to make her feel uncomfortable, so I walked through town to keep myself busy until Beni was through.

I wished Beni's ex and her friends were as considerate. They chose to make a scene in the courtroom by gathering around in prayer and making his ex look like the poor victim. The friends also stayed in the courtroom the whole entire time listening to things that weren't their business. These were the church people who had snubbed Beni after he and his ex separated. I felt so bad for Beni that his old friends had not only turned their backs on him, but they also stuck their noses in his private matters.

During the entire three days of hearings, Beni's ex remained totally unreasonable. The financial matters of the divorce weren't resolved, and a future hearing had to be scheduled. Luckily the judge granted Beni the divorce immediately, and the other matters could be resolved at a later date. Beni was totally drained from the hearings, but extremely happy that he was now legally divorced.

Beni took me out to dinner that evening to celebrate. We went to a fancy Italian restaurant. It was a fun evening, and we had a lot of laughs, too. As we walked into the restaurant we spotted Beni's lawyer at one of the tables with her husband, her assistant and her assistant's husband. We had become good friends with Beni's lawyer and her assistant because they were two nice people whom we got along so well with. Upon seeing them, Beni decided to buy them a bottle of wine and have it brought to their table. They waved to us and said thank you.

Beni and I then had a wonderful dinner together. When it was time to pay the bill, the waiter informed us that the bill had already been paid by the other table (he was pointing to Beni's lawyer's table). We were both laughing and thinking just how sweet it was of them to do that. We smiled and giggled as we thought about how we tried to treat them to a bottle of wine, and they wound up treating us to dinner. It was a cute moment.

After dinner Beni took me for one of our special occasion drinks. While we were sitting there he asked me to marry him. We had talked about marriage before, but we couldn't become officially engaged because Beni's divorce wasn't finalized. I told him yes and that I loved him very much. It was a romantic and special evening. I was truly the luckiest woman in the world.

When Beni and I returned to New York we were sad that the vacation was over, but we looked forward to seeing the kids again. When Kadin and Kazem came back from their father's, they were tired. They said they went camping with him and that Serin and Omer went, too. They liked camping, but complained about things that went on while they were there. Kazem claimed Serin hit him when he tried to unzip the door to the tent. Sahir in turn hit Serin in the head and made her cry. Kadin said his father grabbed his face again when he got angry with him. I knew that although they were things that shouldn't have happened, it was still not enough to start a case against Sahir. I was once again faced with that feeling of helplessness. At least I was confident they would tell me if things got any worse.

Beni and I further discussed our plans to relocate. We knew the process would take months, and by the time we were done, Kayla would be finished with high school. Timmy would still have one more year to go, but he would stay in New York to finish. After talking to both Kayla and Timmy about the relocation, they were both fine with the idea. They said they would miss us, but they would come to visit. They agreed it was in Kadin and Kazem's best interest to move to Arizona. I felt much better after hearing that Kayla and Timmy were okay with the idea. The next step was to find a good lawyer.

CHAPTER 22
Filing For Relocation And Sahir's Threats Of Retaliation

Beni and I searched the Internet in hope of finding a good lawyer who had experience with relocation cases. It wasn't long before we found one who not only had experience, but also won one of the first relocation cases in New York State. We immediately contacted him and set up an appointment to discuss our case.

On September 14, 2004, we met with the lawyer and gave him all the background information pertaining to our case. After we finished giving him the details, he told us we had a good chance of winning our case. He also told us that it was extremely difficult to get a relocation granted in New York, so he couldn't make any promises. I already knew that to be true, but after hearing it from the lawyer my hopes seemed to fade. I also became worried again about what Sahir would do when he found out that we had begun filing for relocation.

The lawyer informed us that the process begins by sending Sahir a letter stating my intent to relocate. He in turn has to write a written objection if he doesn't agree. At that moment I had visions of Sahir reading the letter and blowing his stack. I began trembling with fear knowing that he was going to do something bad to get back at me. Not knowing what it was made it even worse.

I spent the entire day thinking about the relocation letter. The worst part about it was the fact that Kadin and Kazem were going to have a weekend visit right around the time he would be receiving the letter. I was sure he would take it out on the two of them, so I tried to prepare the kids for the worst. I let them know their father was going to get a letter concerning our relocation. They both had the same reaction when I told them. In a nervous tone of voice both said, "Our father is going to be mad!"

I told them both to stay calm if he starts badgering them about the relocation and to say to him, "Please don't discuss this with us. We are only children and this doesn't concern us. This is between you and mom."

It definitely wasn't going to be easy for Kadin and Kazem, but I figured at least they wouldn't be shocked if they knew about it in advance. I wasn't sure exactly when Sahir would receive the letter, but the lawyer said he was going to write it as soon as possible.

The lawyer called me on the 21st of September to tell me he sent the letter to Sahir. Now I was really scared. I kept picturing him opening that letter, and it wasn't hard to paint a picture in my mind of his reaction. The kid's weekend visit was to take place only three days later, so that compounded my fear.

When Kadin and Kazem got ready to leave for their weekend visit, they were both a bundle of nerves. As usual they both closed the front door to kiss me and say goodbye when April pulled up in front of the house. The last thing they said to me before they left was that they were scared their father was going to blow up about the letter. I reminded them about the conversation we had, and I told them not to worry.

The entire time they were gone I kept wondering how Sahir was treating the kids. I prayed he wasn't tormenting them about how angry he was about the letter. It was unlikely that Sahir would keep his rage to himself. This would be another one of Sahir's episodes where he put Kadin and Kazem in the middle. I wish I could have spared them from more pain, but even if Sahir never got the letter, he would have found something else to rage about. That's the type of person he is, and there's nothing you could say or do to make him change.

I anxiously awaited Kadin and Kazem's return. When they finally walked in the door they appeared extremely agitated. They told me their father got the letter, and that he was angry. Their exact words were, "Our father said we're not going to Arizona, and that Beni is going to jail. He also told us that he's taking us to Turkey, and once we're there we'll never have to see our *mother fucking Chinese bitch* mother ever again.

I was upset when they told me what Sahir had said to them. I didn't care what he thought about me. It hurt me that he said such horrible things to the kids and that he also used such vulgarity while saying it. My fear also intensified after hearing his threats directed toward Beni. I now knew for sure that Sahir was going to try to trump up some phony charges against Beni. I had no idea what he was going to come up with, but I knew he would devise some kind of plan. For years Sahir had wanted to get back at me for having him arrested. This was his perfect opportunity, and he was waiting for just the right moment.

My nerves were shot to pieces and the feeling of

helplessness once again overcame me. I held my feelings inside until the kids fell asleep. I then fell apart and cried hysterically. Was there ever going to be a time that my children would have a normal life? Would I have to live in fear for the rest of my life? I was tired of tip-toeing around, writing logs of my children's daily lives and constantly living in fear. I was so mentally and physically exhausted.

There was a time when the anxiety got so bad that I had frequent fluttering in my heart. I thought I was having a heart attack. It got so bad that I consulted a cardiologist. After hooking me up to a heart monitor and doing a sonogram of my heart, he found the symptoms to be a result of extreme anxiety. The stress in my life was definitely taking its toll on my body. Since I had no control over the causes of the stress, the only thing I could do was try relaxation techniques. I began taking deep breaths at times when I felt the anxiety coming on. I then tried to busy myself with other things to get my mind off of my worries. It didn't take away all my stress, but it helped keep me from getting overwhelmed.

During the visitations to follow, it was evident that the badgering had continued. The kids came back extremely agitated after every visit, but they didn't volunteer any information. I could tell that something was bothering them, but I didn't want to question them. All I could ask them was if everything was okay. They would always answer with a yes, but the look in their eyes told me different.

October had just arrived, and the kids made some new friends down the street. They spent the afternoon riding bikes and playing outside. I was happy they could take their minds off of their troubles and have some fun with other children.

While they were playing outside, what should have been just a small accident turned into something much worse. While Kadin was walking on the side of the road, his friend accidentally rode his bicycle into him, knocking him down. Kadin sustained a pretty large bruise on his thigh. Normally this would hurt a bit, but it wouldn't be a big deal. Suddenly Sahir's past threats came into my head, and I had a bad feeling Sahir would use this to pin something on us. It was so ridiculous that I had worry about every cut and bruise the kids got. All kids get cuts and bruises at times. It was a normal fact of life, but in our case it meant that it opened a door for Sahir to trump up false allegations against us.

I felt the anxiety starting to build up, and no matter how hard I attempted the relaxation techniques, it didn't go away. I even tried to convince myself not to worry because Kadin would tell him about the bike accident. Even so, I still had a bad feeling about it.

It was bad enough that Kadin injured his leg, but to make matters worse, he had another accident a day or so later. The builder of our house dropped of a large pile of gravel in the road directly in front of the house. Our basement was leaking, so they planned to dig out our window wells and put gravel in them for better drainage. I instructed the kids to stay away from the pile, especially while they were riding their bikes. I didn't want them to fall and get hurt. No sooner than I told them, Kadin rode his bike too close and fell. Not only did he whack the same bruise, but also hurt another spot on the same leg.

When Kadin came in the house and showed me his leg, I thought, what are the chances of this happening right after the other accident? I can't believe this! I felt like we were on a streak of bad luck. Not only was this true, but things were soon to get much worse.

October 5th was Beni's birthday, so we went out to dinner with my parents to celebrate. We all had a delicious Chinese dinner, and enjoyed spending quality time as a family.

By the time we got home, it was getting late. The kids had school the next day, so they only had enough time for a shower and a quick game, which they usually played with Beni before going to bed. Kazem always liked to lie belly-down on the floor and hold onto Beni's ankle. Beni would then start to walk, and Kazem would hang on for the ride.

Well, going back to the saying, "When it rains, it pours," Beni lost his balance and accidentally stepped back, bumping Kazem's lip. Kazem got a tiny bump on his lip, but nothing serious. He was okay after a few seconds, but in my mind it was now another thing to worry about, just more ammunition for Sahir to use in his devious scheme. Why were we so unlucky? Of all people to have three accidents, one after the other, why did it have to be us? It was like a nightmare!

The next day Beni had to fly back to Arizona to do some maintenance work on his RV Park. I woke the kids up early in the morning so we could drive him to the airport. Just before Beni got out of the car to leave, he gave Kadin and Kazem each $5 to spend in the dollar store. (It was a store that they liked to shop in). On the way home the kids and I spent the entire time talking about how much we were going to miss Beni while he was away. We hated when Beni had to leave, but we knew it was necessary for him to take care of his business.

That afternoon Kadin and Kazem had a four-hour

visit with their father. I tried to tell myself everything would be all right. I knew that even if Kadin was easily manipulated, Kazem would tell the truth about the accidents. Kazem had always told the truth about everything in the past. Kadin, on the other hand, was weaker. He had lied before, especially when it had to do with homework and school. When under pressure, he would tell a lie. Thinking about Kazem's truthfulness put my mind a little more at ease.

I was able to keep busy and not think about things too much while the kids were gone. While I was able to ease my mind, subconsciously I still had a bad feeling, and for a good reason, too. The events to follow were so horribly unimaginable. It was worse than I could ever have expected.

Kadin and Kazem were due back at 8:00 pm. When they hadn't arrived by 8:15 I became a little worried, but I figured they were running a little late. They had been late many times before, so it didn't concern me too much. At 8:30 they still didn't show up. I was a bit annoyed thinking that Sahir was just inconsiderate and didn't bother to call me to say that he was going to be late.

I decided to give Sahir a call to find out what was taking them so long. When I called his house there was no answer, so I decided to try to reach him at his store. A worker answered and said that Sahir should be at home. I told him I already called there and that I got no answer. He said to try calling April. When I called her house, there was no answer there either. I went into a sheer panic at that moment. My first thoughts were that Sahir had kidnapped the kids and left for Turkey. Frantically, I called the worker back, and he told me that he'd try to find where Sahir went.

While I was waiting I quickly called Beni on my

cellphone to tell him what happened. I was crying hysterically and didn't know what to do. While I was speaking with Beni, the home phone rang. Thinking that it could possibly be the kids, I told Beni I'd call him back.

My heart was ready to explode because it was beating so fast. Sahir was on the other end, and as soon as I heard his voice, I asked why the kids weren't home yet. I'll never forget the horrible conversation that I had with him that night. He said, "The kids aren't coming home because your boyfriend beat them up."

I immediately replied, "He did not! Beni is always wonderful with the kids, and he would never lay a hand on them! You bring the kids home or I'll call the police!"

Sahir then started to get into a rage and said that he already called the police. He began screaming at the top of his lungs. Everything that came out of his mouth was nonsense. Half the time I couldn't even understand what he was saying. I began shouting back, and it wasn't long before I realized I wasn't getting anywhere.

My worst fear had come true. Sahir trumped up false allegations of child abuse in retaliation to the relocation letter. He had threatened to put Beni in jail, and now he put his plan in action. I was horrified! I thought that all of Sahir's past actions were as low as a person could stoop, but he managed to step even lower. Words could never describe how I felt at that moment. My entire body felt like someone had sucked the life out of it. I began sobbing hysterically, and the last thing I said to Sahir was that I was calling the police.

The moment after I hung up the phone, I called

the police. They said they would send someone over as soon as a car was available. Waiting for the police was sheer agony. I wanted my two children safe at home with me. I had no idea what Sahir was doing to them or if he was planning to leave the country. I thought that I was going to go out of my mind!

When I got off of the phone with the police, I called Beni back. I was crying so hard that Beni could barely understand me. He, too, was shook up, but he tried to remain calm to help keep me from falling apart. It was evident that Sahir had seized the perfect moment in putting his plan into action. He waited until I was alone and more vulnerable. He also used Kadin's bike injuries and Kazem's bumped lip as a way of tricking authorities into believing that they were abused.

To this day, I still can't understand how someone could be so cruel as to do such an evil act. The worst part about it is that Sahir could care less about how much he hurt his own children while doing it.

About an hour and a half went by and there was no sign of the police. By that time I was frantic. I decided to call back to see what was holding them up. When the police answered the phone, I explained the situation and stressed the fact that it was a real emergency. They once again told me that they couldn't send anyone until a car was available. I couldn't believe it was the only answer that I got! Minutes seemed like days while I was waiting for them to arrive. I began pacing back and forth for a total of two and a half hours before they finally arrived.

When two officers showed up at my door, I let them in and told them the story. I was crying so much that I had difficulty telling them what happened. I told them how dangerous Sahir was and also that I had concerns that he'd try to leave the country with them. I asked if they could please bring my children back home so they would be safe. They told me they wished that they could help, but issues involving custody matters were out of their jurisdiction. They also informed me that they were the ones who responded to Sahir's call and that they had notified CPS.

I couldn't believe that CPS was once again involved! I was unable to get their help when Sahir was committing acts of violence against Serin, attempting to alienate the kids and showing hatred toward Beni and me in front of the kids. Sahir, on the other hand, could make up a bunch of lies and immediately they were involved. It was unbelievable!

The female officer was sympathetic to my situation. She did everything she could, and she truly felt bad that she was unable to help. My mom also came to the house and pleaded with the officers to help bring my children home, but it was of no use.

I was falling apart at that point, and I felt like I was going to collapse. My mom tried desperately to console me. I had no negative feelings toward the officers because I realized that their hands were tied. They could only do what they were allowed to do. They did at least make sure that the kids were still at Sahir's house and not out of the country. I know in my heart that they would have done more if it were possible.

After writing a report, the officers left. My mom stayed around for a while to offer support. After a short while I told her she should go home and get some sleep. I convinced her I was all right even though I was actually ready for a nervous breakdown. I needed to be alone because in my mind I simply gave up. My children were in the hands of an abuser, and the gentle loving man who gave so much to my children and me was now falsely accused of child abuse. Worst of all, there wasn't a single thing I could do right now to help my poor defenseless children. At that very moment I wanted to die! Sahir had put me through hell and back and dragged my children and Beni along with me.

I ran a hot tub to try to calm myself, but I only lay there in the water thinking just how much I wanted my life to end. I begged God to take me away from all the misery I was going through. There were other times in my life when I thought I hit rock bottom, but that night was surely the lowest I ever felt. I cried so hard and kept asking God, "Why? I can't take it anymore! How can Sahir keep getting away with all the cruel and evil things he does? Please take me! I don't want to live anymore!"

Just then, these visions went through my head. All the love I had for my children and Beni filled my body with strength. It was a small reserve of strength that came from deep inside. I wasn't even aware that it existed. As miserable as I was at that moment, I told myself that I couldn't give up. My family needed me, and I was going to fight for them. I prayed to God, asking him to give me the strength to go on. I knew it was going to be hard, but I just had to do it for the sake of my family.

I had no idea what the first step was that I could take or who I could turn to for help. What I did know was that the next day was a holiday, and everything was going to be closed. I'd have to sit on my hands for another day feeling alone and helpless. Never in my life did I suffer as much as I did that night. I cried more tears than I ever did before. This was only the beginning of many heart-breaking days to come.

CHAPTER 23
Many Days In Court

I got up the next morning feeling totally empty, and I constantly fought back tears. The only thing I wanted was to have my family back and for all the nightmarish hell that we were all going through to go away. I pleaded with Beni to come home even though I knew it wasn't possible. He was in the middle of taking care of business, and he also didn't know whether or not it was a good idea for him to return at that point. When it comes to allegations of abuse, it doesn't matter that you've been falsely accused. Unlike normal cases, you're basically guilty until proven innocent. Authorities don't know who you are and even though you're innocent, they don't know that. You have to prove your innocence, and unfortunately it's a long and painful process.

I decided that the first thing I'd have to do was to call the courts and find out how to bring my children home. Beni and I then planned to call CPS and meet with them to tell everything that happened and show that we were falsely accused. Unfortunately I was unable to do anything that day except write a list of everything that I had to do. It was my bad luck that it just happened to be a holiday, and I wasn't going to be able to get hold of anyone until the next day.

I spent most of that day on the phone with friends and family. I called my work to tell them what happened and to say that I was unable to work. I was extremely distraught. I had no idea when I was going to be emotionally ready to return. They were understanding and told me that I could come back when I was ready.

Feeling like I was going to go out of my mind, I kept pacing the floor and crying hysterically. I was in dire need of emotional support. Minutes seemed like hours, and hours seemed like days. I couldn't bear the thought of losing my children and Beni. They were my life, and they didn't deserve to be going through all of this. I knew in my heart that all the time spent trying to help my children recover from Sahir's past detrimental behavior and actions was all for nothing. The progress we made was all wiped away by a single evil act committed by Sahir and his family. It was hard to comprehend how someone could be so evil. I could never deliberately hurt anyone even if it was someone I didn't like. It made me so sad to think that there are people like that out there.

After a long exhausting day I was pretty wiped out of any remaining energy. As tired as I was, I had trouble sleeping that night. That empty feeling created a knot in my stomach. All the bad events that took place the night that Sahir abducted my children repeatedly ran through my brain. I spent most of the night tossing and turning and reliving that horrible nightmare. I couldn't wait until the next day arrived so I could at least begin taking steps to rectify the terrible situation.

I contacted the courts first thing in the morning. After explaining the situation to the clerk, she instructed me to file a Writ Of Habeas Corpus, a court order to force Sahir to bring my children to court. No sooner than she told me, I ran out the door and headed for the court.

When I arrived at the courthouse, the room where you filed the petitions, also known as intake, was extremely crowded. It worked on a first come, first served basis. I was glad I arrived early in the morning because by early afternoon they began turning people away. They could only take so many people each day because they closed at about 5 or 6 pm. I had to wait many hours before I was called in. It took so long that I had a bad feeling I wasn't going to get an immediate hearing as I had hoped. I had no knowledge of what the procedure was concerning the petition I was filing, but it seemed as though it wasn't a speedy process.

When my papers were finished with the filing process, I received a copy along with a scheduled court date. What little hope I had left of getting my children back that day withered away the moment I read the court date. It wasn't for another four days! I told the clerk it was an emergency and asked if they could set an earlier date. She told me that I got the earliest date possible.

I walked out of the courthouse in total disbelief. I was frantic thinking about the danger my children were in. Sahir was unstable and unpredictable. My children could be taken out of the country before anything was done. He had gotten fake passports for his brothers in the past. What was to stop him from getting them for the kids? All his past threats were now being turned into reality. How could I stop him from acting out this threat? There must be something I could do.

When I got back home I called CPS to set up an

appointment for Beni and me to meet with them. After three tries and no answer, I realized that they must have still been closed due to the holiday. I then decided to call Sahir to make sure the kids were still in the U.S. It was also my final attempt to persuade him to stop his cruel game and get him to send the kids home at once.

Sahir did, in fact, answer the phone, but as soon as I demanded that the kids be returned, he refused. I further demanded that he put the kids on so I could talk to them. I just had to make sure they were there and that they were safe. Sahir claimed that Kadin and Kazem didn't want to talk to me. Immediately after he said that, I heard Kadin screaming in the background in an angry tone. All I could make out was that he said he didn't want to talk and that it was his country. Kazem just kept saying, "No!" Something was wrong with Kadin and Kazem's state of mind. I was sure that Sahir had scared them into saying whatever they were saying, and I was also sure that he accomplished it by threatening them.

No matter how many times I asked to speak to the kids, Sahir refused to put them on. I began to cry hysterically once again as I hung up the phone. What had Sahir done to my poor babies? I had such a pain in my heart thinking about what Kadin and Kazem were going through. They were just kids! How could he be so cold and put them through such torture?

My mom came over again to offer emotional support. I was at the point where I couldn't take much more. Both Beni and I were physically and emotionally drained from all the trauma. Just as I thought things were as bad as they could get, I heard a knock at the door. When I opened the door I saw a sheriff standing outside. I was puzzled as to why he was there, but a sense of deja vu suddenly came over me. Flashbacks of being served with a neglect charge back in 1999 entered my head. With an immense knot in my stomach, I opened the door and invited him inside. I looked at him in disbelief when he served me with an Order Of Protection. Sobbing with tears running down my face I asked, "An Order Of Protection against *me*? I haven't done anything wrong!"

He apologized and said he knew nothing about the papers and that he was only there to serve them. I quickly flipped through the papers to find nothing but a whole page of lies that Sahir and his family had trumped up. He accused Beni of everything from repeatedly punching and kicking Kadin and Kazem, to burning them with his cigarettes and even abusing alcohol and Marijuana. He even stated that Beni and I left the kids out in the cold one day without a jacket!

I couldn't believe the lies he made up. First of all, any authority should realize that a child isn't going to have a couple of bruises on his leg or a small bump on his lip if a six-foot man was repeatedly punching and kicking him. And what about the cigarette burns? My children don't have any scars on them! The accusations were so incredibly ridiculous!

My mom and I explained to the sheriff everything that Sahir and his family had done. There was nothing the sheriff could do for us, but he offered some helpful information. He explained that documentation was everything, and that I should document all the beatings Sahir subjected me to while I was married to him. Even if it was too late to press charges, I could still report them. At least there would be a record of it.

At that moment, not only did I think about all the beatings that I was afraid to report in the past, but also all the times Sahir had violated the Order Of Protection. I thought I was saving my children from mental anguish, but in reality all I was doing was letting Sahir get away with it. It's true that Kadin and Kazem got upset the couple of times their father was arrested, but they suffered much more every time he didn't get in trouble.

Sahir knew he could get away with it, so the more he got away with it, the more times he would violate the order. Sahir eventually went on to bigger and better things. Maybe if I had been tougher and shown him that he couldn't get away with all his wrong doings, I wouldn't have been where I was that day. I doubt it. I still think Sahir would have gone through with his evil plan regardless.

While the officer was still at my house, Kayla stopped by with her friend. Seeing how upset I was, she wrapped her arms around me to comfort me. She then proceeded to tell the sheriff that Beni and I were always loving parents and that we would never harm Kadin and Kazem. She also told him all the bad things Sahir had done to our family and how he made up the whole child abuse story.

Kayla's friend also told the officer that Beni and I were loving parents. She spent time at our house in the past, so she knew how we treated Kadin and Kazem. Nothing they said mattered that night because the officer was unable to do anything. It did, however, make me feel good knowing that people loved us and cared enough to stand by us. I needed all the support I could get. I was so fortunate to have my mom there, and when Kayla and her friend showed up, it meant the world to me. Without all of them comforting me, I don't think I could have made it through the night.

I also have to thank Beni because while I was on the phone earlier in the evening, he heard just how distraught I was over everything. He had his friend Jerri contact my mom about my condition. I thank God that I have such a wonderful family. Some people are less fortunate, and it makes me feel sad to think there are others who have to go through similar things all alone.

Two days later I received a phone call from a detective. It was about 10:30 at night, and the reason he called was to update his investigation. I was glad he called because I got a chance to tell him the whole story. I told him that Sahir was still unlawfully holding my children and that he even kept them out of school (I had called the school to see if they had attended). When I asked the detective if he knew how I could get the kids back, he instructed me to drive to a nearby shopping center, which was around the corner from Sahir's house. He then told me that I should call the police and ask for a police escort to the house. I could then safely pick them up.

After hanging up the phone, I drove directly to the shopping center, bringing Timmy with me for safety reasons. By the time the officers arrived it was 11:30 pm. They proceeded to follow me to Sahir's house.

When we arrived, the officers knocked on the door, and when Sahir answered, they went inside to talk to him. When they came back out they told me it was out of their jurisdiction to remove my children from his house! They said the kids were fine, and that it was late. They also added that the kids were playing quietly in the bedroom. I was relieved that they were okay, but upset that they couldn't come home. Why did the detective instruct me to do that if the officers could do nothing?

I was so disappointed and upset that I began crying once more. Thoughts about my two precious children still in the hands of their abusive father were eating me up inside. I asked myself where the justice was in our system. Why can't my children be protected? CPS always questioned me as to why I never left Sahir before that night he was arrested. I think this gives them the answer they were looking for. Sahir made good on his threats of taking my children. He was capable of the unthinkable and that's exactly what he did. He and his family are self-centered and controlling. They didn't care who they hurt, not even their own children, as long as they got their way.

I spent the next day making various phone calls. I managed to finally get hold of CPS to set up an appointment for Beni and me to meet with them. We couldn't wait to tell them what really happened. Beni planned to fly back to New York not only talk with CPS, but also so he could attend the hearing. I also contacted the school social workers from both schools, (Kadin was now in middle school), and the psychologist. They all planned to meet with the CPS case worker.

Having the elementary school social worker and Kadin's psychologist speak with the caseworker was a positive thing. They both had been seeing Kadin for a long time, so they knew a lot about him and everything that had been going on over the years.

I didn't know too much about the social worker in the middle school because I only spoke to her on the phone a couple of times. Early in the school year Kadin was having anxiety over starting a new school year in a different school. I had arranged for Kadin to speak with her. Kadin never opened up to her because she was a woman. He kept hearing so many negative comments from his father about women in general. This had influenced his attitude toward her. He would always complain about speaking with her, and as a result she probably didn't learn too much about him.

Later in the day I stopped by the neighbor's house to see if they witnessed Kadin's bike accident. They were the parents of the boy who accidentally rode into Kadin, causing the large bruise on his leg. Lucky for Beni and me, they had in fact seen the accident and were willing to write a letter to the courts stating that they saw it happen.

I also spoke to a few other neighbors in hope of finding another witness. The mother of another child who was playing with Kadin at the time of the accident told me that her son had seen it happen. She remembered her son telling her all about the incident on the day it happened. She, too, was willing to write a letter to the courts. She even gave me her telephone number in case they had any other questions for her.

I was so grateful to have neighbors who not only witnessed the incident, but were also caring enough to get involved. It was still hard for me to believe that Beni and I had to prove our innocence. We always tried our hardest to be the best parents we could be and provide a loving warm environment for all my children. We always had their best interests in mind. We would never do anything to hurt them. It just didn't make sense that the authorities would trust an abuser like Sahir.

The day of the hearing had finally arrived. I was extremely anxious to see my children, but at the same time I was worried about their state of mind. Sahir kept them out of school the whole time he had them.

He most likely had them isolated so he could brain wash them until the hearing. He had used scare tactics before to get the kids to say and do whatever he wanted. I feared he would do it again.

My mom came with Beni and me to the courthouse. When we arrived, Sahir was there with his three brothers. They sat there glaring at us like they were gangsters and we were little defenseless people who they planned to wipe out. I felt intimidated by them, and I tried to sit as far from them as I could. They may have been able to intimidate me, but Beni didn't let their evil stares get the best of him. At one point we had to walk past them, and when we did, Beni turned around and looked straight into Sahir's eyes. It felt so good to see him stare Sahir down.

Kadin and Kazem were nowhere in sight, which made me wonder where they were. Sahir and Sarim put on a big act trying to look like they were concerned parents. They attempted to put up a false front to gain CPS's trust. It simply made me sick to my stomach. They were all good at putting on an act when necessary. I knew them all too well, and I could see through everything. Sahir spoke and understood English without any difficulty. When he was at his criminal hearing back in 1999, he claimed he needed an interpreter. Now suddenly he had no problems conversing without one. This would later change when the tables were turned.

The courts were busy, and we had to wait until late in the afternoon before our case was heard. It was about 4:30 pm when Kadin and Kazem were finally brought into the court by April. I was so heart broken when I saw them walk in. They both couldn't even look me in the eyes because April sat there constantly watching their every move. It was obvious they were scared to look at my mom, Beni and me because they had been threatened. I felt so sorry for them, and all I wanted to do was give them a big hug. It killed me that I couldn't hold them in my arms and that they were so filled with fear. I could only imagine just how much Sahir and his family had tortured them.

A lady from the court had questioned Kadin and Kazem separately. After they were finished, our case was called. Beni wasn't allowed to enter the courtroom, so my mom escorted me inside. Sarim walked in with Sahir while April remained in the waiting area with the kids.

The judge who was residing was the same judge who had given Sahir so much leeway during the visitation hearings. I had a bad feeling about it because Sahir fooled him in the past. He was a family-oriented judge, and Sahir, being the great actor whom he was, pretended to be a loving father who simply made a mistake. He took the judge for a ride by playing on his sympathies.

I suddenly felt anxiety take over my body. My hope of Sahir getting caught in his evil plan seemed to totally fade away. Sahir and I were then called to the front of the room. As I approached the bench, my whole body began to shake. Just as I seemed to have lost every single hope I had, I caught glimpse of the Law Guardian who was assigned to represent Kadin and Kazem. She was the one who represented my children during Sahir's criminal hearings. She was smart and not easily fooled. Seeing her standing there was like a sign from God telling me not to lose hope. This particular Law Guardian had a lot of knowledge of Sahir's past and based on past experience with her, it was evident she truly cared about my children.

At that moment I knew God had sent an angel down from heaven.

Even though I did get a glimpse of hope, the hearing went almost as bad as it possibly could. Beni was ordered to stay away from Kadin and Kazem! Upon hearing those words I began to cry. Beni had done nothing wrong. The only thing he was guilty of was loving my kids so much. I wanted to die at that moment.

On the positive side, the lady who had questioned Kadin and Kazem told the judge that they gave conflicting answers. It was apparent that someone had been coaching them about what to say. This also showed they were lying. CPS was now in the process of conducting a full investigation.

I was thankful the judge ordered that Kadin and Kazem be released to me. I still couldn't bear the thought of Beni being ordered to stay away. Words could never express the heartbreak I was feeling. The judge adjourned the hearing until a later date so CPS could finish their investigation. As the hearing came to a close and I began heading for the door, I slowly fell apart. Filled with so much pain, I wept so hard that I could barely stand.

I sat in the corner crying my eyes out as my mom tried to console me. Sahir and his brothers passed by with huge smirks on their faces. They all had succeeded in hurting Beni and me, and they were gloating over their victory. Beni remained outside the courthouse not knowing the outcome of the hearing. No matter how hard I tried, I was unable to control my crying. Sahir and his family had once again gotten away with their unspeakable cruelty! I couldn't stand the thought of how much he hurt my children and Beni. I felt like I was going to collapse because I was filled with so much pain. Just before I completely lost it, the Law Guardian came over. She helped me find what little strength I had left by telling me that I had to pull myself together for the sake of my children. She was right. They needed me more than ever at that time. I had to be there for them no matter how much I hurt inside.

Moments after I spoke to the Law Guardian, Kadin and Kazem walked over to me. With tears in my eyes, I gave them the biggest hug that I can ever remember. They both looked at me with such sorrow, and their eyes filled with guilt. I knew Sahir had forced them both to lie to the police and others who questioned them, and that it was eating them up inside. It probably bothered Kazem even more so. I can't even think of one single time that Kazem ever lied. He was always forthright about everything. He must have been under tremendous pressure to lie as he did.

The first two things that the kids said to me were, "Where's Beni? I want to go to Arizona!"

I was ordered by the judge not to discuss the incident with them, and that if they asked questions, to give simple answers. It was quite difficult because the moment we got outside the building, Kadin and Kazem had a meltdown. They began to cry and say, "Our father made us lie to the police. He said that if we didn't say Beni was beating us up, he'd go back to Turkey and never see us again! Where's Beni? I miss him! I'm so sorry!"

The only thing I could tell them was that Beni wasn't allowed to come home because of what happened, and I emphasized how important it was to tell the truth. I also hugged them and told them that it wasn't their fault.

I spoke to Beni on the phone just before we got

into the car to leave. He had gotten the terrible news from our lawyer that he was still not allowed to go near Kadin and Kazem. He was so heartbroken that he, too, was in tears. He told me it was the lowest point in his life. Not only was he falsely accused, but while he was waiting outside, Sahir and his brothers exited the building and laughed at Beni as they stared at him. I felt so sorry for Beni, and I knew just how he felt.

Not only were things emotional that day, but also complicated. My mom, Beni and I had all come to the court in one car. Since Beni wasn't allowed near the kids, he had to get a ride home with the lawyer. He had to leave first so he could pick up his car and stay in a motel. One of the saddest moments was when we passed Beni on the road. As our cars went by each other, the kids and I gazed at Beni, and Beni gazed back. We all wanted to be together again in the worst way.

During the drive home Kadin and Kazem began telling all about the traumatic ordeal. I didn't try to change the subject because I knew they needed to let out their feelings. They talked about how their father made them sit in the hot car the entire day. They arrived at the courthouse about 7:00 am and were in the car until about 4:30 pm. The only food they were given was a little junk food. Lying and getting Beni in trouble weighed heavily on their minds.

Not having Beni at home was upsetting to them. They repeatedly remarked about how their father pressured them into lying and how bad they felt about it. After talking a while, Kadin and Kazem fell asleep in the car. They had been through so much the past week, and they were completely exhausted.

That night was extremely emotional. My heart was

so broken that I had to constantly fight off tears. As I ran bath water for the kids, Kazem completely fell apart. I felt this heart-wrenching pain as I saw my poor little boy fall to his knees. He buried his face in his hands and began weeping. He then cried out, "I have the worst life! Beni's not allowed home, and I miss him so much!"

One of the hardest things a mother can face is seeing her child hurt so much. It had such an impact on me, and it's a painful picture in my mind that I'll never forget. It was just so sad that all my children had to be put through that. I hoped that one day Sahir and his family would have to pay for what they had done. I truly believe the saying, "What goes around comes around."

The next morning Kadin and Kazem were still pretty upset, but they were well enough to go to school. I called the school social workers to update them on the present situation. They both promised to speak with Kadin and Kazem to help them get through the horrible ordeal. The social worker in Kazem's school agreed to meet with him on a regular basis. He never needed therapy in the past, but now that he went through such a trauma, it was more than he could handle.

CPS planned to meet with Kadin and Kazem that week and further question them about everything that happened. They were also going to meet with Kayla and Timmy while they were at their dad's house. Beni and I had an appointment with them later that morning. We both couldn't wait to speak with them so we could tell them what really happened.

When the caseworker arrived, she seemed nice, and Beni and I found it easy to talk to her. The down side to her being the one whom we had to talk to was that she was the same caseworker who found me guilty of neglect back in 1999. I once again had that feeling of uncertainty about whether or not she would see the truth as to what was really going on. Even though CPS had a record of Sahir's past, we started from the beginning when I was physically and mentally abused by Sahir. We continued telling everything that happened right up to that awful night when Kadin and Kazem didn't come home.

During our talk she told us that Sahir had made statements about Beni and me such as, "Beni repeatedly punched and kicked Kazem. He constantly drinks and gets so drunk that he falls asleep with a cigarette in his hand. The children often have to extinguish it themselves. He abuses Marijuana and burns the kids with his cigarettes. Laurie and Beni made the kids go out in the cold without a jacket on a cold day. They also lock the kids in their rooms as punishment."

The ridiculous accusations were endless. Sahir had quite an imagination when it came to making up lies. In addition to Beni rarely ever drinking, he never smoked in the house. I had to laugh when I first heard statement regarding putting my children out in the cold without a jacket. My children all know how I never let them step out the door without proper clothing to keep them warm. If anything, I over-do it with warm clothing. Even my son Timmy laughed when he heard that one. When the kids were asked if and how they knew that Beni used Marijuana, they both sheepishly nodded. Kadin then added, "When I went into mom's closet to find wrapping paper, I found this green goo."

The caseworker asked if I had any green goo in

my closet. I looked at her in such a way as to say, *You got to be kidding, right?* I told her "No" and explained that no one in my home abuses drugs and alcohol. Beni and I even offered to take a drug and alcohol test. We were willing to take a test every day if that's what it took to prove our innocence. All the lies that Sahir made up about us were outrageous.

After talking with the caseworker I was shocked to hear her say that when she met with Sahir he seemed like a nice man. I nearly fell over when I heard her say that. It shouldn't surprise me, though, because as I said earlier Sahir was always good at putting on an act when necessary. He was especially good at charming women so he could fool them. After all, he fooled me many years ago, and I married him.

When the caseworker was finished speaking with us, she politely thanked us for our time. She said she would meet with my four children within a couple of days. After she left, I called the Law Guardian to discuss the situation with her. I also asked if there was anything else we could do to prove that we were wrongly accused. Just as I told the caseworker, I expressed our willingness to take drug and alcohol tests. Her only other advice was for us to cooperate with CPS and let them finish their investigation. All we could do was hope that Kadin and Kazem would tell CPS the truth now that they were no longer under their father's control. Thank goodness, the social workers would be there so the kids would be more relaxed. I still worried about Kadin because he had a new social worker whom he wasn't that close with.

A day or two after Beni and I met with the CPS caseworker, Beni flew back to Arizona. It made no sense for him to stay in New York since he wasn't allowed to come home. I had always been sad when

Beni had to leave, but this time it was much worse. I felt like I was losing my best friend and soul mate. Words couldn't even begin to describe how empty I was inside. Beni was so upset that he couldn't hold down any food. When the kids came back from school the day that Beat left, they were sad to hear that he went back to Arizona. They both became angry at their father for what he had done.

During that week I also brought Kadin and Kazem to the pediatrician for a physical. I explained in detail everything that had transpired, including the false allegations. I needed physical proof that the kids had no signs of abuse. As the doctor examined them, he stated that the two bruises Kadin had on his leg and the little bump Kazem had on his lip weren't signs of abuse. He said that children who are abused typically have multiple severe bruises on their arms and upper body. I now had documentation from the doctor if I needed it. I wanted to take every course of action possible so we could prove that we were falsely accused.

CPS eventually met with all of my children. Kazem admitted that his father had forced him to lie about Beni beating him up and abusing drugs and alcohol. He said his father threatened to go back to Turkey and never see him again if he didn't tell those lies. Kadin also admitted that he was forced by his father to lie about Beni and that he, too, was threatened. Even though he admitted that, the caseworker felt he wasn't being completely truthful about everything. I don't know what else Kadin had said, but I can imagine he made up some stories. Kadin was always good at telling stories, so unless you know him, it's hard to sort out what's fact and what's made up. Nevertheless, Kadin did tell the truth on the important facts.

Kayla and Timmy also told CPS that we had always provided a safe and loving environment for all of them. They had spent a lot of time with Beni and never even heard him raise his voice. They both loved him and always spoke highly of him.

Regardless of all the evil things Sahir and his family had done, Sahir was still allowed to have unsupervised visitations with the kids. It killed me inside knowing that once again they were in danger. The authorities weren't convinced at this point that Sahir had done anything wrong or that he posed a definite risk to Kadin and Kazem.

A short while before April picked up the kids for their next visit, they began talking about the incident again. They both apologized for not talking to me on the phone when I called. They said they had to pretend that they didn't want to talk to me because their father would get mad. He already had made it clear that he didn't want them talking to me.

Kadin and Kazem also expressed how bad they felt because didn't look at my mom and me when they saw us in court. They said that April was watching them, and she would tell their father if she caught them saying hi to us. My mom and I had noticed April staring at Kadin and Kazem in court that day, and we had come to that conclusion. I hugged them both and reminded them that nothing was their fault. I also re-enforced the fact that it was important to always tell the truth, and that people get hurt when lies are told. It was something I couldn't emphasize enough.

When April arrived, Kadin and Kazem looked like two frightened little kids. They did their usual *let me close the door so I can kiss you* routine. The next four hours were going to be long and painful. My nerves would be shot to pieces until they arrived safely home. I was petrified that Sahir was going to pull something else and not bring them back.

Being all alone at home made my anxiety worse. It became so overwhelming that I had to talk to somebody. I had spoken to Beni earlier, and he, too, was experiencing anxiety, so I didn't want to bother him by calling again.

I began thinking about Beni's stress, and I suddenly became insecure. I started to fear that Beni would be scared off by everything he was being dragged into. Most people would have left already. Who would need the headache? I couldn't blame him if he couldn't deal with it anymore. I knew Beni loved me, but he didn't need that kind of stress and he definitely didn't deserve it.

After pacing the floor enough times and feeling that I was going to go crazy, I called Jerri. We talked for a while, and during the conversation I cried so hard it was as if someone was sticking a knife through me. I was hurting so much, and it was more pain than I had ever felt before. Jerri tried to calm me, but at the same time I could sense that she had stress of her own. I decided to cut our conversation short and give Beni a call. I needed to hear his reassuring voice, and it was also best to tell him how I was feeling. Beni was the only person who could make the darkest moments seem brighter. He was always patient even if he was under stress himself.

When Beni answered his phone I was in bad shape. I could barely speak because I was crying so hard. When I told him I was scared that he was going to leave me, he reassured me that it would never happen. Beni expressed how much he loved me and that no matter what, he was going to stand by me. He said that we had to stick together and that in the end, the truth would come out. After hearing his words, I felt a lot better. I still couldn't help worrying about Kadin and Kazem, but at least Beni gave me the strength to go on.

After four torturous hours went by, Kadin and Kazem finally came home. I was so relieved that they came home safely. When they both walked in the door, however, they were distraught. When I asked why they were so upset, they both said, "I don't want to go to a school in Turkey!"

With my eyes wide open and my mouth dropping I asked, "What are you talking about?"

They both replied, "Our father said that he's going to take us to Turkey and put us in a school there! We don't want to go to Turkey!"

My heart almost stopped when I heard them say that. In my mind I was thinking, Sahir is planning to steal them! I had to do something, and fast! It was late, and I knew it wasn't possible to get hold of the Law Guardian, so I planned to give her a call first thing in the morning. In addition to what Kadin and Kazem had just told me, they also said their father kept questioning them about what they told CPS. He also repeatedly bad-mouthed Beni and me, which was another obvious attempt to alienate my children from us.

I was fortunate enough to get hold of the Law Guardian the next day. Out of concern for Kadin and Kazem, she scheduled an immediate appointment to speak with them. Hearing what Sahir had said to the kids during visitation was alarming to the Law Guardian. She, too, took his threats seriously and knew she had to take action right away.

My mom came to the courthouse with me so I wouldn't have to go alone. I was extremely fearful of running into Sahir and his brothers. You never knew where they could turn up, and I didn't want to be confronted by them. They instilled so much fear in me that I was becoming paranoid. Every time I had to go to the courthouse, I spent the entire time looking over my shoulder, and I refused to walk alone.

Kadin and Kazem were questioned individually, first by a social worker, then again by the Law Guardian. After the questioning was completed, the Law Guardian spoke with my mom and me. She told me that based on what Kadin and Kazem told her and the social worker, there was a definite risk of abduction. It was also evident that Sahir was trying to alienate Kadin and Kazem from Beni and me. The Law Guardian planned to take immediate action by petitioning the court for supervised visitation. I was relieved she made that decision. Kadin and Kazem's well being was at risk, so I prayed the judge would grant the petition. She said the process would take a couple of days, but she would call me as soon as she received an answer.

A couple of days passed and I still didn't get word from the Law Guardian. Kadin and Kazem were supposed to visit their father that day, so I was worried. I wanted them to stay home, but I had no legal way of keeping them from visiting. Their safety was my top priority, so I couldn't help worrying about them.

My prayers were finally answered. The Law Guardian called that afternoon and told me she filed the petition and that a court hearing was set for November 4th (three days later). Sahir wasn't allowed to visit the kids unsupervised in the meantime. I could rest easy for the time being because Kadin and Kazem were safe for now. Things also became a little brighter because the truth was slowly coming out.

I decided to go back to work to keep my mind busy. I missed Beni so much, and I wanted my family back together. Staying home wasn't helping because all I did was sit in the house and think about how unfair life was. I knew it was going to be difficult trying to keep my mind on my work rather than my troubles.

The first day back was the hardest. I had to captain a wedding, which was a big responsibility. The toughest part about it was that it made me think about Beni and how hard it was being away from him. While I was setting the tables and getting everything ready for the reception, I couldn't help but wish that it was Beni's and my wedding. Our family could be together enjoying a wonderful celebration, but instead we were apart and miserable.

All the normal little obstacles in life that I thought were so inconvenient in the past suddenly seemed so small compared to what we were going through. Nothing else seemed to matter anymore. I just wanted my family back together. Tears started filling my eyes, and I tried my darnedest to hold back my emotions. It was a couple's special day, and I didn't want to ruin it for them.

Before things got any worse, I asked Joann to tell me something funny so I could stop crying. God knows that once I get started, I can't stop. Joann always had a way of putting a smile on my face. She was always so good to me, and she would do anything to cheer me up. She was so funny that no matter how sad I was, I couldn't help laughing. She succeeded in putting a smile on my face that day even though I was still sad.

While the rest of the staff and I waited for the bride and groom to arrive, Butch and I had a chat. While

275

we were talking, the reverend walked in. She was always so bubbly and as nice as could be. The ceremonies she performed could always bring tears to your eyes. While she stood around waiting, I told Butch that I wished she could say a prayer for my family and me. He told me I should ask her, and that she wouldn't mind if I did. I told him I couldn't because I was much too shy.

Before I could blink, Butch went over to ask her. I was so embarrassed that my face must have turned a bright red. The reverend came right over and told me that she would love to say a prayer for me. The three of us held hands as she said a memorable prayer for me in the middle of the lobby. I may have been embarrassed, but I was happy and grateful that she did.

Her prayer helped me get through the rest of the evening. It also made me think about going back to church. I had wanted to start going again when I was married to Sahir, but he forbid me to practice my religion. Now I was able to go if I pleased, and I knew that I needed every prayer I could get. I felt a bit guilty it took me that long and such a tragedy to make me finally go to church again, but God knows that I've always had faith in him.

On the morning of the hearing I was extremely nervous. I kept hoping the judge would see just what Sahir was doing to the kids and that there was a risk of abduction. I prayed he would keep the visits supervised. When my mom and I entered the lobby outside the courtroom, Sahir and his brothers sat there giving us dirty looks and cursing at us in Turkish. My mom stayed by my side at all times because she knew how frightened I was. Sahir's lawyer was such a weasel. He kept spying on my mom and me to try to hear what we were saying. It was so obvious that we had to laugh. He constantly walked by us, and every time I had to use the bathroom, he would walk over to the pay phones located outside the door. I wouldn't be surprised if he put his ear to the door.

When it was time to enter the courtroom, a thought entered my mind. I began thinking back to a conversation I had with one of the girls I worked with. We were discussing my situation, and she asked which judge I had. She apparently had a boyfriend who had some run-ins with the law. After I told her the name of our judge, she told me that she was familiar with him. She said he was a good judge. Her exact words were, "He's a good judge. He's fair and gives you a chance, but if you cross him, he'll be hard on you!"

This was encouraging because Sahir had definitely been given a lot of leeway, and he had definitely crossed the judge. I hoped the girl was right. I held my breath as the hearing began.

It wasn't a surprise that Sahir's lawyer approached the judge claiming that Sahir needed an interpreter. Now that the truth was coming to light and the tables were turned, Sahir suddenly had trouble understanding and speaking English. Luckily, there was an interpreter available, so our hearing wasn't delayed.

The Law Guardian then proceeded to state all the facts as the judge listened. Sahir and his brothers didn't like to hear the truth about themselves, and of course they would never admit it, so they claimed that the Law Guardian was prejudiced against them. Not only was what they were saying pure nonsense, but I noticed they always accused others of things that were true about themselves. In addition to telling the judge all the bad things Sahir had done to the kids, the Law Guardian also let the judge know that the allegations of child abuse made against Beni were unfounded.

Upon hearing her say that, the judge asked why Beni was still out of his home. I was so happy to hear the judge ask that question. He came to realize that Beni was innocent. Unfortunately for us, CPS stepped in and said that they weren't finished writing their report. As a result, the judge wasn't able to grant Beni permission to return home. I was extremely disappointed and sad that things turned out that way. I had my heart set on having our family together again. Kadin and Kazem were going to be upset, too. They had cried nearly every day from missing him so much.

While that part of the hearing didn't go as well as I hoped, the part concerning Kadin and Kazem's welfare went much better. After all the facts were presented to the judge, he felt that the kids were at great risk, so he ruled that the visits remain supervised until the completion of the trial. He offered Sahir a supervised visit after the hearing that day, but Sahir refused it. He said he did nothing wrong and he didn't deserve that. This was one of the many ways that showed the judge just how Sahir only cared about himself. He didn't take into consideration the feelings of his own children. His true nature was beginning to show, and in future hearings it came out more and more.

The next hearing was set for December 2nd. I hoped we could get an earlier date, but because of the holidays approaching, the courts and our lawyers were busy. Having to wait another whole month meant being away from Beni that much longer. The separation was killing us! All I could think about was holding Beni in my arms once again.

All four of my children were extremely upset that Beni still wasn't allowed to come home. They all decided to write a letter to the judge stating how they felt. I told them that I didn't know if he would be willing to read the letters, or if he even had the time, but in any case I felt it was a good idea. It was therapeutic for them to write their feelings down on paper, and at the same time it could possibly help our case.

While reading their letters I had tears in my eyes. It meant the world to me that my children had so much love for Beni and me. They put a lot of effort into their letters to show the judge how false the accusations were and just how good we were to them. One of Timmy's best friends also wrote a letter. Beni and I were so touched by the letters that I just had to include them in my story. The first four letters are from my children and the last one is from Timmy's friend Mark. They are as follows:

Kayla's letter

I am writing this letter in response to the allegations brought against my mother Laurie and her boyfriend Beni. Beni is the most laid back and kind man. In the couple of years I've known him he has never so much as raised his voice to me or my three brothers. I'm a teenager with an occasional attitude, and as nasty or mean as my attitude gets he has never lost his temper with me. I look up to him very much, and Kadin and Kazem, my two younger brothers, do as

279

well. Not only is this accusation false but is outrageous. Sahir, the accuser, has brought nothing but grief to my life since the day I met him. He beat my mother more times than I can count and then threatened to flee the country with Kadin and Kazem if she so much as asked for help or tried to leave him. The night he was arrested for the domestic violence incident, he beat my mother, almost killing her and when I tried to protect her, he threw me to the floor, injuring my arm. He then proceeded to scream in my face that "now my mother, stepmother and father could all have sex together." Upon receiving the Order Of Protection against Sahir he continued to harass me and my family. One night my mother went to a movie with my grandmother. Sahir called repeatedly and would not leave me alone, interrogating me about the whereabouts of my mother, insisting she was out with another man. When my mother returned I was in tears from being harassed. Kadin and Kazem mean very much to me and I have been thinking about them non-stop. If Child Protective Services is supposed to protect children, then why are my two brothers in the care of an abuser and liar? I feel as if my family's and my rights have been violated. I worry about them day after day and wonder if they are o.k. This is my statement from my heart.

Thank you.

Sincerely, Kayla

Timmy's letter

I have been informed of the charges placed against my mom Laurie and her fiancé Beni. I can immediately tell you, for a fact, that they are false. When my mom was with Sahir, I did all I could to protect her from him and I called the cops on him. My mom's current fiancé Beni, is the total opposite. I've known him for two years now and he is one of the calmest people I've ever met. I've seen him with my brothers Kadin and Kazem, and he has never given me a reason to worry about him hitting them. Beni and my mother would never raise a hand to my brothers. They both know how to discipline the kids in a calm and rational manner. As for the charge of leaving my brothers in the cold with no jacket, this is absurd because my mother has always made it imperative that they dress warm, with a jacket and all clothing necessary before the kids would ever leave the house in the winter. I'm sure that Beni and my mother have never laid a hand on the kids or have ever punished them in an irrational manner. If I ever saw Beni or my mom treat my brothers in a violent or irrational manner, I would immediately take action and inform the police, but I've never seen or even had to worry about my mom and Beni ever abusing the children or treating them hurtfully. Sahir has said plenty of things about my mother and

281

Beni that are lies for a fact because I was always there to witness the truth.

Sincerely, Timmy

Kazem's letter

Dear Judge,

I really want Beni home. I'm so sad when Beni is not here. It's not good without Beni. I wish Beni was here right now. I wish Beni was here for my birthday. I want him for all the holidays. He's the best one in the family. I really miss Beni. I hope our family will come back together. Can you please bring Beni back? I cannot sleep when he is not here. I hope he will walk in the door and say hi family. He is very nice to me. I hope I will pick up the phone and Beni will say I'm comeing home. He is the best. That is true. I really love Beni. I hope he will be back with me. I like what he cookes for me. I hope he will be home again. He is the nicest one in the family. He is really nice to my family.

From Kazem

Kadin's letter

Dear Judge

I really want Beni to come home. I miss Beni. I can't sleep drink or eat because I miss him so much. Can you please send him home?

From Kadin

Mark's letter

To Whom it may concern,

I'm writing this letter on behalf of Beni and Laurie. I have slept at their house numerous times. I feel that they are good parents. I have not seen any abuse or even as much as unnecessary yelling at the kids. I feel that they try to make Kadin and Kazem's life as good as they possibly can.

Sincerely, Mark

At this point in time Beni and I decided to file our relocation petition in Family Court rather than Superior Court. We already had a court date set for December 2nd, so it would be faster to do it all in the same hearing. It also helped that the Family Court judge was already familiar with our case. This was now one huge hearing involving custody, false allegation charges and relocation. Now I was even more nervous knowing that we would soon find out whether or not we could relocate to Arizona. Our family's life was in the hands of one judge.

I needed any proof I could get to show the judge Sahir's true nature and things he had done in the past. I decided to go to the hospital and get copies of my records. I thank God that I had confided in two of my doctors concerning the abuse inflicted on me by Sahir and the injuries I sustained. I remembered what the sheriff had told me concerning just how important documentation was. These were the only records I had that proved just how violent Sahir was and what he was capable of doing. Even though it was only a small fraction of what he had done, it was still proof. Sahir probably had no idea such records existed. He instilled so much fear in me that he probably believed I'd never tell anyone.

As I read the medical records I began experiencing flashbacks from all the beatings Sahir had subjected me to. Reliving the physical and mental abuse he inflicted on me was extremely painful. I wondered just how I survived all those years living in so much fear day to day. I felt myself barely breathing while I was reading, and before I knew it I was gasping for air. It was a miracle that Sahir had never killed me. The beatings were so severe that I must have had a guardian angel watching over me. The force of Sahir smashing my head repeatedly on the floor was so great that it alone could have ended my life. It's a scary thought that I might not have been here today writing this story.

Thanksgiving slowly arrived, and I was much too

depressed to spend it with my relatives. Not having Beni home to spend it with us took all the fun out of it. Kayla and Timmy planned to spend Thanksgiving with their father and Betty, so Kadin, Kazem and I were home alone. I tried my best to cheer up Kadin and Kazem and provide them with some kind of holiday spirit regardless of how sad I was. I decided to make a turkey just for the three of us. While the food was good, our hearts were so empty. We all sat there holding back the tears as we looked at Beni's empty chair. The three of us only talked about how much we missed Beni. Kazem also told me how much he hoped that Beni would be home for his birthday. I told Kazem that we all hoped he could make it to his birthday, but that I couldn't make any promises.

In addition to all the letters written on Beni's and my behalf, two more were written. One was by the elementary school social worker and the other by the psychologist. They spent many years meeting with Kadin, so they knew exactly what was going on. I had kept in close contact with both of them in a joint effort to try to help Kadin. They also knew Beni because he became involved in Kadin's therapy. Not only did Beni bring Kadin to therapy on numerous occasions, but he also met with the social worker several times. During his sessions, Kadin also talked about how positive his relationship was with Beni.

I appreciated the fact that the social worker and therapist truly cared about Kadin's well being. They went above and beyond, and till this day Kadin speaks positively about both of them. They both have a special place in Kadin's heart.

Toward the end of November, I decided to Have Kazem start meeting with the psychologist. Even though Sahir had pressured Kazem into lying about

Beni, Kazem was still laden with guilt. He also had so much anxiety from all of his father's threats, and he was having difficulty dealing with the trauma caused by his father. Kazem liked the idea of speaking with the psychologist because he had met him many times when we took Kadin for therapy. He felt comfortable talking with him, and he knew that he was in dire need of venting his problems. Kazem was always strong, but even he had his limits. He worried me all the more because he was always so quiet and tried so hard to please everyone. He never wanted anyone to know he was hurting inside. I could feel that he was holding in so much, and after talking to him a while bits and pieces slowly came out. This was the first time that Kazem was beginning to open up.

CHAPTER 24

Custody And Relocation Hearings And Brighter Days To Come

In the months to come, many days were spent in court. The courts were so busy that there were some days we spent nearly the entire day just waiting around. It was extremely frustrating, not only because of the long waiting, but also because every moment wasted meant more dollars spent on paying the lawyer.

There were many witnesses who had to testify during these proceedings, so we needed ample time for our case to be heard. Most of the time it seemed as though we only had about an hour and a half per day by the time our case was called in. Sometimes it was even less than that. This meant that we were paying the lawyer to sit around for about seven hours. I'm sure our lawyer was frustrated, too, because not only was it boring just sitting there, but also by our case dragging on, it kept him from other cases.

Being that there were so many witnesses, it's extremely difficult to remember exactly who testified first. I can only say for sure that Sahir's family went first, and that it finished with me, my mom, Beni and finally the rebuttals. In between those testimonies were the testimonies of the school social worker, the psychologist, CPS and the court social worker.

December 2nd was the first of these proceedings. Kayla was off from school that day, so she decided to come with my mom and me to the hearing. She was so angry at Sahir and hated everything he had done. I think she had to come to court that day not only to offer support to me, but also as a way to stand up to Sahir. She so desperately needed to see justice served. In addition to everything he did to hurt all of us, he never admitted to hurting her that last night he and I were together. This bothered her. It's bad enough when someone hurts you, but it's even worse when they refuse to admit it.

The Law Guardian subpoenaed the elementary school social worker and the psychologist. The social worker didn't show up that day due to miscommunication in the school. Knowing just how crucial his testimony was, I panicked out of fear that he may not come. He would only be allowed to testify if the school approved it. My mom and I talked on the phone with several school officials, and after much pleading with them, they agreed to let him testify. He would only be allowed one day, so we had to make sure a certain day was set for him to testify.

April was among the first to testify. She lied through her teeth the entire time. I knew without a doubt she'd been coached what to say. She was using words that were definitely not in her vocabulary. If someone had asked her just what those words meant, she wouldn't be able to answer. She denied making threats to Kadin and Kazem or preventing them in any other way from showing affection toward me. She also claimed I had never driven Sahir to and from work even though I had done it for years. With the exception of her stating her name and who she was, everything that came out of her mouth was a lie.

I think the judge didn't have any difficulty figuring out that she wasn't truthful. The shifty look in her eyes made it obvious. When asked if she brought the kids to the doctor when she saw the bruises on Kadin's leg and the bump on Kazem's lip, she answered, "No. I called my lawyer."

My attorney then asked her why she didn't bring them to the doctor if she felt they were being abused. Her answer to that one was, "Because they were closed."

I was actually surprised that Sarim and Sahir used her as a witness. Even though she was normally a chronic liar, she wasn't good at it. She was also not very bright, so even if someone had spent hours coaching her about just what to say, it wasn't hard to make her slip while she was lying.

Sahir's wife Serin was the next to get up on the stand. She didn't speak a word of English, so the translator had to assist her. Serin looked scared to death while she was being questioned. I felt sorry for her, knowing the pressure she was under. She probably feared for her life because she knew that if she didn't say exactly what she was told, she would be beaten up.

As expected, of course, she didn't admit to ever being abused by Sahir. Even though the kids had witnessed the incident in Florida, she still denied it. I can only imagine the fear she was experiencing, so I can't blame her for lying about the abuse. Serin's testimony was short because of the little time she had spent with the kids and her lack of knowledge concerning our case.

When Sahir took the stand he spent the entire time looking down. He never once looked the judge in the eyes, and he evaded every question he was asked.

Never once did he give a straight answer because he knew he was guilty. All of his testimonies were total lies. He even went as far as saying that my mom had a mural of the Great Wall hanging in her home and that she used it to ridicule him. He claimed that she would make him sit in the corner alone during family gatherings and say, "See this wall? It was built to keep people like you out!"

When I heard him say something so ridiculous as that, I just had to laugh. How could he make up such a story? My mom is the sweetest and most loving person in the world. In addition to her not being capable of being mean to anyone, the story was so absurd. It was apparent that even the court officials had to hold the smirks back on their faces.

Sahir also came up with other crazy stories. He claimed I never loved him because I wanted to marry a model. I don't know how he thought up such stories, but he made our hearing into a side show act. The list goes on.

When he was questioned about the abuse he put me through, he denied everything. He claimed that on the night he was arrested he simply pushed me out of the way because he wanted to have a cigarette. Sahir also denied throwing Kayla to the ground and hurting her arm. Kayla was furious when she heard him lie under oath. I could tell she was holding back tears as she listened to everything Sahir said while he was on the stand. I gave her a supportive hug and told her not to worry because justice would be served.

Sahir continued to tell one lie after another, and he even brought out pictures to try to convince the judge that he was a good father. It was frustrating having to sit back and listen to all of his lies. I felt like crying, but I knew I had to stay strong. I also dreaded going up on the stand when it was my turn to testify. Not only was I extremely shy, but I knew that Sahir and his family would be glaring at me the entire time I was up there.

Sahir's evasiveness and ridiculous stories definitely hurt his credibility. On top of all that, he lied so much that he caused himself to slip up. While being questioned by the Law Guardian, he forgot to wait for the translator to translate one of the questions asked of him. He immediately answered the question, and not only did he answer it, but also he answered it in English. Previous to that question and all those thereafter, everything had to go through the translator first. This made it obvious to the court that he was dishonest about needing an interpreter.

Sahir also told the judge that he agreed to the third degree assault charges back in 1999 because he had trouble understanding what was said to him. He claimed he was under the impression that he had to plead guilty because it was the only way he could see his kids. Contrary to those claims, he still refused to see his kids supervised while these hearings were going on because "he didn't do anything wrong and he didn't deserve it."

Sahir contradicted himself so many times that the judge had no problem seeing that Sahir wasn't being truthful. It was evident by the tone of the judge's voice that he was becoming tired of Sahir's dishonesty.

Sahir's testimony took so long that it had to be continued on the next court date. It was a long, stressful day. Never in my life had I heard so many lies told. I was totally drained and exasperated. At least the day ended on a positive note. The law Guardian made a motion requesting that Beni be allowed home. Thank goodness CPS had finally finished their report. The allegations of child abuse were unfounded, so the judge vacated the order of protection and Beni was allowed to come home.

We had been apart for two long months. I couldn't wait to call Beni and tell him the great news! I knew my children were going to be so happy to finally be a family again. I was still so angry that Sahir's cruelty caused us to be apart in the first place, but I was so happy that Beni could come home. Rather than dwelling on the injustice done to us, I used my energy to enjoy the good news.

When I called to tell Beni the wonderful news, he was extremely happy. He booked the earliest flight possible so he could be home in time for Kazem's birthday. When Kazem found out Beni was coming back on his birthday, he told me that it was the best present he ever got. The sadness that had filled our home for the past two months quickly vanished into thin air.

Having Beni back home was like the sunshine after the rain. Our prayers were answered, and we were a family once again. Kadin and Kazem kept apologizing to Beni about lying to the police and other authorities. We both reassured them again that it wasn't their fault, and we once again gave them the reminder about how important it was to tell the truth.

Sometime after Beni returned back home, we attended another hearing. Sahir had to finish his testimony from where he left off. He was only a little more than half way through last time we were in court. He continued to tell lies and once again was evasive during the questioning.

After Sahir's testimony was finally finished, the

school social worker and the psychologist testified. They were both credible witnesses who told the judge about all the years they worked with Kadin, and how they were now meeting with Kazem. They said that Beni and I got involved with the kids' schooling and therapy, and that both kids spoke highly of us. Both children told them how their father constantly bad-mouthed me over the years and how he forced them to lie about Beni hitting them. During therapy they also talked about how scared they were because their father threatened to take them to Turkey and put them in school there. They also mentioned how much they wanted to move to Arizona.

After hearing all the false testimony from Sahir and his family, it was refreshing to hear the testimony of two professionals. They painted a true picture of what was going on in the lives of my children. It felt good to finally see the truth starting to come out and the wheels of justice beginning to turn.

The next one to be called to the stand was the CPS caseworker. She looked extremely nervous, which made it difficult for her to answer the questions. She also remained fooled by Sahir's manipulating charm. Regardless of anything Sahir did, she still thought he was a nice man. Even the Law Guardian seemed to have serious doubts concerning her judgment. I think the caseworker was also frightened of Sahir and his family due to an incident that oc-curred in the lobby prior to the hearing. My mother did nothing more than say hello and introduce herself to the caseworker when April suddenly ran toward them screaming, "Sarim! She's talking to her! She's not supposed to do that!"

The caseworker looked over in fear and pro-ceeded to walk away. Seeing the caseworker's state of mind during her testimony, it's my belief the judge didn't weigh her testimony too heavily.

The court caseworker was the last to testify before it was my turn. The kids had been open to her about how their father forced them to lie about Beni and about his threats of abduction. They also had told her what good parents Beni and I were and how much they wanted to move to Arizona. They said that they would miss their father if they moved, but they would visit him. Like the school social worker and the psychologist, she testified in a professional manner. She, too, painted a real picture, and she came across as a credible witness.

Christmas fell in between the many hearings. The courts were closed for the holidays, so our family finally had some time to relax. Since being apart delayed our wedding plans, we decided to get married after the New Year. After speaking with all my relatives and finding out when everyone was free, we set our wedding date for January 14, 2005. Everyone was so happy for us, and they all looked forward to attending our wedding.

I only had a few weeks to get everything ready, but since I had a lot of experience with weddings from work, I wasn't worried in the least. We planned to have a small wedding reception at the catering hall where I worked. We also decided to have the ceremony there as well. One reason I wanted to have the wedding at my work place was because everyone there had always put a lot of effort toward making every party a memorable one. Another reason was because the people I worked with were like family to me. I thought it would be nice to have some of them not only work at our wedding, but also celebrate our special day with us.

My favorite reverend, (the one who said the prayer for me in the lobby of my work) agreed to perform the ceremony. We also were able to get my favorite DJ, Jack. He was a sweet man who always performed at the senior parties. He had a wonderful personality and he was always entertaining, so I was thrilled when he said he would do it for us.

I was sad at that time knowing that no one in Beni's family would be able to attend. They lived all the way in Switzerland, and they all had jobs there, so it would be difficult for them to take off at such a short notice and fly to New York. While I was sad, I completely understood their situation.

Just days after wishing that Beni's family could attend, Beni and I received a wonderful surprise. Beni's two nieces and their boyfriends, along with Beni's nephew and his girlfriend, arranged to fly out and attend our wedding. It meant the world to us that they went so much out of their way to be with us. In addition to his family being able to attend, Beni's friend Jerri was also able to come. Her boyfriend Dan was nice enough to offer to take care of the RV Park while she was away. They all planned to fly out to New York a few days before our wedding.

My boss, along with other friends I worked with, helped organize everything. Joann looked forward to being our mai'tre D, and Francine was excited to be our bartender. Butch went out of his way to leave his calendar open so he could be our bridal captain. He had another job, so this meant a lot to us that he reserved that day so he could be there. We were having about thirty people, including ourselves, so we only needed two waitresses. My two good friends Kerri and Mable were happy when we asked them.

Since the staff that was going to work our party

was like family, we asked if they could sit down and eat dinner with us and join in the fun when they had time. We were also going to be the only party in the house that night, so my boss had no problem letting the staff join in the party. Everyone looked forward to having a blast with us. They all knew the hard times Beni and I had gone through. They loved us both and were so happy we found each other and that we were becoming a unity. Everyone at my work had seen just how much we went through together in the past several months and how our love got us through it all. It meant a lot to them that they could be a part of it. We were fortunate to have such wonderful friends who cared so much about us.

I told Beni earlier in the year that the only two things I wanted for Christmas were to marry him and to be able to relocate to Arizona. I didn't yet know about the relocation, but I was so thankful I was marrying the love of my life. My heart was filled with so much love for him, so I looked forward to our special day.

The next few weeks went by quickly. Jerri and Beni's relatives arrived safely at our house. All of the preparations for our wedding were complete, so we were able to spend some time with family and friends. I enjoyed sitting around the table talking with everyone. Beni has a nice family. They're all warm and friendly, and I always felt comfortable talking to them from the day I met them.

On the morning of our wedding, the weather wasn't too nice. It was cloudy, and by midday it was snowing. I was worried the weather would get worse as the day went on. Some of my relatives were driving in from the city, so I hoped it would clear up. In addition to having bad weather, Kadin wasn't feeling too well, and he had a fever. Even though the early part of the day started out rocky, I wasn't going to let that spoil our special day. All I could do was pray that everything would turn out okay.

By early evening the weather cleared up, and Kadin didn't get any worse. He still had a fever, but he was well enough to enjoy our celebration. Things seemed to be finally going smooth until about an hour before we were supposed to leave. Timmy was nowhere to be found. He was supposed to be at our house already, but he never showed up. Kayla told me that she would call around and try to find him while I got ready. After several attempts, she finally found him. The bad thing was that when he got about half way to our house, he realized he forgot his shirt. We were leaving in 45 minutes, and not only did Timmy have to go back to get his shirt, but he also still had to change into his suit. I was beginning to panic at that point.

About ten minutes before we planned to leave I heard the sound of a limousine wedding horn. It couldn't be for us, I thought. We had rented a large van to take to the wedding, so I was puzzled. With a smile on my face, I suspiciously asked Beni if he had called a limo. I was surprised and even more puzzled when he told me that he didn't. I knew someone had given us a big surprise, but who? When the driver got out, he said that the people at my work paid for a limo for us! I was so touched by the thoughtful gift they gave us. It was quite a surprise.

We were all ready to leave, with the exception of Timmy. Just as I was about to lose hope about him showing up, he pulled up the driveway. Luckily, Timmy is a fast dresser. We left about ten minutes late, but at least we made it. Even though it was a stretch limo, we still had too many people, so Beni's nieces drove the van and followed behind us.

It was neat riding in a fancy limo. Kadin and Kazem were having a ball along with everyone else. The atmosphere was filled with joy and excitement, but as we were just pulling into the parking lot of the hall, Kadin and Kazem suddenly had a fearful look in their eyes. They must have caught sight of their father's gas station, which was visible from the parking lot. It was apparent they still had a tremendous fear of what their father might do. Before I could ask what was wrong they both blurted, "What if our father sees us? He's going to be mad if he finds out you got married!"

I was pretty shocked to hear them say that because my mind was so filled with bliss that day. Worrying about Sahir was the farthest thing from my mind, so it took me by surprise. In a reassuring voice I told them both not to worry because their father couldn't do anything. I also reminded them how dark it was outside and that he probably couldn't see us anyway. Joann and Butch gave us a warm, loving welcome as we pulled up to the door. As they helped us out of the limo, Kadin and Kazem became distracted by the beauty and excitement of the catering hall. They quickly forgot about the fear they had just moments earlier.

The room was set up beautifully for our ceremony. Being that I worked there, I had seen it set that way many times, but that day it was even more special. As I looked at the room I felt like crying because this time it was there for us. I couldn't believe that it was really happening. Months earlier I had felt like my life was over, and now it was one of the best days of my life. I had the best man in the whole world right next to me, and we were soon about to become one.

My Uncle Albert gave us the wonderful gift of taking all the photos. He was a great photographer, and we were appreciative he did that for us. My Cousin Jacob was also thoughtful. He was my uncle's back-up photographer. He, too, was great at taking pictures, so we were fortunate. One of my friends who I grew up with named Mary gave us the special gift of taking a video of our ceremony and reception. Having such a beautiful memory of our day was a priceless gift. I knew Beni and I would spend much time looking at the beautiful photos and video, reliving that special moment in our lives.

As I walked down the aisle toward my handsome groom, I gazed into his gorgeous eyes. They were filled with tears of joy and contentment. I, too, had to hold back the tears as Beni and I joined hands. The reverend performed the most beautiful ceremony with her heart-felt words. Beni and I did a family candle lighting with Kayla, Timmy, Kadin and Kazem. All of us were so touched that we almost started to cry as we lit the candles. We were all blessed with having such a wonderful family. It was truly a memorable moment that brought tears to everyone's eyes. Even my brother, who doesn't usually cry at ceremonies, cried at ours.

Our reception that followed was the best I had been to. Not only was it ours, but never in my life did I have so much fun. Beni and I, along with everyone else, danced nearly the entire evening, except when we ate dinner and cut the cake. The room was filled with more love and excitement than any other wedding I had ever been to, and from working at the catering hall, I had seen a lot of weddings. Even Kadin danced non-stop, and with the way he moved around, you would never know that he was sick.

We had a lot of memorable moments that night. One in particular that I'll always remember was the dance I had with Timmy. He was usually a bit on the shy side. He wasn't the type to get out on the dance floor, but on that night it was different. Not only did he get out there, but also he did a slow dance with me while others watched. It meant the world to me that he had the courage and the will to do that for me.

Toward the end of the evening Beni gave a moving speech. He thanked my family for letting him into their lives, and he promised to take good care of me. He also thanked family and friends for spending our special day with us. After he was finished, I made a quick speech. Being the shy person that I am, it was difficult to get up in front of everyone and speak, even if they were my own family. It definitely wasn't the best speech in the world, but I tried my best, and the words came from my heart.

We had a wonderful time that night. The DJ Jack kept us fully entertained, and the food was great. Everyone at my work took good care of us. Most importantly, Beni and I were united together in the company of people who were dear to our hearts.

Being that we were in the middle of many court hearings, we weren't able to go on a honeymoon after our wedding. We would have to plan that at a later date. Kayla offered to baby-sit Kadin and Kazem the next day so that we were able to at least take a trip to Manhattan with my mom, Jerri, Beni's nieces and nephew and their boyfriends/girlfriend. We still had the van we rented, so it was nice driving there and spending the day sightseeing. It was pretty cold that day, but we had a good time anyway.

In addition to all the fun we had spending time

together, we also experienced moments of great sadness. We visited Ground Zero to pay our respects to those who lost their lives during that tragic day of September 11, 2001. As I looked at the vacant spot where the World Trade Center used to stand, a feeling of pure emptiness filled my body. My heart cried out to all the people who died and the families that were left behind. Seeing the sight that day truly left an impact on me.

Several days after our wedding, Beni's family and Jerri had to return home. I was sad to see everyone leave, but I knew they had to go back to work and that Beni and I would soon be back in court. I dreaded returning to court and seeing Sahir and his family again, but at least we had spent the past weeks full of total bliss. Being stress-free for a while helped us regain our strength for the oncoming final battle.

Even though we had some time to recuperate from the months of stress and lack of sleep caused by Sahir and his family, it still took its toll on my health. The day before I was to testify, I came down with the flu. I was so weak and cold that I couldn't even get out of bed. In previous years I always got a flu vaccination, but that year due to the shortage, I was unable to get one. Lucky for me I must have had a little resistance left because even though I still didn't feel well the next day, I was able to get back on my feet. I also think my adrenaline was so high that it kept me going the entire day.

It was now my turn to get up and testify. Standing up to Sahir and his family was one of my biggest fears. They were sitting directly across the room from where I was seated, so I was petrified. I told myself not to look in their direction and to only focus on the person questioning me. My children's lives depended on me, so I had to remain strong. All the words of encouragement that my mom and Beni gave me helped me stand tall.

As my testimony began I felt my body shaking in fear as I sat there all alone. I could feel the evil stares coming from Sahir and his family, but I didn't dare look their way the entire time I was sitting there.

Sahir's lawyer played dirty by trying to intimidate me with his antagonistic loud voice. Knowing that I was completely honest and I had nothing to hide made answering his questions quite easy. The only things that made it difficult were my fear of Sahir and his family and my shyness. To my amazement, even though I was so nervous, I even remembered dates that were asked of me which is normally difficult for anyone.

Sahir's lawyer became annoyed that he couldn't rattle me. He was surprised by my response when he questioned my abuse accusations against Sahir. When he asked if I had medical records to back my claims, he was totally shocked when I actually had medical records to show. After he looked over the records and saw that my doctor had documented the abuse, he suddenly responded by saying that they were no good because they weren't certified.

It felt good that I had the chance to not only talk about things of the present, but also about the past abuse Sahir had put me through while I was pregnant and while my children were present. His lawyer attempted to stop me from telling the judge, but thanks to a good judge who saw all the danger that Sahir subjected my children to, I was allowed to finish.

Sahir's lawyer went as far as to show ridiculous photos of Kadin's bruise from the bike accident and the little bump on Kazem's lip. I didn't in any way deny the fact that they had those small injuries, but I explained to the judge just how they got them. I also explained that they were active, and that it wasn't uncommon for them to get hurt during play. I don't think there's a child in this world who didn't get some cuts and bruises while playing. If needed, I also had the letters from my neighbors stating that they witnessed Kadin's accident with the bike. I don't believe that the judge ever asked me for the letters because it was obvious I was telling the truth.

Being up on the stand seemed like forever. Between having the flu and being a nervous wreck, I was exhausted by the time I was finished.

The court took a recess after my testimony. As I stepped out of the courtroom, I was so filled with emotion that I took one look at Beni and broke down into tears. He held me in his arms and immediately I felt a sigh of relief. All the emotions that built up inside slowly went away. I had a difficult time being in the courtroom because all my support was sitting outside. He and my mom had to wait in the lobby because they were both witnesses. They weren't permitted inside the courtroom until they were called in to testify. As hard as it was, I was proud of myself that I didn't let Sahir and his family get the best of me.

My mom was next to be questioned. She, too, was harassed by Sahir's lawyer, and she became the next victim to have preposterous allegations thrown at her. He insisted that she had a "Great Wall Mural" that Sahir spoke of hanging in her house. My mom had a look in her eyes as if to say *are you nuts?* Regardless of the way she felt, she politely told him the truth that she didn't own such a thing.

In addition to coming up with such ridiculous accusations, the lawyer had a way of making a fool of himself. There were many times when it seemed as though everyone had difficulty trying not to laugh at him because of his sleazy manners and ruffled attire. It didn't surprise me that Sahir and his family had chosen such a lawyer. He seemed to fit in perfectly with their clan.

My mom also had the chance to talk about the past abuse I endured when I was married to Sahir. She became all choked up and fought back tears as she spoke. It was also hard for her to talk about the mental abuse Sahir had been inflicting on Kadin and Kazem. She talked about how fearful they were that their father would hurt her and me. She said that while she was baby-sitting them, they told her he was saying bad things about us and that he threatened to smash my mother's car and hurt her.

When our lawyer asked her how she felt about Beni and the relocation, she answered by saying that he was a great man. She also mentioned what incredible patience he had and how wonderful he was to all my children. She also included the fact that he spent a lot of time helping the kids with their homework. Concerning the relocation, she stated that she would miss all of us, but she knew it was in Kadin and Kazem's best interest. She promised to visit, talk on the phone and write letters to us on a regular basis.

After my mom finished testifying, she was upset at herself because she felt that she could have said more. She kept remembering things she wanted to say. I told her she did a great job, and that she talked about all the important things. Being on that stand was nerve-wrecking. I knew just how she felt having everyone staring, especially Sahir and his family, and to have his lawyer antagonizing her. It was definitely no picnic.

Beni was last to be questioned that day. Even as calm and collective as Beni is, he was nervous. He answered questions about himself and presented the entire relocation plan. He showed pictures of the lot that he purchased and the house that would be built if we were permitted to leave New York. Beni had visited the schools in Arizona and spoke with the administration. He even brought back photos to show the judge how nice the schools were. Sahir's lawyer tried to antagonize Beni just as he did the rest of us. Beni, being as levelheaded as he was, didn't get rattled in the least. The lawyer became annoyed and began making gestures that made himself look like a clown. Many times during the hearings I thought about just how glad I was that he wasn't our lawyer.

Our case just seemed to drag on because of the little time we had each day due to the court's overload. Not only did the judge still have the rebuttal testimonies to hear, but he also wanted to have an in-camera with Kadin and Kazem. He planned to speak to them with only the Law Guardian present.

Sahir's lawyer requested permission to be present during the in-camera. The judge denied his request. I think the judge knew that his lawyer would try to intimidate the kids. Kadin and Kazem already knew the lawyer because their father brought them to his office when he filed the false charges against Beni. There's no doubt in my mind that if Kadin and Kazem were to see the lawyer while they were being questioned, they would be scared to talk. The judge made a good decision, and I was thankful for that.

To keep our case from dragging on further, the

judge was nice enough to clear his calendar for our next hearing, so we would have the entire day to finish. The hearing was scheduled for February 14, 2005.

It wasn't long before our final hearing date arrived. It was coincidental that it just happened to land on Valentine's Day. I suggested to Beni that it might be a good sign because two years prior on that same day, Sahir had signed the divorce papers. It was also then that I got to take my first trip to see Beni in Arizona. I knew it was coincidence and wishful thinking, but something inside still felt good about it.

There's not much to say about the rebuttal testimonies. They were nothing more than a bunch of repeated lies coming from Sahir and his family. They denied each and every allegation and tried to convince the judge that they did no wrong. Sahir still refused to see Kadin and Kazem supervised because he claimed he did nothing wrong and didn't deserve that.

While the rebuttals finished, Beni drove home to pick up Kadin and Kazem from school. He brought them to the court for the in-camera. When he got inside, he brought them in a back entrance so they wouldn't run into anyone from Sahir's family. The Law Guardian instructed Beni to go that way so the kids wouldn't get frightened. She knew that if Sahir and his family saw the kids, they would give them dirty looks to keep them from talking.

In the late afternoon the final testimony was finished. The judge waited until Sahir and his family left before he brought Kadin and Kazem into the room. Sahir's lawyer lingered around the entire time the kids were being interviewed, and at times I saw him peeking through the crack in the door. It appeared as though he wanted to be in that room so badly that if he was able to squeeze through the crack without being seen, he would have.

After about an hour or so, the interview was complete. Kadin and Kazem came out of the room looking totally relaxed. The judge had a warm personality, especially when it came to children. It was evident that the kids were comfortable around the Law Guardian and the judge. My mom, Beni and I were relieved that we were finally finished in court. The only thing we could do was wait. The Law Guardian said that we wouldn't receive the decision for at least one month.

After making sure that Sahir and his family left, the security guard walked us to the door just as he did after each hearing. The Law Guardian knew the hostility Sahir and his family had toward us, so she wanted to ensure our safety. I appreciated her concern because I had a lot of fear knowing that they could be waiting in the parking lot. As we got to the car, Beni and I thanked my mom for all her support. It had been a long, agonizing four-plus months, so it felt good we got through it all and that the truth finally came to light.

When we got home we called my dad to thank him for watching the kids during all the court hearings. Every time we had a hearing he would pick up Kadin and Kazem from the bus and stay with them until we got back. We were truly thankful for all of his help. We all decided to go out for dinner to celebrate the happier times we were now in and the rocky road that we made it through.

CHAPTER 25

The Decision

Having to wait one month for the decision seemed like a long time. I felt like I was in a limbo. I didn't know whether or not to start packing or to just sit tight. One thing I knew for sure was that if we received the decision in the mail and it was in our favor, we'd have to drop everything and leave that day. The lawyer instructed us to do that because if Sahir filed an appeal, he could keep us from leaving. We'd have to wait until the appeal hearing, and we could still only leave if that hearing was won. If an appeal was filed after we left, it would be much harder for him to bring us back once we've moved.

After thinking it over a bit, I decided to pack all the things that we weren't presently using. We had many things that were just sitting in the cabinets, so that's where I decided to start. I figured the worst that could happen would be that I'd have to unpack everything if we weren't allowed to move. At best, it would be a head start if we were granted the relocation.

A few months back I had decided it would be a good idea if we looked for a real estate broker. Even if we weren't sure about the move, we could line one up instead of waiting until the last moment. There was one agent in particular whom I had in mind. She had sold more houses in our neighborhood than any other agent had. I knew she had a lot of experience and that she was successful in her sales, so I contacted her first.

When I spoke with her at that time I had explained how we were in the middle of filing for relocation, and that it would be months before we knew anything. She told us to keep in touch and let her know how things were progressing. She called many times after our conversation, but each and every time I had no new information for her. I figured now that we were at least finished with the hearings, it would be a good time to call her back.

While I was eager to get things rolling, that sad feeling of uncertainty entered my mind once again. It was the same feeling I got when Beni purchased the land in Arizona and also when we looked at some houses there. I felt myself wishing again that I knew for sure that we were permitted to move.

As soon as I was able to push my feelings aside, I gave the agent a call. For someone who didn't get a definite answer, the agent was extremely excited about the opportunity. She even made an appointment to come over to see the house. I liked that she was ambitious about selling houses, but at the same time she also came across as being too pushy. In the months before, she called excessively. She also had a voice that was so loud that I had to keep the phone away from my ear. It actually got to the point of being annoying, but I decided to give her a try because of her success rate. I also figured I'd get to know her a little better if I met her in person.

When the agent arrived she gave Beni and me the same impression as she gave us on the phone.

She was just as pushy in person, and her voice was even louder. I felt myself wishing I had earplugs the entire time she was there. I still felt, however, that her pushiness could be to our advantage. I had seen houses listed on the market by other agents that sat there indefinitely. Unlike those agents, she seemed to quickly sell the houses she listed. Some were listed only a couple of weeks before they were sold. This made me optimistic, so we decided to fill out all the paper work. If we were granted the relocation, we'd sign a contract with her. We both agreed that it was definitely worth putting up with a loud, crackly voice if it meant selling the house quickly.

As the weeks went by, everyone at work asked me if we heard anything. Some friends even asked, "You're still here?"

Francine and Butch always gave me a boost of confidence. They kept telling me that in their hearts they felt we were going to be able to move. They knew we wanted to move for all the right reasons. Beni and I both knew our intentions were good, and that it was in Kadin and Kazem's best interest, but we also knew that everything didn't always turn out the way it should. Hearing positive attitudes always helped in making us feel better.

In addition to all my friends at work, senior guests also asked how everything was going. During the years I worked at the catering hall I became close with the senior citizens who held their parties there. I enjoyed dancing with them and spending time talking to them. It meant the world to me when I was able to put a smile on their faces. It didn't take much to make them happy, and they were appreciative of everything.

I guess spending time with them brought back

memories of all the time I spent with my grandmother. Many of them knew about everything Beni, the kids and I had gone through and how we were waiting for our court decision. Some even promised to say prayers for us. I told them that if they didn't see me there one day, it meant we were granted the relocation. As much as they didn't want to see me leave, they hoped things turned out in our favor. I was extremely touched by their concern for me, and I knew I was going to miss them if I left.

By the beginning of April I began to get antsy. A month and a half had gone by and we still didn't hear from the courts. I knew that any day we could hear something, so my nerves were on edge. It was now at the point that I had to tell my boss to only schedule me as an extra. I didn't want to leave them short-handed if I suddenly had to leave. They were understanding about the fact that I might have to drop everything and go. I was so thankful that they still gave me work considering my situation.

About a week and a half later the suspense was killing me. I could no longer stand not knowing whether or not we could go. I decided to call the courts to at least see if a decision was in. Each and every time I called I got the same answer. I was told that there was no decision yet, but that I could call back.

On April 14, I called the courts again and this time the man who answered told me there wasn't a decision yet, but that it was on the calendar for the day. After hearing that I became so nervous that I was shaking. I thought, this is it! Please let the judge have ruled in our favor!

I couldn't think about anything else that entire day. Beni and I were on the edges of our seats waiting to hear the news. By mid-afternoon I decided to call back to see if a decision had been reached. To my disappointment the courts were so busy that they were unable to get to our case. I couldn't believe I'd have to wait another day.

The minute I woke up the next morning I began thinking about the decision. At about mid-morning I gave the courts a call again. The man who answered told me that our decision was on the calendar again, but he couldn't guarantee they would get to it that day. He said I could call back in the afternoon to check. It seemed as though there was never going to be an end to our waiting. For all I knew this could go on for weeks. I hated to keep calling the courts because I didn't want to annoy the court clerks. I kept hoping someone different would answer the next time.

I called again at 2:00, and when another man answered I was relieved at first. As it turned out, the man wasn't as friendly. I would have been better off talking to the man I spoke with earlier. This clerk told me the decision wasn't in and when I asked if I could call back later he answered in a snappy tone, "This isn't something that happens overnight! I'm not telling you to call back today, tomorrow or the next day! It takes time!"

I must have been desperate at that time because even though he was nasty, I still politely asked, "But I can still call back later if I want to, right?"

He then snapped back by saying, "You can do what you like!"

My hope of hearing anything in the next few days was shot to pieces after that last phone call. I was doubtful that I was going to call back even though I had asked if I could. I told Beni all about the phone call, and he agreed that we probably wouldn't hear anything for a while. Not more than thirty minutes after I got off the phone with the courts I received a phone call from the Law Guardian Bureau. As I picked up the phone and heard the Law Guardian's voice, I became extremely nervous. I had no idea what she was going to say. I usually feared the worst, but at that moment I didn't know what to think. Her first words were, "Laurie, pack your bags."

I was so surprised and extremely elated! Here I was thinking that we wouldn't hear anything, and suddenly the other half of my Christmas wish came true!

I was so happy that I was shaking. The excitement made it difficult to pay attention to everything else the Law Guardian had to say. I tried to control myself and listen carefully because I knew that everything she was telling me was important. The Law Guardian said I should receive a copy of the decision in the mail, but that she would also fax one copy to me and one to my lawyer. Beni walked into the room while I was on the phone. When I gave him a thumbs up with a huge smile on my face he knew right away that we were granted the relocation. He smiled back at me, threw his arms in the air and said, "Yes!"

I thanked the Law guardian for everything she had done for my children. In my heart she'll always be the guardian angel who watched over my children. She holds a place not only in my heart, but also the hearts of my children. They still talk about how nice she was to them and about how much she cared.

We contacted the lawyer to give him the great news and to tell him to look out for a fax from the Law Guardian. We thanked him for a job well done. He was a great lawyer, and we're both happy we found him. He's quick thinking and smart. He was easy to get hold of, and whenever we left messages he would get right back to us. Unlike Sahir's lawyer, he never followed anyone to the bathroom to spy on him or her.

Shortly after finishing our conversation with the lawyer, the fax from the Law Guardian came in. It was a long eighteen page fax that we just couldn't wait to read. As we both sat down to read the decision, I became extremely choked up. After stating all the facts about our case, the judge went on about his findings. He was not at all fooled by Sahir and his family's game playing. He saw all the mental cruelty that they subjected my children to. All the lies they told in court were obvious to the judge, and he knew that Beni and I had been good parents to Kadin and Kazem. He also knew that Beni, my mom and I had all been truthful about everything.

The judge ordered that I retain custody of Kadin and Kazem and that it was in the children's best interest that we relocate to Arizona. He also ordered that Sahir go to parenting classes and individual counseling.

I had tears in my eyes by the time I finished reading the decision. The girl at my work was exactly right about the judge. He was a good judge. He was fair and gave you a chance, but if he caught you lying to him, he was tough! I waited a long time and I went through hell, but justice was finally served.

We called my mom and dad to tell them the wonderful news. They were both happy for us, but at the same time sad. It was the first time in their lives that such a great distance would separate them from me. I had always lived within ten minutes from their house, and we always had a close relationship. It was difficult for not only them, but for me as well. Even though I was happy about moving to Arizona, I was going to miss them.

It was also going to be extremely hard to say goodbye to Kayla and Timmy. I had wished that they could come with us, but I knew it was better for them to stay and finish high school. At least I had the comfort of knowing that they were in good hands with their father and Betty. I also knew we could all visit and call each other regularly.

When I spoke to both of them on the phone, they, too, were happy for us, but like my parents, they were also sad. Before they got off the phone, they promised to stop by to say goodbye. We planned to meet at my parents' house so we could see everyone before we left. Kayla became emotional on the phone right before we hung up, and I felt an empty space in my heart.

Kadin and Kazem came home from school about an hour later. We shouted the news as they walked toward the house. They were so excited that they shouted for joy and began rolling on the grass. The smiles on their faces were so big that they went from practically one ear to the other. It was a great day for all of us.

Now that the kids were home and we had time to enjoy our excitement, we had many things to take care of. We had little time to do it because we had to be out of New York that day. We planned to pack the bare necessities along with Rusty in our van and take the 8:00 pm ferry. It was difficult to figure out where to start. I was so excited that I was completely unorganized. Thank goodness Beni was always organized regardless of how he felt. He helped direct the kids and me, and once we got started it was a lot

315

easier. We needed extra room in the van so we pulled the back seat out and left it in the living room. It must have looked like pure chaos at that time because of all our running around and pulling things out. Rusty looked so funny sitting there with his head cocked to the side. He must have been thinking, what the heck are they doing?

After everything was packed and loaded into the car I called my work to tell them we were leaving and to say goodbye. I was sad that I didn't have time to go down there. Both Joann and Francine were crying on the phone, but they were so happy for us. Francine told me she knew we were going to be able to move. I also said goodbye to the cook. He, too, always looked out for me. Anytime I had something bothering me he would listen. He also made me the best omelets in the world. I was going to miss his friendship and his delicious food.

Not everyone whom I wanted to say goodbye to was at work that day. I was disappointed that I didn't get the chance to say goodbye to them. I'd be back to visit, though, so maybe then it was possible to see them. I was also going to miss my senior friends. They used to refer to me as the skinny waitress with the long black hair who danced with them. They were special people who will always be dear to me. I'll always cherish the fun times I spent with all of them.

The last call I made that evening was to the real estate broker. She was positively thrilled. She especially loved our home because it was only five and a half years old, and I kept it super clean. We were in a nice neighborhood, too, so she knew she would have no trouble selling our house. I was sad about the thought of selling our home. The kids and I had a lot of good memories in that house because we made our new start there. There were also sad memories as well, and some that happened not long ago. The whole ordeal with Sahir taking the kids and filing false allegations of abuse will always be a haunting memory. We were soon going build a new home where we'd be able to start fresh and make new memories. I looked forward to starting a new chapter in our lives.

On our way to the ferry we stopped at my parents' house as planned. Saying goodbye to Kayla, Timmy and my parents was the hardest thing I had to do. It hurt because I loved them all so much and being apart was going to be difficult. My mom was usually good at hiding her emotions, but on that day it was extremely hard for her. It reminded me of the time she cried when I left for college.

I guess that leaving for school wasn't the only time she cried before. Sahir and his family gave my mom more stress than she could handle over all those years I've known them. She always feared for my safety and the safety of my children. Now at least she knows we're all safe and that Beni will take good care of us.

As I gave Kayla a big hug she began to cry. She told me that us moving was better for Kadin and Kazem and that she was only crying because she would miss us. We all promised to visit each other and keep in touch.

As we drove away from my parents' house we were sad, but at the same time we were looking forward to our new life. We could finally leave all the bad memories behind and keep the precious ones in our hearts. Our journey to another place was just beginning.

CHAPTER 26
Moving To Arizona And Rebuilding Our Lives

We arrived at the port in plenty of time to take the 8:00 pm ferry. We were starving because we didn't have time to eat dinner. We planned to grab a bite on the ferry because it would be too late by the time we arrived in Connecticut. Kadin was so hungry that he was beginning to get moody. I couldn't blame him because in addition to being late, we had been running around non-stop all evening. Everyone had worked up quite an appetite. Once I told him that we would buy something on the ferry he was a little better.

To our great disappointment, the 8:00 pm ferry was the only one that no longer served food. When Kadin heard that the snack bar was closed, he wasn't a happy camper. He started getting an attitude, and all I could think about was how it was going to be a long trip. Knowing just how hungry and tired he must have been, I couldn't get too annoyed with him. I tried talking to him calmly so he wouldn't get into a tantrum. Other than a few mumbled words and rolling of his eyes, he pretty much kept his self-control.

The ferry ride was smooth and relaxing. When we reached the shore we stopped at the first restaurant we could find. It was nearly 10:00 pm and we were famished. We all looked like a hungry pack of wolves who hadn't eaten in a week. Kadin was in a much better mood after eating. Beni and I were even more tired after we ate, but the kids seemed to get their second wind. They were jumping around having the time of their lives. As tired as I was, I was still filled with so much excitement.

We stayed at a nearby motel because it was pretty late by the time we finished dinner. We had to make an early start the next day because we had a long drive ahead of us. We planned to take our time driving to Arizona so the kids wouldn't have to sit too many hours each day. This would also give us a chance to do some sightseeing. It had been a long day, so I don't think any of us had trouble sleeping that night.

During the next seven days we traveled through many of the middle states. We took the same route that Beni and I had taken the last time we drove to Arizona. One of our favorite stops was Amarillo, Texas. We stayed at this hotel that had a huge swimming pool and an atrium inside. It was a beautiful place and we knew about it because Beni and I stayed there the previous time that we visited Amarillo. The kids loved the swimming pool. They both loved to swim, so whenever we traveled, we tried to always stay where there was a nice pool.

We also went to a nice Texas steakhouse. They had a cool contest that you can either participate in or just watch. They serve a 76 ounce steak, and if you can eat the entire steak, they will let you have it for free. Needless to say, none of us even attempted that one! We did, however, get to see one man attempt such a feat. He sat in a chair on stage and in front of him was a 76 ounce steak, potatoes and a salad. I was becoming ill just watching him! He had to not only eat the entire steak, but also every last mouthful of the side items. Can you believe that he actually did it? He struggled a bit at the end, but when everyone counted down to the last second, he finished just in time. Oh yeah, I forgot to mention that he had one hour to do it. It was pretty funny and quite entertaining.

By the time we reached Arizona our butts were pretty sore from sitting. It was a nice trip, but it was good to finally be there. We stayed in Beni's house in the RV Park. Jerri was living there at the time, but she agreed to stay in Beni's trailer temporarily until we purchased a home for our lot.

I still couldn't believe we made it to Arizona. What seemed so uncertain to me for so long actually came to pass. For the first time in Kadin and Kazem's lives they were so relaxed. They had no more mental badgering or threats from their father and his family. They could now enjoy life the way a child should. Things were so quiet and peaceful, and what better place to enjoy the relaxation than Arizona.

Now that we were many miles away I didn't have to be scared that Sahir and his family were spying on us or planning to destroy our property. I had lived in fear for so many years. I can't say that all those fears vanished, but my anxiety was a lot less. I still worried that he was going to call and harass me. Just the sound of his voice made my hair stand up. I decided it was best to put those thoughts aside and deal with things as they come.

We immediately enrolled the kids in school. Since we had to leave New York so quickly, my mom stopped by the kid's old schools to pick up their work. She also requested that their records be faxed over to the new schools. Arizona schools start the school year in August and end in May, so Kadin and Kazem only had about one month left of school.

They both liked the new school, and they met a lot of new friends. They also liked the idea of being in the same school together. That would change the following year, though, because Kadin would be going to the junior high at that time. He was a little anxious about starting another new school, but it was nothing more than what every other kid feels.

Kadin's behavior was starting to improve. His outbursts were less frequent, and he no longer got totally out of control. We were starting to see a difference in him since he had been away from his father's negative influence. Kadin was also becoming self-conscious about his weight. Being only about 4 feet 9 inches and weighing 132 lbs., he was at an all-time high. He desperately wanted to get in shape, so we promised to help him reach a goal. He had gained so much weight from all the junk food his father had been giving him. It was going to be difficult for him to shed those pounds. At least he was maturing and starting to care about himself.

About two to three weeks after we arrived in Arizona the real estate agent found a prospective buyer for our home in New York. We were relieved that she found one so fast. I hated the idea of having to worry about the house, being that we were so far away. The idea of selling our home still made me sad, but at least the couple who was interested seemed to be nice people who would take good care of it. I dreaded the thought of having to return to New York to pack up everything. It's amazing just how much a person can collect in five years! Probably 80% of everything we owned was Kadin and Kazem's things.

They had too much stuff.

Lucky for us the buyers were approved for a mortgage, and they wanted to move in quickly. They wanted to close in June, which turned out to be the same as what we hoped for. Kayla had her prom and graduation around the same time, so the timing was just perfect. We planned to pack up the house, see her off to her prom and attend her graduation all on the same trip. Jerri agreed to watch the kids for us while we were gone. Beni and I didn't feel like it was a good idea to bring them back to New York so soon. It would also add to the confusion of trying to sort everything out. It was much faster if the two of us went alone.

We left for New York a couple of weeks later. I had a bit of anxiety going back there that soon. I felt like I had finally gotten far from the place where Sahir and his family kept us victims of his cruelty. Being back there gave me flashbacks of all the torture that he inflicted on all of us. I was also extremely afraid that I would run into Sahir and his family. I hoped they would never find out we were there.

As it turned out I didn't have much time to spend worrying about Sahir. We were busy the entire week. In addition to seeing Kayla off to her prom and attending her graduation, we had tons of packing and cleaning to do. We only had three days to pack the entire house because on the fourth day, the truck would be there.

We worked from morning until late at night. I never realized just how much stuff we had. There were times I thought we wouldn't finish. I was fortunate that Beni was strong and that he kept me going. When it got late, I felt like quitting because I was so exhausted. Beni helped me push myself a bit more each day so that we were able to finish. My mom was also helpful. She came over to the house to help us pack. It would definitely have been easier to sell everything, but we just didn't have the time. The last night we stayed up until about one or two in the morning, but we finally finished and were ready for the truck the next day.

The truck showed up first thing in the morning. We were pretty worn out from the night before, but we had to push ourselves because we were responsible for loading everything onto the truck. It was the kind of truck where you load and they drive. Lucky for us we were able to pay the two guys to help us. It was much too big a job for just the two of us, especially since we were so tired from packing for three days straight.

By the end of the day we loaded the last few things into the truck with nearly no room to spare. We definitely wouldn't have fit everything in if we didn't give one of my friends at work some furniture. We were trying to help her out, and as it turned out she helped us in return.

The truck planned to arrive in Arizona a few days after us, which worked out well. We were going to have to put everything in storage until our house was ready. This would give us enough time to find a place to store it.

I was pretty weary about having to store all our things for a couple of reasons, the first being that I didn't know how our furniture would hold up in the heat. Jerri had told us that she had some furniture in storage at one time, and the heat melted all the glue. All her furniture was destroyed. We had quite a bit of laminated furniture, so I had a bad feeling about it. My second big problem was my OCD and phobias. One of my problems with my OCD had to do with cleanliness. I hated the idea of our things being in a dirty storage. I've seen how disgustingly dirty people can be, so using a storage that someone else used before was a big turn-off for me. I also have a terrible phobia of bugs, especially when it comes to the creepy crawly ones. They're the worst, but I still hate them all! They make my skin crawl, and they totally gross me out! I have a great fear of creatures that might decide to lurk in our things. Regardless of how I felt, I knew we didn't have a choice.

We spent the last two days cleaning the house. I wanted the house to be spic and span for the new owners. They would have a lot of moving in to do, so making everything spotless would probably help them a lot. When I finished cleaning everything, it was so sparkling clean that you could eat off of the floor, (although I wouldn't). The new owners were surprised by how clean it was, and they were appreciative. It always made me feel good inside knowing that I could make someone else's life easier. I was so happy when we were finally finished and were able to return to Arizona.

Shortly after we got back home, the closing on our house in New York took place. Even though I was still sad about selling the house, it felt good not having to worry anymore about it sitting there empty. Now that it was sold, we could actually purchase a new one. We had been looking at manufactured home dealers in the area for quite some time. We saw some that were nice, but none stood out in our minds. Beni and I had both agreed that we would know when we found the one that was perfect for us. It would have to be a house that when you walked into it, you got that *at home* feeling and could say without a doubt, "Now that's the house!"

It wasn't until we visited a dealer in Las Vegas back in May that we found our dream home. It was a beautiful four bedroom, three bathroom 2500 square foot home! We both immediately agreed that it was the one we wanted. It was twice the size of the one that we had in New York and only a fraction of the cost. We couldn't commit to it back then because we didn't know when our previous house would sell. We did, however, fill out all the paperwork so that everything would be ready when the time was right. Now that our previous home was sold, we were finally ready to purchase our new home. We were looking forward to finalizing our contract.

The only thing we had left to do was store the furniture. Things went exactly as scheduled. The truck arrived on time, and we were fortunate enough to get a storage unit that was located next door to Beni's RV Park. It was convenient having it so close because anytime I needed something, I could just walk next door and get it. To my surprise the unit was clean. It was actually a boat storage, so that was probably the reason why it was so clean. I still worried about the bugs, but I tried not to dwell on it. Beni found a couple of guys to help us load everything into the storage. With all of us working together, we had everything moved quickly.

Things were slowly falling into place, and just as I thought how wonderful life was getting, things got even better. I received a letter one afternoon from the Fair Hearing Bureau concerning the neglect charge that CPS had filed against me back in 1999. It had been a few years since I heard anything from them, so I had basically given up any hope of getting a fair hearing and amending the report.

When I opened the letter I was surprised to find

that they scheduled an initial meeting with me. It was like a pre-hearing, which would take place before the actual hearing. The downside to it was that I would have to fly back and forth between Arizona and New York. That would not only be costly, but also difficult since the kids would be in school at that time. I still had to home tutor Kadin. He was doing much better in school, but he still needed my help in some areas.

I decided to write a letter explaining my situation and requesting an over the phone hearing. I was skeptical that they would allow me to have a hearing over the phone, but I figured that it wouldn't hurt to ask. If they didn't agree to it I would have no other choice but to withdraw my request for the hearing. My children came first, and they needed me to be home with them. After mailing the letter there was nothing more I could do for the time being. Like I had done many times in the past, I had to wait.

We began taking Kadin and Kazem to the river nearly every day to swim. The water was so incredibly cold, but being the two little fish that they were, they never minded. Not only was swimming one of their favorite things to do, but it was a great way for Kadin to get in shape. As the months went by, not only did Kadin grow, but he also dropped down to 118 lbs! In addition to getting so much exercise, he ate healthy and cut down his portions. He became a lot more active and began feeling better about himself. Beni and I were so happy for him, and we were extremely proud.

Before the summer was over Beni and I had to make one final trip. Beni's family was having a reunion in the Alps in Switzerland. Beni's father was 94 years old and his health was slowly deteriorating. I had never met his parents, and I wanted to meet them while I had the chance.

We wanted to bring Kadin and Kazem with us, but were afraid we'd have trouble at the border. Even though I had all the court papers and their father never contacted the kids, the border patrol might not let us through because we didn't have his consent. We didn't want to risk having to turn back and losing all that money, so Jerri agreed to let them stay with her.

We decided to make a short ten-day trip versus the three weeks that we would have liked to spend there. We didn't want to leave the kids too long, especially since we had just gone to New York a short time before.

We felt so bad that we couldn't take Kadin and Kazem with us, so we promised to take them to Disneyland, Universal Studios, Sea World and Hollywood if they behaved while we were gone. They were a bit sad that we'd be leaving, but our plan to take a family vacation sure made things a lot easier on them.

I was looking forward to meeting Beni's parents and the rest of his family. I had heard so many nice things about them, and I had talked on the phone with them, so it was nice to finally get to meet them in person.

One of his brothers, Max, along with his family, I had met before. He and his wife Resli had visited Arizona the same time that I did back in February of 2003. Three of their children attended our wedding and their other daughter had visited us in New York on a different occasion. They were all nice people, and they were family-oriented. They were easy to talk to, and I enjoyed their company, so it was going to be exciting to see them again.

Max and Resli invited us to stay at their house during our visit. I was touched by their generosity and willingness to open their home to Beni and me, and I was also extremely grateful.

Our friends Horst, Alicia and their three girls were also planning to visit. They, too, were invited to stay there, so it was going to be a lot of fun. We were all attending the reunion together, which was to take place for three days in a rented house in the Alps.

It was a long eleven-hour flight to get to Switzerland, but we were fortunate to have a smooth flight. The flight attendants were extremely friendly and the food was good, so it made the trip enjoyable. Max came to pick us up at the airport. His mother also stopped by to give us a warm welcome and to say hello. She, too, was a sweet person. Being that she was 85 years old, I was amazed by her incredible energy and how alert she was. Like Beni, she had a heart of gold and a high level of intelligence. It was impressive how she fluently spoke seven different languages, one of them being Chinese. She actually spoke to my mom on the phone in Chinese on one occasion. I thought it was neat that they could converse in my mom's native language.

Max took us back to his house, and on the way there I had the pleasure of enjoying the beautiful scenery in Switzerland. Many people had farms with cows, so it was no wonder how they kept their grass so green. People in New York always struggled to get their lawns that green and usually without success. I always tried so hard to have a nice lawn, but it seemed like a losing battle. I guess that manure is the secret. The only downside to the drive was the twisting, turning roads. Max lived in an area where the roads turned so much that I began to get queasy. I was relieved once we got to his house because I don't know how much more my stomach could have taken. I guess I had even less tolerance than normal because we had just taken a long plane ride.

Max and Resli had an amazing house! It was an old house that once belonged to Beni and Max's maternal grandfather. Max put a lot of energy into restoring the house. He also made apartments inside for each of his three daughters. It was also a big house, which enabled him and his wife to accommodate many guests. Some of those guests included troubled teens, whom they opened their hearts to. Max and Resli are special people who do a great thing by helping those troubled teens get their lives back on track. I admire them for doing such a wonderful thing.

Beni's nieces had given Beni and me a memorable wedding gift when we stayed at their house. They knew just how special the song, "The Rose," was to us. One evening they sang the song for us while playing the piano. Their beautiful voices brought tears to my eyes. They had wanted to perform for us on our wedding day, but were unable to use the piano that night. It was truly a heart-filled gift that we'll both remember.

I finally got the chance to meet Beni's oldest brother Rey and his wife Verena on the first day of the reunion. They, too, were friendly and made me feel welcome. I had spoken to Rey many times on the phone, and he always made me laugh. Not only was he an outgoing person, but he always had a great sense of humor. I enjoyed the time I spent talking to him while I was in Switzerland. He always had a lot of interesting things to talk about, including his snorkeling adventures. He also gave me a ride in his "Smart." It was definitely the smallest car that I ever rode in, and it was fun. It was so small that you felt like you were flying in it.

I also got to meet many friends of the family during those three days. Max's son Eric and his girlfriend, both of whom came to our wedding, also joined us in the fun. It was wonderful to have Horst, Alicia and the three girls there with us. We all had a great time talking and going on walks together.

During our trip I even had a chance to entertain everyone with my crazy daredevil personality. Maybe sometimes I'm a little too crazy. During one of our walks we came across a stream. It was made passable by a railroad tie that was used as a small bridge. It was basically a piece of long metal with raised sides. I asked Beni if he dared me to do a handstand on it. I don't know what compelled me to think of such a thing or to even think I could do it without falling in the water. In any case, Beni did in fact dare me, and wouldn't you know it, I went along and tried it. Fearing only about the chance that I might fall into the water, the thought of possibly hurting myself never entered my mind. As it turned out, my legs went too far over my head and my thigh came crashing down on the metal. Boy, did that hurt. It hurt so much that I felt like crying. Knowing that everyone was watching, I tried hard not to cry. As a result I began laughing, and I hobbled along for quite a while. I was fortunate enough that I didn't break my leg, but I sustained a large bruise and a bump that lasted for months to come. I don't think I'll ever try that again. What the heck was I thinking?

One of Beni's friends cooked a fabulous Chinese meal. She and her husband had a catering business where they specialized in Chinese food. She was not only Chinese like my mom, but also had a knack for cooking such delicious Chinese food. Everyone enjoyed the wonderful feast.

While enjoying all of the festivities, I wished that Kadin and Kazem could have been there. They would have had a great time because there were other kids, and we did many fun activities. We even did a scavenger hunt, which I know they would have enjoyed. I hoped that maybe one day we could take them there.

After the reunion we drove to Zurich to visit Beni's parents. It was nice that I got to meet his father and see his mother again. After meeting Beni's father I came to realize where Beni got his calm and patient personality. His father was a kind man who greeted me with a warm welcome into his home. I was amazed by his determination. He was 94 years old and regardless of how difficult it was to move, he never gave up. He took a pretty long walk with us and even took a trip on the ferry. Both of Beni's parents were happy we came to visit. The feeling was mutual, and the only regret we had was that we wished we had more time to visit.

We eventually stopped to visit Beni's other brother Henri. Like Beni's parents, he was involved in missionary work. He traveled quite a bit, and he and his wife Chloe ran a hostel for exchange students. They lived close to Beni's parents, so we all got together and went out for a nice dinner. Seeing the huge smile on Beni's father's face was something I'll never forget. He was so happy to be there with all of us, and seeing that gave me such a warm feeling inside.

After dinner it was getting late so Beni and I drove his parents home. Saying goodbye to Beni's parents was extremely hard. As they waved goodbye from the kitchen window I felt such sadness. I knew that

Beni's father was old and that he was slowing down. I had the sad feeling that it was the first and only time I would ever get to see him. I prayed that I would get the chance to see them both again.

Beni and I spent the rest of the evening walking through Zurich. I enjoyed seeing all the different people who sat outside either eating dinner or having a drink and talking with friends. Not only did we have a lot of fun talking with people, but it was also a romantic evening as well. We sipped a little wine and enjoyed each other's company and we also strolled through the city in the warm summer breeze.

At one point in our walk we passed by a woman in her sixties. By the way she was dressed and the amount of makeup she had on, it was obvious that she was a prostitute. She sat there looking lonely and as though she was wishing that she had a different life. It was sad to see, and it makes you appreciate even more just what you have.

Henri and Chloe let us stay in one of the rooms at the hostel that night. I could understand why the students liked it there. It was a nice place, and the bed was comfortable. We giggled as we told Henri that we had to rearrange the room a bit. It had two twin beds, and us being the lovebirds that we are, refused to sleep apart. The both of us squashing into a small twin bed was out of the question, so we did a little redecorating. We moved things around and pushed the two beds together. Problem solved. The look on his brother's face was priceless. It was pretty funny.

The trip quickly came to an end, and we headed back home. We were so thankful for everyone's warm hospitality. I was truly grateful to all of Beni's relatives for welcoming me into their family and for treating us with such kindness. I was happy to get back to Kadin and Kazem, but I was going to miss everyone.

The kids were extremely happy when we arrived back home. They had missed us so much that they counted down the days until we were back. We had gotten an excellent report from Jerri and Dan about the kids' behavior. We were proud of Kadin and Kazem for being so good while we were away, so we took the kids for a family vacation just as we had promised.

We needed some time to rest up and to get over the jetlag, so we left about four days later. We first went to Hollywood, which was nice. The kids and I had never been there, so it was a neat place to visit. We had only seen the Hollywood signs in movies, so we were excited to see it with our own eyes.

I did, however, expect to see more when we went to Hollywood. I guess it was one of those childhood fantasies that I had ever since I was young. I always thought of it as a big glamorous city full of bright lights and movie stars. It's true many famous people have been there and they make lots of TV shows and movies, but when you see it, it's just another city. Regardless, it was still an exciting place to visit, and I had a great time.

Our next two stops were Disneyland and Universal Studios. I am a kid when it comes to rides, especially roller coasters. They are my absolute favorite! The kids are lucky to have a mom who loves crazy rides. While they are my favorite, I'm sad to say that I also have my limits unlike before I met Sahir. Certain rides can trigger the vertigo that he left me with. I get queasy and dizzy after too many rides, and there are certain ones that I have to avoid altogether. It was heart breaking to me, but I still keep on trying. I refuse to totally give up. I try to do as much as possible, and I just accept my limitations.

What I love about these two parks is that they not only have rides, but also great entertainment for the whole family. Disney is a place where an adult can feel like a kid again, and where all the rides have a theme to go along with it. In Universal we enjoyed all the movie-themed rides and the fabulous bus tour. I didn't expect the tour to be too interesting, but to my surprise it was great! It was cool to see the set where the movie *War Of The Worlds* was filmed. It was amazing! King Kong also attacked us along the way. He had real banana breath. At the end of the night we enjoyed the beautiful fireworks.

After running around for several days nonstop, we became a bit tired. We decided to take it easy on the follow day, so we took a drive to Venice Beach. A movie was being filmed there that day, so we stood by and watched. It was interesting to see just how it was done. I was kind of hoping they would need a few extras because I would love to appear in a movie. As shy as I am, I can still be a real ham. We also decided to take a walk on the beach. It was too cool to go swimming, so we only stuck our feet in the water. We all took deep breaths and enjoyed the serenity of the beach.

The tranquility of the past four months of our lives suddenly came to a halt right in the middle of our walk on the beach that day. My cellphone suddenly rang, and when I checked the caller ID, a strange number appeared. I didn't recognize it, but I didn't think too much about it. As I answered, I got a huge knot in my stomach. It was Sahir! He hadn't called in months, and out of the blue he decided to call. Had I known it was he, I would have let Beni answer my *phone.* I definitely didn't want to talk to him. Now that I had already answered, I knew I'd have to talk to him one way or the other.

He started the conversation off by trying to play the poor victim. He told me he divorced his wife and moved back to Turkey. He also tried to make me feel sorry for him by saying that he was all alone, it didn't work, obviously. I asked if he wanted to talk to the kids and he said yes. I knew I had to listen closely to everything he said to them just to make sure he didn't try to manipulate them as he had always done in the past. Before I gave the kids the phone, they asked where their father was, and I told them he had moved back to Turkey. They didn't seem at all disappointed, which didn't surprise me since not only did he hurt them in the past, but he had also abandoned them for the past nine months.

Sahir quickly changed his story and told the kids that he was only visiting Turkey. It was now evident that he lied to one of us. He then proceeded to tell more lies to the kids. He told them that the judge said he wasn't allowed to see them until they were eighteen. I was upset that he was trying to disrupt the stability in Kadin and Kazem's lives again. They had both been doing so well, and now Sahir had to come along and toy around with their minds.

When he finished talking with the kids, I got back on the phone. I told him he shouldn't lie to the kids and reminded him about the programs that the judge ordered him to do. He flat out refused to do them, and he attempted to point the finger at Kadin, Kazem and me. He tried to blame us for everything. I didn't want to start arguing with him because I knew it was futile. The last thing I said to him was that the courts already decided who was at fault, and that I didn't even want to get into a discussion about it with him. I then told him that I had to go.

After hanging up, my anxiety level was extremely high. The fear of Sahir starting trouble again had always sat in the back of my mind. I guess I knew that the peace we had for so many months was too good to last. At least we were many miles away, so it would be hard for him to do us physical harm. Then I thought, what if he comes here, or sends someone else to do his dirty work? Sahir and his family were always dead set on revenge, so the thought of what he might do frightened me.

I began having flashbacks of all the things he did the year before. The only thing I knew for sure was the fact that he really was in Turkey. After closely examining the phone number on my caller ID, I was sure that he was, in fact, calling from there. Even though he was in Turkey at the moment, he could return at any time.

For the sake of my kids I had to put the worries out of my mind for the time being. I didn't want them to start worrying about the situation. We all agreed to focus on the rest of our vacation and have a good time.

Before returning home, we made a final stop at Sea World. The four of us were real animal lovers, so going there helped take our minds off of our troubles. We spent the entire day seeing all the different animals and taking a lot of pictures. By the end of the day we were all pretty exhausted. It had been a long trip, so we were ready to head home the next day.

Aside from Sahir's phone call, we had a nice trip. Spending family time together was special to the four of us. Now that we were home, our next family project would be to concentrate on building our new home. We planned to take another drive to Las Vegas to speak to the manufactured home dealer and sign the contract.

On the day we drove to the dealer we looked forward to ordering our new home. We loved the house so much that we had to take another walk through the model home on the dealer's lot. We had never seen one that we loved as much as that one.

We then proceeded to speak with the dealer. The only thing we had left to do was go back over everything. We had already made all our color choices and picked out the siding, roof, carpeting, etc. the last time we met with him. We had also changed a few details of the construction, one being that we wanted the mirror image of the house. Being that it's so hot in Arizona and the fact that the kitchen has six large windows, we wanted the morning sun on that side.

After going back over everything, the dealer informed us that he had to send the changes to the manufacturer before we could finalize the order. We were under the impression that he had already taken care of that months ago, so we were a bit disappointed that he didn't have the contract ready for us. He assured us that he'd get back to us shortly so we could put a down payment on the house and sign the paperwork. As disappointed as we were that we'd have to wait a bit longer, it still felt good knowing that our house would soon be built.

Just two weeks after Sahir's unpleasant phone call, I received another. This time I recognized the phone number, which was the same as the last time. I asked Beni to answer because I could no longer deal with Sahir's lies and harassment. When Beni answered, Sahir asked where Kadin and Kazem were. Beni explained that the kids weren't home because they were at the Boys and Girls Club. Sahir became angry and demanded that he put the kids on the phone. Beni tried a second time to explain that they weren't home. Sahir then became furious and said, "You mother fucker! Who the hell are you?"

Beni warned Sahir that he'd hang up if the cursing continued. Sahir then demanded that he put me on the phone. Sahir was screaming so loud that I could hear everything he was saying. The sound of his raging voice never failed to send chills up my spine. Sahir continued to swear when Beni didn't put me on the phone. In addition to using bad language, Sahir also threatened Beni. Beni responded by hanging up the phone. Sahir called back immediately, and when Beni answered the phone, Sahir once again began swearing. He was given another warning about the foul language, and when Sahir ignored it, Beni hung up again.

The phone calls continued and, on some of the calls, Sahir would curse, and other times he would say nothing. Many phone calls later, April finally called. Beni politely told her the same thing that he told Sahir concerning the whereabouts of Kadin and Kazem. He even told her what time they would be back. When she didn't respond, Beni felt that maybe she didn't hear him. When he repeated himself, April gave a nasty response by saying, "I'm not stupid you know!"

Since it was only April on the phone I decided to talk to her. I made sure she was clear on all the facts about where the kids were and when to call back. Speaking to me rather than Beni didn't change her tone of voice at all, but she claimed that she understood.

Minutes later the office phone rang. Not recognizing the phone number, and not being aware that Sahir and his family had the office number, I answered. Hearing Sarim's voice, I froze from shock and fear. I let Beni know who it was, and I then gave him the phone. Just as Sahir had done, Sarim began using profanity and threatening Beni. Beni immediately hung up.

Sahir and Sarim then proceeded to keep calling back. They took turns calling, and during those calls they sometimes said nothing and other times they would swear. After about fourteen phone calls, we decided to call the police. Sahir just happened to call back while the police were talking to us. I answered on one phone while the police answered the other. I knew if Sahir heard my voice he would start talking, and this would show the police that it was, in fact, him. It was obvious that Sahir had no idea the police were there because when the officer asked who he was, he replied in a sarcastic tone, "Well, who are you?"

When the officer identified himself and repeated his request for Sahir to identify who he was, Sahir softened his voice and said, "Oh, I'm sorry. I must have the wrong number."

It was so typical of Sahir to change his demeanor just like that to avoid getting into trouble. He would only push things as far as he could without getting caught. Even though he refused to say who he was, hearing his voice and seeing the caller ID was enough proof for the police.

The officer wrote a report, and the next day Beni and I went down to the court. I filed for three Orders Of Protection for my children and myself. One was against Sahir, and the other two against Sarim and April. Beni filed for three injunctions against harassment against them. Beni had to file separately because he wasn't related to them. Lucky for us the courts where we live aren't crowded like they are in New York. We didn't have to wait too long before our case was heard.

In addition to the police report, we gave the judge the court decision from New York along with the Law Guardian summary. She was shocked after she read about all the trouble that Sahir and his family had caused. After reviewing all the information she immediately granted us the orders. From past experience I knew that they were only pieces of paper, but I also knew that if Sahir, Sarim or April violated them I wouldn't think twice about calling the police.

We hired a server in New York to serve the court orders to Sahir, Sarim and April. After a couple of attempts, the server was able to locate them and serve the papers. The fact that we provided her with pictures of all three of them and suggested they be served simultaneously probably made it easier for her to get the job done. When the server called to tell us that she was successful in serving the court papers, she added one comment, "When I gave the papers to Sarim, he took one look at them and threw them on the ground."

I told her that what she told me didn't surprise me. I was happy for her that throwing the papers was all that he did.

That night I discovered a message on my cellphone from Sarim. He left it the day before, but I didn't find it until then. After hearing the message I was just as glad that I didn't hear it sooner. I was in an emotional state the day before and the message that Sarim left was filled with anger and hatred. Sarim had called me names such as "a hooker", and "a slut." He also called Beni a faggot and kept talking nonsense about the two of us. When I first heard the message I began to cry, but then after thinking about it, I realized that Sarim wasn't worth getting upset over. He was nothing more than a big evil bully, and I wasn't going to waste my energy worrying about his ridiculous message.

Things soon quieted down, and Kadin and Kazem started another new school year. Kadin had a bit of difficulty adjusting to the junior high. He complained of stomach aches, and his grades slipped during the first three weeks. Kadin had finished the last year with excellent grades, so we knew that he was capable of much more. We suspected that hearing from his father might have had something to do with his behavior. Kazem was still in the same school, and he had no problems, as usual, but we knew he was also in the habit of holding his feelings inside.

Beni and I decided to put them both in therapy. After everything that happened with the phone calls, we wanted to make sure they weren't harboring any troubled feelings. For their safety we had to tell them about the threatening phone calls and the Orders Of Protection. We didn't get into too much detail, but we explained to them that if Sahir or his family ever were to approach them, that they should walk away and tell us immediately. I also gave the schools a copy of all the court papers. I was terrified that Sahir would try to abduct them. After speaking to Kadin and Kazem about the situation, they didn't seem too upset. I think they actually felt more secure knowing they were protected.

Kadin and Kazem liked speaking with the new therapist. Even though she was a woman, Kadin enjoyed talking with her. Now that he was no longer influenced by his father's negativity toward women, Kadin seemed to have a more positive attitude. The kids expressed how they missed their father, but that they felt abandoned by him. They also talked about how angry they were about all the bad things he did. The therapist planned to meet with both of them once every two weeks. Kadin and Kazem liked the idea of having an outlet so they could vent their feelings.

Beni and I decided to have a long talk with Kadin. We gave him time to talk about his anxieties, and we suggested things he could do to relieve the stress. We also boosted his confidence and set up a reward system for good grades. We figured it would be an incentive for him to do well in school. After our talk, Kadin seemed relieved. Seeing just how effective the talk was made me realize that I should sit down with him on a regular basis.

In time the talks proved to be positive. Kadin began getting excellent grades, and the anxiety he was feeling soon diminished. Homework could still be a battle at times, but he was doing much better overall.

To add to the list of positive things going on, I received a phone call from the Special Hearings Bureau at the end of August. I was extremely surprised when they told me that they were calling to hold my hearing over the phone at that moment! I couldn't believe it, and on top of that I was so nervous.

After answering a few simple questions, just like you would in a regular court hearing, CPS stated that they weren't going to present any evidence to support their neglect finding. I then got an immediate decision right there and then. They amended the report to show that I was no longer a subject of the maltreatment report!

I knew in my heart all these years that I had tried everything I possibly could at that time to keep my children safe. Hearing that I was finally cleared of the neglect charge meant the world to me. For so long I had felt like I was victimized all over again, and on that day I once again felt like justice was served. Sahir was the only one who should be blamed for his actions. After getting the wonderful decision I became emotional, and tears filled my eyes. It was truly a memorable day.

At this time we were still waiting for the home dealer to call. We called him a few times only to get the same answer each and every time. He claimed he was still waiting to hear from the manufacturer. We were starting to lose our patience. After repeated calls to him and no results, we finally decided to give the manufacturer a call.

When we got through to them, we spoke to the customer service supervisor. We told him just how much we loved the house, but explained how we were having a problem with the dealer's incompetence. The dealer was an extremely nice man, but he was too slow in getting things done. We asked if their company had another dealer we could purchase the house from.

The supervisor was nice, and he took care of the problem right away. He set us up with a dealer located in Utah. The dealer drove out to meet us at a half way point. She immediately took all the information down and filled out the paper work.

All the things the previous dealer was unable to accomplish even after several months was completed by the new dealer in no time. It wasn't long before she had the contract ready to be signed. Not only was she quick at taking care of everything, but the price of the house was $15,000 less! We were impressed by her friendly personality and outstanding customer service. After signing the contract, we were told that the house should ready in a few months.

The holidays were rapidly approaching once again before we knew it. There hadn't been anymore phone calls since we got the court orders. I was so thankful that things were nice and quiet. Even though it had been eight months since Sahir had stopped paying child support, I was reluctant to file for child support enforcement. I didn't want to stir things up, but then I remembered all the times that I kept quiet just to keep peace. Where did that get me? Those words of wisdom concerning documentation spoken by the sheriff in New York also ran through my head. I decided to file, not because of the money, but more for documentation purposes.

Getting the correct information concerning child support enforcement was difficult. The fact that we lived in a different state made filing more complicated. It was difficult to find someone knowledgeable on interstate filing. When I called the courts in New York and in Arizona everyone gave me a different answer. No one was sure what to do. It took many phone calls before I was given the correct information. I was finally able to file the papers just before we left for New York to celebrate Christmas.

Our house was supposed to be delivered by this time, but because the manufacturer was so busy, there was a delay. They rescheduled the delivery for after the New Year. This worked out better for us anyway because we wanted to be there when it arrived. When we returned from the holidays we could start setting up the house so we could move in.

About a week or so after we came back, the

house arrived just as scheduled. Aside from having the wrong color shutters, it came just as we had ordered it. We were all excited to see the house being driven down the road. It arrived in three parts, which had to be put together once it was placed on our lot. I remember the first time that I saw a house being driven down the road. It was actually in New York. I thought it strange back then, but over here it was a common thing, especially these days. They make the manufactured homes sturdy and beautiful, unlike years ago when they looked more like a trailer.

Getting the home onto our lot posed a lot of problems for the drivers. Not only was the house huge in size, but the ground was soft. The wheels of the truck kept digging into the loose sand, getting stuck. The driver also lacked the skills needed to put the house in the right position. After struggling for hours without success, the worst was yet to come. During one of the attempts the driver accidentally hit the trailer that one of the three parts was sitting on. This caused the trailer to fall off the concrete block that was used to keep the right side propped up. I didn't see it happen because I was sitting in my car, which was parked in the street. All I heard was this loud crash. I thought, Oh my gosh, what was that?

I was afraid to look. It was so loud that I knew it must be bad. When I looked and saw the right side of the trailer on the ground, I knew they dropped the house. Lucky for us it didn't clunk from a great height. There were some cracks in the walls inside our bathroom, and some tiles that had to be glued back on, but as far as we could see, there was no major damage. We were still concerned, though, because it was possible that there was structural damage that wasn't visible. The manufacturer documented the accident and agreed to repair any related problems in the future. Just before it got dark the drivers finally got the house in place. If getting the house into our lot was that difficult, I hated to think what kind of deal putting it together was going to be. I figured I'd worry about that when the time came.

Aside from little obstacles here and there, the contractor didn't run into any major problems putting the house together and completing the hook-ups. He finished everything in a reasonable amount of time. By the beginning of March we were ready to start moving the furniture into the house. We decided to take our time since we could live in Beni's park as long as we wanted. This way everything would be finished before we actually started to live there.

Taking the furniture out of storage was a bit upsetting. Just as I feared, the glue had melted and much of the laminate had lifted. The mover also damaged some pieces. I had to chew on the fact that our nice new furniture was in pretty bad shape. As much as it hurt, I realized that dwelling on it wasn't going to change a thing. I decided to spend my energy just thanking God for helping us be in Arizona. Looking on the bright side, I didn't find any creepy crawlers in my things. That was a relief!

By mid-April we finally moved into our beautiful new home. We were pleased with the job they did putting it together. Having all our things put away already made things a lot easier. All we had to do now was settle in and start making new memories.

Looking back at the long road we had to take simply amazes me. It's hard to believe we made it this far. To think how many bumps in the road we hit, but yet we still made it is unbelievable.

Kadin and Kazem are now both doing well in

school. Kazem got straight "A"s last year and Kadin had a high "B+" average. He also made the honor roll. Kadin has lost a lot of his excess weight, and he exercises daily to keep in shape. He no longer has the outbursts, and he's turning into a fine young man. Kazem is a well-adjusted ten-year-old who has a pleasant personality.

Kayla and Timmy have both grown up to be fine young adults. Like the rest of us, they, too, still have scars from the past, but they're at peace now knowing that we're safe in Arizona.

I'm extremely thankful to all those people who have made a difference in the lives of my children. Many people helped in different ways, and I'm grateful to all of them. I especially owe so much to my parents and my husband Beni. My parents gave up so much of their time helping my children and me. Their unconditional love and support got me through some tough times. Beni is my soul mate who picked me up and rescued me when I was at the end of my rope. He stood by me regardless of how rocky the road became, and he gave my children and me so much love and support. He helped guide my children into becoming who they are today.

Today I may still be dealing with my physical and emotional scars, but with a smile on my face I can say, "I was once the silent victim, but now I'm running free."

DEDICATION

This book is dedicated to my husband, children, mom, dad, brother and the rest of my entire family. They all gave me their unconditional love and support during the worst of times. I would also like to dedicate it to the caring people who touched the lives of my children.

Printed in the United States
113443LV00006B/15/P